THE DAUGHTERS OF CHARITY
OF ST VINCENT DE PAUL IN IRELAND

In grateful tribute to the four courageous Daughters of Charity who arrived in post-Famine Ireland in November 1855: Sister Josephine de Virieu, 37, of Côte-d'Or; Sister Amelia Ellis, 31, of Wales; Sister Gabrielle de la Moussaye, 28, of Paris; Sister Jeanne Morris, 21, of Skryne, County Meath; to serve those who were poor, destitute and abandoned in a spirit of humility, simplicity and charity with compassion, respect, devotion, creativity and daring.

Edited by
Jacinta Prunty CHF & Louise Sullivan DC

The Daughters of Charity of St Vincent de Paul in Ireland

THE EARLY YEARS

the columba press

First published in 2014 by

the columba press

55A Spruce Avenue,
Stillorgan Industrial Park,
Blackrock, Co. Dublin

Cover image: *The Breadline 1916*, permission kindly provided by the
Crawford Art Gallery, Cork.
Cover design by sin é design
Origination by The Columba Press
Printed by Bell & Bain Ltd

ISBN 978 1 78218 177 4

Acknowledgements

Sincere gratitude to all those who by their collaboration have made this publication possible:

To Catherine Prendergast DC, provincial of the Irish province of the Daughters of Charity, for initiating this project as part of the 150th anniversary of the arrival of the Daughters of Charity in Ireland. We thank her for her inspiration and support throughout the writing of this collection of essays.

To Joseph McCann CM for proofreading the final draft.

To Dr Daire Keogh for writing the preface.

To Ms Anne Boddaert of the Crawford Art Gallery, Cork for permission to reproduce *The Breadline 1916* in this publication.

To Bernadette Mac Mahon DC for her assistance in researching and preparing material for the chapter on North William Street.

To Áine O'Brien DC for her assistance in researching and preparing material.

To Maeve O'Sullivan DC for her interest and help.

To Tom Davitt CM, archivist for the Congregation of the Mission, St Paul's Raheny, Dublin, for his help in translating documents from the original French and for sharing his expertise with the authors.

To Mr Ned Byrne for his help in accessing information on St Vincent's Hospital, Fairview, Dublin.

Thank you to the archivists in the various institutions for making material available for the project: Claire Hermann DC and her assistant archivists in the Mother House of the Daughters of Charity, rue du Bac, Paris; Judith Greville DC, Joan Conroy DC, and Bernadette Ryder DC, archivists, Provincial House, Mill Hill, London; Kevin McAlinden DC, and Áine MacNamara DC, archivists in the Provincial House, St Catherine's Dunardagh, Blackrock, Co. Dublin; Betty Ann McNeill DC, archivist in Emmitsburg Maryland, United States; Martin Dehlinger DC, archivist and provincial secretary in Taiwan; Ms Noelle Dowling, archivist for the Archdiocese of Dublin, Clonliffe Road Dublin; Alice Aylward CHF, archivist for the Holy Faith Sisters, Glasnevin, Dublin; The staff of the National Archives of Ireland, Kildare Street, Dublin; Marie Bernadette O'Leary RSC, the archivist for the

Religious Sisters of Charity; Teresa Delaney RSM, the archivist for the Sisters of Mercy Western Province, Galway; the archivist for the Down and Connor Diocese; Patrick Crowley SSC, archivist of the Missionary Society of St Columban; Mr Brian McGee and staff, of the Cork Archival Institute, Blackpool, Cork.

The librarians of the following libraries for their help: the Staff of Pearse Street Library, Dublin; Ms Teresa Whitington and the staff of the Central Catholic Library of Merrion Square, Dublin; Ms Katherine McSharry and the staff of the National Library of Ireland, Kildare Street, Dublin.

To Carmel McArdle DC and the sisters in St Catherine's Provincial House, Dunardagh, Blackrock for their hospitality, support, encouragement and consideration of the authors

To the Daughters of Charity in the local communities who supported the authors.

To Mr Fearghal O'Boyle and the staff at the Columba Press, for their unfailing courtesy and professionalism in the publication of this book.

Contents

Appedices

Glossary

Company of the Daughters of Charity of St Vincent de Paul: The official title of the Daughters of Charity since their foundation in 1633.

Conferences of St Vincent de Paul: During his lifetime, Vincent shared his spiritual reflections with the Daughters of Charity and the Congregation of the Mission.

Congregation of the Mission (CM): A community of Roman Catholic priests and brothers founded by Vincent de Paul in 1625; also known as the Vincentian Community, Vincentian Fathers or Lazarists.

Constitutions and Statutes: These are laws that govern the life of the Company of the Daughters of Charity and have received the approval of the Church.

Cornette: The official headdress of the Daughters of Charity from the seventeenth century until the 1960s.

Director/Provincial Director/Father Director: A priest of the Congregation of the Mission, appointed by the superior general, who promotes the Vincentian spirit in collaboration with the visitatrice/provincial of the Daughters of Charity and her council.

Dunardagh, Blackrock, Co. Dublin: The administrative centre of the Daughters of Charity in Ireland since the formation of the Irish province in September 1970.

Filles de la Charité: The official name of the Company of the Daughters of Charity in French.

French Sisters: A name given to the Daughters of Charity in Ireland to distinguish them from the Irish Sisters of Charity, now known as the Religious Sisters of Charity.

Lazarists: The title given to the members of the Congregation of the Mission in France because their motherhouse was the Priory of St Lazare.

Mill Hill, London: The administrative centre of the Daughters of Charity from April 1885 when the province of Great Britain and Ireland was established.

Missioned: The term used when a sister is asked by the provincial to move from one local community to another, sometimes at short notice.

Motherhouse: It is situated at 140 rue du Bac, Paris and is the central administrative centre of the international community of the Daughters of Charity since 1815.

Prise d'habit/Sending on Mission: The ceremony at the end of the seminary period of initial formation that marks the sister's missioning to a ministry within the Company.

Postulant: The name used to describe the first stage of initial formation that a candidate to the Company experiences for a period of time ranging from six months to one year.

Province: An administrative division of the Company which does not necessarily follow political boundaries. It is composed of a number of local communities and is under the leadership of a visitatrice.

Provincial/Visitatrice: The leader of a province who is assisted by a provincial assistant and a group of provincial councillors.

Provincial Council: The group of sisters who support the provincial in the administration of the province.

Provincial House: The administrative centre of a province, where the provincial resides.

Renewal of Vows: The vows taken by the Daughters of Charity are 'non-religious' and are renewed annually on the feast of the Annunciation during the celebration of the Eucharist.

Renovation: The term used for the renewal of vows.

Seminary: The term used for the initial period of spiritual formation of the Daughters of Charity.

Sister Servant: The appointed leader in every local community (house) of the Daughters of Charity.

Sœurs Grises: A name given to the Daughters of Charity in France because of the grey/blue colour of their dress until the 1960s.

Superior General: The superior general of the Congregation of the Mission is also the superior general of the Daughters of Charity. This practice has been maintained since the time of Louise de Marillac and Vincent de Paul.

Superioress General: The successor of Louise de Marillac and the international leader of the Daughters of Charity.

Visitation: An official visit made by the superioress general or provincial to all provinces or local communities at regular intervals. These visits are concerned with the various aspects of life within the province and local community.

Foreword

When the first Daughters of Charity arrived in Ireland in November 1855, they were continuing to fulfil the vision of the founders of their Company, Vincent de Paul and Louise de Marillac:

> Our vocation is not to a parish or a diocese, but to the entire world. And what are we called to do? To do what the Son of God did … spread fire upon the earth so that it might be inflamed with his love.[1]

The arrival of the first sisters in Ireland was part of the expansion of the Company of the Daughters of Charity in the half-century following its re-establishment in Paris after the French Revolution. The decade of the 1850s was post-Famine Ireland and the indigenous religious communities and the newly introduced foreign orders were all engaged with the care of the most deprived of the country.

The journey from France to Ireland was one of faith, courage, hope and determination rooted in the belief that all was being undertaken for the glory of God and the salvation of people. The sentiments expressed by St Paul to the people of Galatia – 'yet it is no longer I, but Christ living in me. The life I am now living, subject to the limitation of human nature, I am living in faith, faith in the Son of God who loved me and gave himself for me'[2] – come to mind when considering the journey to Drogheda and the subsequent expansion of the Daughters of Charity in Ireland. This foundation was a venture into the unknown, into another culture, language and people: an opportunity to inculturate the charism of the community in a new land.

The spirit of these founding sisters is expressed in the lines from Patrick Kavanagh:

> God cannot catch us
> Unless we stay in the unconscious room

---

[1] P. Coste CM, *Saint Vincent de Paul: Correspondence, Conférences, Documents*, XII, ed. and tr. Marie Poole (New York: New City Press), p. 215.

[2] Gal 2:20.

of our hearts. We must be nothing,
Nothing that God can make us something.
We must not daydream to-morrow's judgement–
God must be allowed to surprise us.[3]

In their lives of prayer, *the unconscious room of our hearts,* the sisters found the courage, strength and conviction to undertake their mission. It was in leaving all that was familiar to them that they became *nothing.* This sacrifice allowed their mission and works to expand and develop into services for people who were the weakest and most marginalised in Irish society in the nineteenth century. As we read this collection of essays let us *not daydream to-morrow's judgement* but *allow [God] to surprise us,* as He has done to the Daughters of Charity in Ireland since November 1855.

This collection tells some of the story of the intervening 158 years with their joys, sorrows, successes, difficulties, expansion and rationalisation among a group of faith-filled women and the various groups with whom they collaborated. This book is a testament to the work, dedication and service of the pioneer sisters, in particular during the first fifty years of their ministry in Ireland. It is equally a testament to the commitment and dedication of the sisters who have researched, written and edited it. Each essay is directly related to the areas of work in which the sisters became involved during the first fifty years. Each of the authors had either direct experience of the ministry, or a particular interest in the work that they researched.

I am indebted to Dr Jacinta Prunty CHF, for her guidance, support and encouragement. Her vast knowledge of Ireland, and in particular Dublin, in the latter half of the nineteenth century proved to be invaluable in the sourcing of primary documents and the compilation of the various essays.

Dr Louise Sullivan DC guided the authors in preparing the essays for publication. Her expertise in Vincentian studies, her attention to detail, her unfailing encouragement and her knowledge in preparing material for publication have made it possible to complete this project.

I offer a very sincere word of thanks to Dr Daire Keogh for undertaking to write the preface to this collection of essays. I sincerely thank Dr Joseph McCann CM for his wonderful contribution in proofreading the final text.

Thanks is extended to each of the authors for their efforts and commitment. It is with special gratitude that I remember sisters Mary Dixon and Sheila Mathews DC, both of whom played a central role in the researching and writing of this book and who died before its completion. May they rest in peace.

---

[3] P. Kavanagh, 'Having Confessed', *Collected Poems* (London: W. W. Norton, 1973), p. 149.

Finally, I want to thank my five companions, sisters Anna Byrne, Breege Keenan, Anne Neylon, Carmel Ryan and Claire Sweeney who during the past eight months have worked tirelessly to bring this collection of essays to a conclusion. Their generosity and dedication is truly in the spirit of the founding sisters and the final text is a worthy tribute to all who have gone before us.

Catherine Prendergast
Provincial of the Daughters of Charity
St Catherine's Provincial House
Dunardagh, Blackrock, Co. Dublin
April 2013

Preface

In 1855 the River Boyne was spanned by a great viaduct at Drogheda. In that same year, a pioneering company of sisters arrived in the town, beginning a tradition of care, which has endured for over a century and a half.

This volume is a testament to that service, an account of generations of women who lived a life of charity faithful to the spirit of their founders Vincent de Paul and Louise de Marillac. Indeed, the constant motif of this collection is the recourse of the contributors to the commandment to love, which is the cornerstone of the Christian faith. The collection is set within a discussion of the charism of the congregation, as sisters driven by the charity of the crucified Christ. The Daughters embrace the poor as 'his sacrament' and this history records how they served them as 'their Lords and Masters' in contexts as varied as schools, refuges, workhouses, prisons, and the factories of Belfast where they ministered to girls James Connolly characterised as 'linen slaves'.

The Daughters of Charity were pioneers in every sense. Indeed, the determination of the founding group, welcomed to Drogheda by Archbishop Dixon, was mirrored by their successors as their ministries evolved to meet the needs of the age. The sisters regarded nothing as 'foreign to their spirit' and while they displayed an amazing adaptability it is notable that at every juncture they sought to be informed. They were never amateurs, but professionals who availed of international expertise which they applied to their ministries. The account of St Vincent's Hospital in Fairview reflects this and the chapter recalls the evolution of the institution from a humane asylum in the nineteenth century to the modern community-based psychiatric service it is today.

There is a tendency in religious history to focus excessively on the character of the founder. The distinct contributions of Vincent and Louise have prevented this in the Vincentian tradition, but this volume makes a particular point of emphasising the importance of the group as opposed to the heroics of any individual. From the outset, the chapters emphasise the energies and enthusiasm of the 'founding circle' in Ireland, a group which included Cardinal Cullen and some of his closest collaborators, Fr Philip Dowley CM and the indomitable Margaret Aylward, whose biographer has co-edited this collection. Later chapters, too, reflect the instinctive disposition of the Daughters towards collaboration, in a range of projects which produced great effect. One such venture was the vision of sisters Louise Burke, Gertrude O'Callaghan and Fr Donal Cregan CM which led to the foundation of the Special Education Department at St Patrick's College. As Ireland's first such department, its foundation represented an important milestone in the inclusion of children with special needs in the education system.

This collection reflects the fidelity of the sisters to their founder's passion for faith and good works. We are grateful to the editors, Jacinta Prunty and Louise Sullivan and their contributors who have prepared this labour of love, especially the late sisters Mary Dixon and Sheila Matthews who did not live to see the volume published. The characteristic 'cornettes' of the Daughters of Charity may have long gone, but the poverty, exclusion and spiritual hunger which brought them to Ireland remains. If, as Anne Neylon notes, an institution that forgets its own past will have difficulty finding and defining its future, this history will contribute greatly to the remembrance of the Daughters of Charity's past and, therefore, the defining of its future.

Dr Daire Keogh,
President, St Patrick's College,
Drumcondra, Dublin 9.
May 2013

Prologue

Vincentian Spirituality: Source of the Energy of the Early Daughters of Charity in Ireland for the Service of those who were Poor

Christina O'Mahony DC

The Company of the Daughters of Charity of St Vincent de Paul, a society of apostolic life in community, was founded in France in the seventeenth century by Vincent de Paul and Louise de Marillac. Its beginnings were simple and unexpected. 'Who would have thought that there would be Daughters of Charity? … I did not think of it. God thought of it for you.'[1] Attentive to the voice of Divine Providence and responding to the promptings of the Holy Spirit, Vincent de Paul (1581–1660) became conscious of the material and spiritual poverty of his time and devoted his life to the service and evangelisation of poor people.[2] For this purpose he founded the Confraternities of Charity (1617) and the Congregation of the Mission (1625). Providentially, he met Louise de Marillac (1591–1660), who collaborated closely with him in his charitable works.[3]

---

[1] Pierre Coste, IX, p. 113 (Vincent de Paul speaking to the Daughters of Charity). Coste refers to the fourteen-volume French edition of St Vincent's works, edited by Pierre Coste CM (Paris: Librairie Lecoffre, J. Gabalda, 1920–5). (Henceforward Coste; Roman numerals refer to the volume and Arabic numbers refer to page numbers.)

[2] The use of the word 'poor' throughout this chapter is a generic term covering all forms of poverty.

[3] Wife, mother and widowed when she collaborated with Vincent de Paul in the work of the Ladies' Confraternities of Charity and in the foundation of the Daughters of Charity in Paris, 1633.

On Pentecost Sunday, 4 June 1623, Louise received the grace of envisioning what would be for her a new community:

> On the feast of Pentecost, during Holy Mass or while I was praying in church … I was made to understand … that a time would come when I would be in a position to make vows of poverty, chastity and obedience, and that I would be in a small Community in which others would do the same. I then understood that I would be in a place where I could help my neighbour, but I could not understand how this would be possible because there would be much coming and going.[4]

Then a simple young woman from the country, named Marguerite Naseau (1594–1633), inspired by true evangelical love, presented herself to perform the menial tasks which the Ladies of the Confraternities of Charity were unable or unwilling to assume. Vincent would later say of her, 'Marguerite was the first sister who had the happiness of showing others the way although she had almost no other teacher but God.'[5] Her example was contagious. It was in this way that, imperceptibly, in the manner of things divine, the Company of the Daughters of Charity was born. As early as 1630, Vincent de Paul entrusted to Louise de Marillac the first young women who were devoting themselves to the work of the various confraternities. On 29 November 1633, six of these young women, later joined by others, gathered around her to live their ideal under her guidance in community. They nursed the sick poor in their homes, in the towns and villages and later cared for the sick in hospitals, involved themselves in education, work for foundlings, galley convicts, wounded soldiers, refugees, the aged, and others. The Vincentian charism means the gift that the Holy Spirit gave to the Church through Vincent de Paul and Louise de Marillac. It is a missionary charism. Availability and mobility are its fundamental attitudes – going wherever the needs are greatest and to the most deprived.

---

[4] L. Sullivan DC, ed., *Spiritual Writings of Louise de Marillac: Correspondence and Thoughts* (Brooklyn: New City Press, 1991), p. 1. Translated from French by Sr Louise Sullivan DC. Henceforward SWLM.
[5] Coste, IX, p. 77.

In 1855, another branch of the Vincentian tree of charity took root in Irish soil when superiors in Paris missioned a group of sisters to Ireland.[6] Their story is recounted in this book. They were popularly called the 'French Sisters' and were conspicuous by their traditional dress which evolved from the French peasant dress of the Ile de France. They were deeply imbued with the spirit of their founders, Louise and Vincent, and had a wealth of experience in serving the poor in that spirit. The energy and driving force behind their way of life, i.e. their Vincentian spirituality, was based on the gospel message, taking Christ, evangeliser of the poor, as exemplar, and nurtured by the teachings and rules of their founders. Louise and Vincent emphasised the importance of a deep prayer life – both personal and liturgical – and the vital role of mutual trust and acceptance in a community modelled on the life of union within the Blessed Trinity. For these first Daughters of Charity in Ireland and those who would come after, their prayer life and their community life nourished and animated their encounters with the poor, which in turn enriched their prayer and union with God.

Just as there are multiple strands of varying hues and radiance adorning and adding lustre to the texture of the multicoloured tapestry that expresses Vincentian spirituality, so there are various opinions as to what constitutes its core. In order to understand the driving force animating the lives and works of Vincent and Louise, we will outline briefly the spirituality of each of them and some of the main strands of Vincentian spirituality. Each of these strands expresses an element of truth but they are but a pale and partial representation of the riches and radiance of what the entire tapestry expresses.

Vincentian spirituality is 'more a lifestyle in which to be engaged than it is a subject to be studied'.[7] It is more appropriate then, to describe rather than define it since Vincent de Paul was not a systematic theologian and did not speak or write about Christology as such. Rather, he developed a

---

[6] The Vincentian priests, and brothers (Congregation of the Mission), the Association of the Ladies of Charity and the Society of St Vincent de Paul were already established in Ireland.

[7] J. Prager CM, 'Reflections on the Renewal of Vincentian Spirituality' in *Vincentiana* 1981, pp. 366–83, at p. 383.

way of following Christ and taught it to his followers since, for him, praxis was more important than theory. It is a spirituality of service, rooted in charity which leads us progressively to becoming identified with Christ the servant. 'It is essential to empty yourself in order to put on Jesus Christ.'[8] The spirituality that underpins the service of the Daughters of Charity is derived from the particular way the founders understood Christ's incarnation and mission. 'In order to be good Daughters of Charity, you must do what the Son of God did while he was on earth.'[9] The strand of Marian spirituality richly adorns the Vincentian tapestry.

The Vincentian family understands the expression 'Vincentian spirituality' to mean the spiritual path along which the Holy Spirit led the founders to sanctity through a specific way of following Christ and continuing his mission.[10] It is most of all characterised by a spirituality of first-hand encounters. It is rooted in Vincent and Louise's discerning of the finger of God in these through prayer. Their paths to holiness began when they became attentive to God acting through people and events. For both of them, encounters with the poor were decisive factors in their lives. Attentiveness to providence and to the will of God are the hallmarks of their spirituality. Listening to the Holy Spirit enabled them to recognise God speaking and acting through their personal experiences.

Vincentian spirituality espouses a holistic approach, embracing the corporal and spiritual, bringing bread and catechesis to the needy, knowing that the gospel without bread will remain sterile and bread without the gospel will create dependency. The Vincentian emphasis is on concrete, practical charity. 'When I was hungry, you gave me to eat and when I was thirsty, you gave me to drink.'[11] Living a simple lifestyle, followers of Vincent and Louise strive to serve the needy by personal contact and in a simple, humble manner, with a love that is affective, effective, compassionate and

---

[8] Coste, XI, p. 343–4.

[9] Ibid., IX, p. 15.

[10] The Vincentian family today includes many lay organisations such as Ladies of Charity, Society of St Vincent de Paul, De Paul Trust, Vincentian Marian Youth, Association of the Miraculous Medal, as well as The Vincentian Partnership for Social Justice, Daughters of Charity and Vincentian Priests and Brothers.

[11] Mt 25:31. (Scripture quotations are from the New Revised Standard Version (NRSV).)

inventive, considering them as their 'lords and masters' and allowing themselves to be evangelised by them.[12]

Spirituality of Vincent de Paul

While Vincent de Paul was influenced to a certain degree by the Christological principles which he learned from Pierre de Bérulle, Francis de Sales and André Duval, his vision was significantly different from that of his teachers and mentors, and from the adherents of the French School of Spirituality. A study of his writings reveals and makes explicit the Christological vision which underpins Vincent's thought and action, and that lies at the heart of his spirituality. There was only one driving force, the person of Jesus Christ. 'Remember that our life ought to be hidden in Jesus Christ and full of Jesus Christ, and that in order to die like Jesus Christ it is necessary to live like Jesus Christ.'[13] Characterised by an active thrust, it is a Christocentric and missionary spirituality, drawing its impetus from the mission of Christ. Bérulle and the adherents of the French School of Spirituality taught that the Christian life is an attempt to reflect on the states of Christ's life and to imitate his attitudes. For Vincent, the pre-eminent disposition of Christ was charity.[14] The life of Jesus incarnate is characterised by love of the Father and charity towards the neighbour. The Vincentian way of living a Christian lifestyle consists in continuing the mission of Christ.[15] Vincent makes the universality of Christ's vision his own. Before the end of his life he had sent missionaries to Madagascar, Poland, Italy, Algeria, Tunis and Ireland. He dreamed also of sending them (or of going himself) to the Indies. Like Christ, he had a universal outlook.

> Our vocation, then, is to go, not into one parish, nor even to one diocese, but throughout the whole world to inflame the hearts of men and women, to do what the Son of God did. He came to cast fire upon the earth, to inflame it with his love.[16]

---

[12] Vincent and Louise continually remind us in their writings that the poor are our 'lords and masters'.

[13] Coste, VI, p. 295.

[14] Cf. Coste, VI, p. 393; XII, p. 108.

[15] Cf. Coste, II, pp. 207, 133, 343; XII, pp. 132, 262, 264–5, 366–7.

[16] Coste, XII, p. 262.

A study of Vincent's work reveals that his vision focuses on the *missionary* Christ, coming from the Father and returning to him, emptying himself of his condition as Son of God in order to bring integral liberation to the *anawim*, his chosen ones, to the ends of the earth.

> To make God known to the poor, to announce Jesus Christ to them, to tell them that the kingdom of heaven is at hand and that it is for them. Oh, what a great thing it is that we should be called to be sharers in the plans of the Son of God.[17]

But Vincent also remembered that Jesus came to 'save his people from their sins'.[18] Both these aspects of Christ's mission lie at the heart of Vincent's ministry. In his conferences and letters, he envisions a Christ who reaches out to sinners,[19] frequently focusing on the heart of Jesus, 'let us look at the Son of God. O, what a loving Heart! What a flame of love!'[20]

The Constitutions of the Congregation of the Mission give a schematic description of their spirit, which offers a good, if incomplete description of Vincentian spirituality. The following is a brief outline of that description:

> The Vincentian spirit is the spirit of Christ as sent to preach the good news to the poor (C5), as evidenced in the Gospel sayings explained in the common Rules (C4), concretised particularly through: love and reverence towards the Father, compassionate and effective love for the poor, docility to divine Providence (C6), simplicity, humility, meekness, mortification, zeal for souls (C7) … 'Jesus Christ is the rule of the mission' and the centre of its life and activity (C5).[21]

This spirituality flows from a vision of Jesus Christ as the Evangeliser of the Poor. Vincentians are called to follow Christ in the very terms of St Luke's Gospel (4:18) with which Jesus begins his public ministry:

> The spirit of the Lord is upon me; therefore, he has anointed me. He has sent me to bring good news to the poor, to proclaim liberty to

---

[17] Coste, XII, p. 80.
[18] Mt 1:21; Cf. Luke 1:77.
[19] Cf. Coste, XII, p. 190.
[20] Ibid., p. 264.
[21] R. P. Maloney CM, *The Way of Vincent de Paul: A Contemporary Spirituality in the Service of the Poor* (New York: New City Press, 1992), p. 14.

captives, recovery of sight to the blind and release to prisoners, to announce a year of favour from the Lord.

It was this Christ that Vincent contemplated and from whom his spirituality flowed. He expressed it in love and reverence for the Father, compassionate and tender love for the poor, in docility to providence and in the five virtues characteristic of the Congregation of the Mission. It is this Christ who is the Rule of the Mission. The Christ of Luke 4:18 (applying to himself the words of Isaiah 61:1–2) stands at the core of the spirituality embraced by members of the Vincentian family.[22]

Spirituality of Louise de Marillac

Although the word 'Vincentian' is derived from the name Vincent (Vincentius), we cannot consider the special characteristics of the Vincentian charism as referring just to the person of Vincent de Paul. The charism cannot be understood without reference to the original contribution made by Louise de Marillac. The more we study the relationship between Vincent and Louise, the more difficult it is to ascribe to either one alone the inspiration behind the Vincentian charism.[23]

The general framework of Louise's spirituality is Trinitarian, Christocentric and Ecclesial. Although like Vincent, the primary focus of her spirituality is the incarnate word of God, the humanity of Jesus, we also discover the Trinitarian foundation of her spiritual life from her letters and writings. There are frequent examples of her devotion to the Trinity as a unity as well as to the individual persons of the Father, Son and Holy Spirit. She writes, 'I wish to honour the three Persons separately and also together in the unity of the divine essence.'[24] She repeatedly echoed in her letters to the sisters the theme of unity in the Trinity and exhorted them

---

[22] Vincent also cites Matthew frequently, especially Mt 25:31–46 and draws on significant themes from John; emphasis on Jesus' communion with the Father and on practical love of the neighbour.

[23] C. Delgado CM, 'Marian Spirituality and the Vincentian Charism' in *Echoes of the Company*, no. 6 (June, 2003), p. 370.

[24] SWLM, A. 31b, p. 831.

to be devoted to the Trinitarian God.[25] During her pilgrimage to Chartres in 1644, Louise prayed that 'Jesus might be the strong and loving bond that unites the hearts of all the Sisters in imitation of the union of the three divine Persons'.[26] In her spiritual testament, she implicitly suggested the Trinity as she exhorted the Sisters to 'live in great union and cordiality, loving one another in imitation of the union and life of Our Lord'.[27]

Louise's spiritual reflections on and notations of her life experiences indicate the importance of the Holy Spirit in her life. She constantly invoked the aid of the Holy Spirit for direction in her decisions, for comfort in her trials, for light in her spiritual darkness and for strength in overcoming her weaknesses.[28] Major experiences in her faith journey occurred at the time of Pentecost – a significant witness to God's providential care of her and the community at Pentecost 1642 when the ceiling in a room which they were about to enter collapsed[29] and her great spiritual *Lumière* or 'Light' of 1623 which she termed her 'profound interior conversion'.[30] At this time, Louise was overwhelmed by great doubts and anxieties because she had failed to fulfil the vow to 'give herself to God' which she had made before she married. She wondered if she should leave her husband and she had serious doubts about the immortality of the soul and her choice of a spiritual director. All this plunged her into a 'dark night of the soul' and she could find no escape from her anguish. On Pentecost Sunday, 1623, when she was praying in the church of St Nicholas des Champs, she received what she called the 'Light' that assured her that she should remain with her husband and one day she would find herself in a community where there would be much coming and going and that God would send her a new spiritual director. At this point she did not yet know that in God's plan for her, this spiritual director would be Vincent de Paul. Meanwhile, she was to live in peace because it was God who had revealed all this to her. All her doubts disappeared immediately. To mark these Pentecostal

---

25 Cf. SWLM, L. 248, p. 289; L. 429, p. 353; L. 447, p. 478.
26 Ibid., L. 111, p. 121.
27 Ibid., p. 835.
28 Cf. SWLM, A. 26, p. 819; L. 118B, p. 339; L. 102, p. 74.
29 Cf. SWLM, A. 75, p. 768.
30 SWLM, p. 1.

experiences, Louise encouraged the sisters to have a great devotion to this feast. She later wrote to Vincent, 'I then thought that our entire family should have great devotion to the Feast of Pentecost and total dependence on divine providence.'[31] She instructed the sisters to prepare for the feast of Pentecost with great attention, by means of novenas and interior recollection. If possible, those at the motherhouse were to make their annual retreat at this time. She herself made an annual retreat in preparation for Pentecost. 'It is true that I have a special affection for the feast of Pentecost and this time of preparation for it is very dear to me.'[32]

Louise's spirituality was Christocentric, being focused on the Word Incarnate, her model of holiness, who empowered her and her sisters to live out their baptismal call and their call to serve Christ in the poor. The many works of charity and services to the poor which she initiated and directed were seen in the context of the Church continuing the mission of Christ, the Lord of Charity. She saw the Church as the source of her sacramental life and liturgical prayer and she prayed in harmony with the liturgical year. She recognised especially the role of the laity and of women in the Church.[33] Central to her sacramental life was the Eucharist through which she experienced her Lord and Spouse intimately. She highlights love of God in the Eucharist, esteem for it, frequent reception of Holy Communion and due preparation for receiving it.[34] Louise's prayer reflections reveal that God guided her and gifted her with the love and union of mystical prayer.[35]

Seal and Motto

The seal of the Daughters of Charity used by Louise de Marillac to attach to her letters since 1643 is one of the expressions of the importance of the cross in the minds and lives of Vincent and Louise. It represents a heart

---

[31] SWLM, A. 75, p. 768.
[32] Ibid., L. 118b, p. 339. (Writing to Vincent.)
[33] She would certainly be in tune with recent Church emphasis on the role of the laity. Cf. Pope John Paul II, *Christifideles Laici:* Post-Synodal Apostolic Exhortation (1990), nos 23, 25.
[34] Cf. SWLM, pp. 766–77.
[35] Frequently the descriptions of her spiritual experiences echo the reflections of St Teresa of Avila and St John of the Cross.

encompassed by flames, with the figure of Jesus crucified superimposed and surrounded by the motto: *The Charity of Jesus crucified urges us.* The charity of Jesus crucified, which is to animate the heart of a Daughter of Charity and set it on fire, urged them to hasten to the relief of every type of human misery.[36] The crucifix is the symbol of God's love as revealed in Jesus. Both Vincent and Louise often dwelt on God's love as the source of all reaching out to others in love. In their reflections on the cross and on the heart of Jesus, both often reminded their followers of the depth and immensity of God's love for each one of us. The final twenty-seven years of Louise's life were totally dedicated to the formation of her Daughters in preparation for their service of the sick poor. The words of St Paul, 'the charity of Christ urges us on', became the underpinning which she adapted to include the *crucified* Christ.[37] Louise possessed a keen awareness of the infinite love of Jesus and a deep realisation that as her model and way to the Father, He is the centre of her heart and love. Here she chose the two most significant symbols of Jesus' love for people: the heart of fire with love and the crucifix. Both symbols are central to Christian spirituality as they point to the deeper reality of God's limitless love for humankind, in having his Son live, die and rise to reconcile the divine–human relationship. The love that enflames the heart of a Daughter of Charity is nothing less than the love of Christ and it is this love that impels them to serve the poor. The motto that Vincent gave to his Vincentian priests and brothers was *Evangelizare pauperibus misit me* (He sent me to evangelise the poor), taking as exemplar the missionary Christ.[38] Vincent and Louise came to see that their charism, the gift given to them by the Holy Spirit for the building up of the Church, the Mystical Body of Christ, was to make the love of God a reality in the lives of the poor.

Contemplatives in Action

Few saints have been as active as Vincent de Paul but his contemporaries regarded him as a contemplative. Louis Abelly, his earliest biographer,

---

[36] Cf. Constitutions of the Daughters of Charity, p. 15 (Henceforward D. C. Con., 2004).
[37] 2 Cor 5:14.
[38] Cf. Lk 4:18–19; Isa 61:2.

writes, 'His spirit was continually attentive to the presence of God.'[39] The union of contemplation and action is one of the most important keys to Vincentian spirituality; the Constitutions of both the Vincentians and the Daughters of Charity testify to this. It is an apostolic spirituality, holding prayer and action in creative tension. 'The same love inspires and directs their contemplation and their service; in faith they know that God awaits them in those who suffer.'[40] When the Vincentian moves from prayer to service and vice versa, he or she is 'leaving God for God'. In this way the followers of Louise and Vincent are called to live in 'uninterrupted dialogue with God', which helps to maintain unity of life. Contemplatives in action, Vincentians are called – as indeed are all Christians – to pass on the fruits of their contemplation to others. It is through contemplative prayer that Christians learn to discern events in the light of the gospel.

In an appropriate echo of what Vincent has taught, Pope John Paul II understands contemplation as 'fixing our gaze on the face of Christ'.[41] Unless the person of Christ is contemplated it is not possible to see through the lens of faith, nor is it possible to see the face of Christ etched in the suffering members of His Mystical Body.[42] 'The Christ encountered in contemplation is the same Christ who lives and suffers in the poor.'[43] Vincent described prayer as 'an intimate conversation between the soul and God'.[44] Prayer and apostolic life must be integrated.[45] Since we cannot love God abstractly, compassion moves us to share this love in concrete situations with our sisters and brothers. In prayer a person discerns the will of God and God's presence in the poor. 'To leave one work of God to perform another, either of greater obligation or greater merit, is not to

---

[39] Louis Abelly, *The Life of the Venerable Servant of God: Vincent De Paul: Founder and First Superior General of the Congregation of the Mission,* 3 vols., iii, Ch. VI, p. 49.

[40] D.C. Con., 2004, 7b.

[41] Cf. Pope John Paul II, *Novo Millennio Ineunte (At the Beginning of the New Millennium):* Apostolic Letter (2001), par. 16.

[42] Cf. Pope John Paul II, *Starting Afresh From Christ: A Renewed Committment to Consecrated Life in the Third Millenium:* Instruction for Institutes of Consecrated Life and Societies of Apostolic Life (2002), par. 25.

[43] Pope John Paul II, *Vita Consecrata: The Consecrated Life and its Mission in the Church and the World* (1996), par. 82.

[44] Coste, IX, p. 419.

[45] Cf. Coste, XI, p. 40; III, pp. 345–7.

leave God.'[46] This explicit statement and lived reality of the correspondence between finding 'God in the poor' and 'God in prayer' may well
be Vincent's most original and distinctive contribution to the history of
spirituality.[47] The Daughters of Charity are to honour the humanity of Jesus
through their service of the poor. That is why Vincent counselled them to
'leave God for God':

> My Daughters, remember that when you leave prayer and Holy Mass
> to serve the poor, you are losing nothing, because serving the poor
> is going to God and you should see God in them.[48]

Vincent's model was Christ who is constantly before the Father in prayer.
He was utterly convinced of the importance of the union of action and
contemplation that he saw in Christ. He told his followers that stability in
their vocation and the ongoing vitality of their works depended on prayer.

> Give me a man of prayer and he will be capable of everything ... The
> Congregation will last as long as it faithfully carries out the practice
> of prayer which is like an impregnable rampart shielding the
> missionaries from all manner of attack.[49]

Several times he alluded to the fact that Jesus prayed so frequently
especially on all the important occasions in his ministry. 'The apostolic
action of the Daughters of Charity draws its strength from contemplation,
after the example of the Son of God, who, intimately united with his Father,
often went aside to pray.'[50] Vincent urged Louise to form the young Sisters
very well in prayer.[51] He himself gave several practical conferences to them
on the subject. 'Prayer is for the soul what food is for the body ... it is
refreshment in the midst of difficult daily work in the service of the poor.'[52]

---

[46] Coste, III, p. 83.
[47] Cf. Kathryn B. LaFleur SP, *Louise de Marillac: A Light in the Darkness* (New York: New City Press, 1996), p. 162.
[48] Coste, I, p. 284.
[49] Ibid., III, p. 535; Cf. also IX, p. 416; X, p. 583.
[50] D.C. Con., 21a.
[51] Cf. Coste, IV, p. 47.
[52] Coste, IX, p. 416.

Vincent and Louise repeatedly urged the sisters to make prayer a priority: 'Always do what you can so that prayer being your first occupation, your mind may be filled with God for the rest of the day.'[53] The Daughters of Charity were to witness by their prayer as well as by their service. Vincent stated, 'The spiritual life is important, we have to cultivate it; if we fail in this matter, we fail in everything.'[54]

For the Daughters of Charity, prayer before all else is to be the contemplation of Christ in the self-emptying of his redemptive Incarnation: contemplation of the concrete circumstances of the life of Christ who in a spirit of profound humility, washed the feet of his disciples. 'The sisters contemplate in Christ those dispositions which will draw them closer to the most deprived, endeavouring to make them a part of their lives.'[55] Their lives are an act of worship, which reflects their commitment to the poor. 'In praising God, listening to God's word, entreating God, they act not only in their own name but in the name of all humanity, whose joys, hopes, sadness and anguish they bear. They offer themselves with Jesus Christ in the memorial of his Paschal Mystery.'[56]

Divine Providence and the Will of God

Reflecting on the principal events that have taken place in this Company, it seems to me, and this is quite evident, that if they had taken place before they did, they would not have been successful. That is why I have a particular devotion to following the adorable providence of God step by step. ... I think Our Lord alone has carried on and is constantly carrying on the business of the Little Company.[57]

Trust in divine providence and seeking the will of God in all things are the hallmarks of the spirituality of Vincent and Louise. Their letters and

---

[53] Coste, I, p. 29.
[54] Ibid., XII, p. 131.
[55] D. C. Con., 13.
[56] Ibid., 19c.
[57] Coste, II, p. 208. (Referring to the Company of the Daughters of Charity.)

writings allow considerable insight into how they understood providence and God's will in their lives. 'What great hidden treasures there are in holy providence and how marvellously Our Lord is honoured by those who follow it and do not try to get ahead of it!'[58] Vincent was utterly convinced that for those who love God and seek to do his will, 'all things work together for good' (Romans 8:28). 'Let us place ourselves in complete dependence on God, with confidence that in doing that, everything which people say or do against us will work out for the good.'[59] The two foundations of Vincent's teaching on divine providence are confidence in God and indifference. Indifference for him was detachment from all things that would keep us from God.[60] 'We should have great confidence in divine providence seeing that it takes care of all that concerns us, just as a nursing mother takes care of her baby.'[61] Indifference frees us to be united to God,[62] disposing us to will only what he wills. It is indispensably linked with trust in providence: 'What a happiness to will nothing but what God wills, to do nothing but what is in accord with the occasion providence presents.'[63] Vincent is profoundly convinced that because God loves us deeply, he exercises a continual providence in our lives. 'Follow the order of providence. Oh! how good it is to let ourselves be guided by it!'[64] The close link between doing the will of God and following providence is a recurrent theme in Vincent's letters and conferences. We must 'will what divine providence wills' is one of the ways he puts it, combining the two themes.[65] He tells his missionaries, 'Perfection consists in so uniting our will to God's that his will and ours, properly speaking, form only one will.'[66] His writings are replete with references, both implicit and explicit, to the providence of God for his children. 'The things of God come about by themselves and wisdom consists in following providence step by step.'[67]

---

58 Coste, I, p. 68.
59 Ibid., IV, p. 393.
60 Cf. Coste, XII, p. 228.
61 Ibid., X, p. 503.
62 Cf. Coste, XII, pp. 229–30.
63 Ibid., III, p. 193.
64 Ibid., I, p. 26.
65 Ibid., VI, p. 476.
66 Ibid., XI, p. 318.
67 Ibid. II, pp. 472–3.

He spoke frequently to the Daughters of Charity about the importance of seeking and doing the will of God and trusting in divine providence. 'Give me a Daughter of Charity who does for her whole life the will of God ... She begins her paradise even in this world.'[68]

A desire to imitate Jesus in doing the will of his Father was also an underlying theme in many of Louise de Marillac's writings.

> I choose your holy will as the directing force of my life. I shall recognise it by reflecting on the life which your Son led upon earth, to which I shall strive to conform my own ... May your will alone be the rule of my life.[69]

Louise endeavoured to imitate two specific qualities of Jesus: his desire to do the will of God and his trusting abandonment to the providence of God. These characteristics were the hallmarks not only of Louise's attitude to suffering but also of her entire spirituality. Three months before her death, she wrote,

> If you completely entrust everything to the guidance of divine providence and love the most holy will of God, this will contribute greatly to your peace of mind and heart. This is one of the most essential practices I know of for growth in holiness.[70]

Louise knew that abandonment to providence required a great leap of faith, 'If I were not being led in this matter by divine providence, I would be most apprehensive.'[71] Her union with Jesus on the Cross was to be with an attitude of submission to God's will and trusting in his loving providence. In many of her letters, the will of God, the cross and providence were united as one theme. She believed, not in suffering for its own sake but in redemptive suffering, sharing in the Paschal Mystery of Christ. She counselled the sisters to seek the will of God and to find it in a special way in obedience to legitimate authority. Both Louise and Vincent were convinced that God was at work in the events that occur and saw the cross

---

[68] Coste, IX, p. 645.
[69] SWLM, A. 15, p. 713.
[70] Ibid., L. 643, p. 662.
[71] Ibid., L. 267, p. 309.

as a part of God's providence. Both of them bore their crosses as part of God's providence.

> Grace has its moments. Let us abandon ourselves to the providence of God and be on our guard against anticipating it ... it seems to me that we have tried to follow divine providence in all things and to put our feet only in the place it has marked out for us.[72]

Identification of Christ with the Poor – Our Lords and Masters

'He who has a *why* to live for can bear almost any *how*.'[73] Grounded in a realism born of personal experience, Vincent de Paul did not have a romantic vision of the poor. Through the lens of faith, he saw them as sacraments of Christ. It was this faith vision that motivated the *why* and the *how* of his service of them. He recognised that sometimes they present a repulsive exterior but he took this to be the presence of Jesus within each person.[74]

> I should not judge poor peasants, men or women, by their exterior nor by their mental capacities. All the more is this so as very frequently they scarcely seem to have the appearance or mental capacity of reasonable beings, so gross and earthly are they. But turn the medal and you will see by the light of faith that the Son of God, whose will it was to be poor, is represented to us by these creatures.[75]

The faith vision of Vincent and Louise moves beyond the outward appearance of every disfigured face in order to discover therein the icon of Christ:

> Christ – for Christ plays in ten thousand places,
> Lovely in limbs, and lovely in eyes not his
> To the Father through the features of men's faces.[76]

---

[72] Coste, II, p. 453.
[73] V. E. Frankl, *Man's Search for Meaning: An Introduction to Logotherapy* (New York, 1946), p. 121.
[74] Coste, IV, pp. 42–3; IX, p. 252; X, p. 332, pp. 679–80; XI, p. 32.
[75] Ibid., XI, p. 32.
[76] G. M. Hopkins, 'Sonnet 34' in *The Major Poems*, W. Davies, ed., (London: Dent, 1979), p. 88.

The first motive to serve the poor is that God loves them and they are sacraments of the suffering Christ – a motivation which is theological and Christological and not just humanitarian. Because the poor are sacraments of Christ it is not a question of bringing Christ to them since he is there already. Evangelisation means helping them to become aware of his presence. That is why Vincent held out an alternative world, a world where the poor are the real 'lords and masters' and the sisters are their servants, a world where the key attitudes are humility, simplicity, and charity and where the cross is the royal road.[77] It is an upside-down world where the last are first and the first last. In drafting the Rule for the Daughters of Charity, Vincent wrote, 'They should cherish the poor as their masters, since Our Lord is in them, and they in Our Lord.'[78] He repeated the same theme to the priests and brothers of the Mission:

> Let us go then, my brothers, and work with a new love in the service
> of the poor, looking even for the poorest and the most abandoned,
> recognising before God that they are our lords and masters and that
> we are unworthy to render them our small services.[79]

While the Christ of Vincent is 'Lord' and 'Son of God', he lives in the person of the poor and continues to suffer in them. Vincent frequently cited Matthew 25:31–46 to reinforce the identification of Jesus with the poor:

> So this is what obliges you to serve them with respect, as your
> masters, and with devotion: that they represent for you the person
> of Our Lord, who said: 'Whatever you do for one of these the least
> of my brethren, I will consider it as done to me.'[80]

Louise's letters and counsels to her sisters attest to her deep conviction that the poor are indeed the continued incarnation of Christ in the world and must be treated as he himself deserved:

> Where is the gentleness and charity that you must preserve so
> carefully when dealing with our dear masters, the sick poor? If we

---

[77] Cf. Coste, IX, p. 119; X, p. 332.
[78] Coste, XIII, p. 540.
[79] Ibid., XI, p. 393.
[80] Ibid., X, p. 332. Cf. also, X, pp. 679–80; XIII, pp. 805–6.

deviate in the slightest from the conviction that they are the members of Jesus Christ, it will infallibly lead to the weakening of these beautiful virtues in us.[81]

Jesus led Louise to the poor suffering members of his Body and they in turn led her to a deeper union with Jesus. All of her service to the poor was centred in Jesus, in imitation of his ministry to them and in seeing him in them: 'Oh, how true it is that souls who seek God will find him everywhere but especially in the poor.'[82]

The Spirit of Humility, Simplicity and Charity

Jeanne, you will soon discover that Charity is a heavy burden to bear … heavier than the soup pot or the basket of bread … But you must always keep your gentleness and your smile. It is not everything to give soup and bread. The rich can do the same. It is only because of your love, because of your love alone … that the poor will forgive you for the bread you give them.[83]

The most characteristic feature of the Daughters of Charity was not to be their service of the poor, as there are numerous associations whose objective is the assistance and promotion of underprivileged and marginalised groups, but the distinctive spirit which their founders gave them and which consisted of the practice of the virtues of humility, simplicity and charity:

I repeat once more Sisters, that the spirit of your Company consists in the love of Our Lord, love for the poor, love of one another, humility and simplicity. It would be far better that there should be no Daughters of Charity if they lacked these virtues.[84]

This 'spirit' of the Company is something which Vincent perfected over a period of twenty years. The Company had a very precise aim from the

---

[81] SWLM, L. 104b, p. 113.
[82] Ibid., L. 292, p. 431.
[83] These words from the script of the film *Monsieur Vincent* are a paraphrase of similar statements made by Vincent in various contexts.
[84] Coste, IX, p. 596.

first moment of its existence in 1633, yet the three conferences to the sisters on their spirit were given by Vincent only in February 1653. Therefore, he tried to motivate them to live this spirit before he defined and explained it in precise terms. The Constitutions faithfully reflect the thinking of the founders when they state:

> The evangelical virtues of humility, simplicity, and charity are the path along which the Daughters of Charity should allow themselves to be guided by the Holy Spirit. The Sisters contemplate in Christ those dispositions which will draw them close to the most deprived and they endeavour to make these dispositions a part of their own lives.[85]

These virtues are apostolic, oriented towards service. They are to be the soul which animates the body, empowering the Daughters to live an incarnational spirituality of 'servants'. Their exemplar is the humble, simple and charitable Christ. 'They are particularly attentive to the person of Christ and to his attitude towards the humble and oppressed. In focusing on Jesus Christ, they are guided by the example and teaching of their Founders.'[86] This specific spirit is to be the distinctive mark that distinguishes the Daughters as 'Servants of the Poor'. There is a close connection between the three dispositions of Christ – Adorer of the Father, Servant of his loving plan, Evangeliser of the poor – and these three virtues. Vincent saw the adoration Jesus pays to his Father as a sign of his humility. The virtue of humility was an invitation to increasingly imitate Jesus and become 'Adorers of the Father' through prayer and through encountering people and events.[87] Vincent urged his followers to contemplate 'that admirable model of humility, Our Lord Jesus Christ'.[88] Humility, which Christ teaches by word and example, entails the recognition that all good comes from God,[89] an acknowledgment of our own lowliness and faults and a deep confidence in God.[90] It involves loving the hidden life, avoiding worldly applause and taking the last place. It is the origin of all the good

---

[85] D.C. Con., 13.
[86] Ibid., 22a, 22b.
[87] Cf. Coste, XI, p. 394.
[88] Coste, I, p. 182: VII, pp. 98–9.
[89] Cf. Coste, III, p. 279; V, p. 165.
[90] Cf. Coste, IX, p. 674.

that we do;[91] entails having a 'servant' attitude, ready, in imitation of Jesus, to wash one another's feet[92] and called like him to 'serve and not to be served'.[93] The Daughters of Charity witness to it by allowing themselves to be evangelised by the poor.

For Vincent, simplicity consisted in purity of intention, referring things to God alone and was closely linked with humility. This virtue challenges all to become more and more servants of the Father's loving plan. It implies living authentically and transparently.[94] 'Simplicity is my gospel.'[95] Simplicity is 'the virtue I love most'.[96] Charity is a path which leads to becoming 'evangelisers of the poor'. Vincent, Apostle of Charity, and Louise, Patroness of all Social Works[97] witnessed to charity in its threefold dimension: 'Love of Our Lord, love of the poor, love for one another.'[98] Vincent compared these three forms of charity to a robe that should adorn the Company: 'Love of God is the top part; the middle part is love of one's neighbour and of the poor; and the lower part is the love you have for one another. Ah! what a beautiful wedding garment.'[99] Charity is a theological virtue. We are to love God and our neighbour because God first loved us with an unconditional love.[100] For Vincent, Christ was the source and model of all charity.

> The principal end for which God has called and established the Daughters of Charity is to honour Our Lord Jesus Christ as the source and model of all charity; serving him corporally and spiritually in the person of the poor.[101]

Vincent affirmed that all Christians must practise these three virtues but 'Daughters of Charity are bound to practise them in a very special manner', in order to live in conformity with the name they bear.[102]

---

[91] Cf. Jn 13:12–15.
[92] Cf. Mt 20:28.
[93] Cf. D.C. Con., 18b.
[94] Cf. Coste IX, p. 606.
[95] Ibid., I, p. 284.
[96] Ibid., p. 285.
[97] Proclaimed by Pope John XXIII, 10 February 1960.
[98] Cf. Coste IX, pp. 595–6.
[99] Ibid., X, p. 473.
[100] Cf. 1 Jn 4:10, 16, 19; Rom 5:5; 8:15.
[101] D.C. Common Rules (1866), 1.1.
[102] Coste, IX, p. 59, 593; XI, p. 364.

Integral Liberation: Corporal and Spiritual Welfare

Vincent taught that two characteristics of the service of the poor should be to have a holistic approach, serving them corporally and spiritually[103] and with a love that is both affective and effective.[104] Repeatedly, he spoke of evangelisation by word and work. He told the Daughters of Charity that their works must be accompanied by words of faith, so that as well as tending to the bodily needs they must share their faith by witness and words.[105] Vincent also reminded his priests and brothers that they must not think of their mission in exclusively spiritual terms, 'Let us love God, but let it be in the strength of our arms and the sweat of our brow.'[106] The evangelist, Matthew (25:31–46) proclaims that the central criterion for judgment is whether or not we have actually shared with the poor when they were hungry, thirsty, homeless, naked, or imprisoned. That is why the Church and the Vincentian groups call their members to solidarity with the poor and challenge them to make a preferential but not an exclusive option for the poor.[107] When discussing the spirit of the Company with the sisters, Vincent emphasised the necessity of 'affective and effective' love:

> The affective love of God passes on to effective love which is the service of the poor ... The love of Daughters of Charity is not only tender, it is effective, because they serve the poor effectively, both in body and soul. You are bound to teach them how to lead a good life ... this is what marks you off from many religious who tend the body only ... You should bring two sorts of food to the sick poor: food for the body and food for the soul ... you should speak a few words to them, the fruit of your mental prayer, for their instruction ... and there, my dear Sisters, you have the essence of affective and effective love; to serve Our Lord in his members both corporally and spiritually and to do so in their own homes, or indeed in whatever place to which providence may send you.[108]

---

[103] Cf. Coste, IX, p. 475, 592, 599; XI, p. 40.

[104] Cf. Coste, IX, p. 59, 593; XI, p. 592, 364.

[105] Cf. Coste, XI, p. 40; Cf. Pope Benedict XVI, *Porta Fidei:* Apostolic Letter (2012), No. 14.

[106] Coste, IX, p. 364.

[107] Today, we find our founders' preferential option for the poor echoed in several contemporary Church documents. Cf. Pope John Paul II, *Redemptoris Mater* (1987), no. 37; *Sollicitudo Rei Socialis* (1987), no. 42; Pope Benedict XVI, *Deus Caritas Est* (2005), nos 17, 18.

[108] Coste, IX, p. 364.

The emphasis in the Vincentian tradition from its origins to the present day is on practical, concrete charity with the accent on effective love which draws its strength from the affective love experienced through union with God, in Jesus through prayer. Without this dimension one is merely engaging in horizontal humanism. Vincent gives pride of place to charity as 'queen of the virtues'.[109] Genuine charity goes beyond the limits of strict justice, embracing broader horizons. A social order based solely on justice lacks heart. For Vincent, these two virtues were indissolubly linked, 'In what does our perfection consist? ... in doing all our actions well ... speaking well to our neighbour and acting justly towards him.'[110] Vincent was moved by charity to help innumerable people but also by a sense of justice to champion their rights by challenging the status quo, 'in helping them [the poor], we are doing an act of justice and not of mercy'.[111] For members of the Vincentian family, love and compassion which are immeasurable are always to hold the primacy over justice which is measured. Before being advocates for justice, the followers of Vincent and Louise must speak to people of the boundless, gratuitous love of a Trinitarian God for each one. Words of good news will be credible only to the extent that they are accompanied by works of justice, love and peace.[112] Catholic social teaching today states that action on behalf of justice is a constitutive element in the preaching and living of the gospel.[113]

Vincent and Louise saw evangelisation and human promotion as complementary, a vision which is mirrored in Catholic social teaching today as the Church, in committing itself to the 'new evangelisation' strives to become more a church of the poor.[114] Focus on and commitment to Christ as Evangeliser of the poor is at the heart of Vincentian spirituality. One of the great gifts of Vincent and Louise was the ability to mobilise others to

---

[109] Coste, IX, p. 286.
[110] Ibid., XII, p. 77.
[111] Ibid., VII, p. 98.
[112] Cf. Coste, VII, pp. 98, 620, where Vincent speaks of the importance of works of justice.
[113] Cf. Pope John Paul II, *Dives in Misericordiae* (1980), nos 12, 19; Pope Benedict XVI, *Deus Caritas Est* (2005), no. 20.
[114] Today the unity between evangelisation and human promotion is one of the lynchpins in the Church's social teaching. Cf. Pope John Paul II, *Sollicitudo Rei Socialis* (1987), no. 46; *Centesimus Annus* (1991), nos 5, 26.

serve Christ in the poorest. To this end they gathered together rich and poor, women and men, clergy and laity. For both of them, the *quality* of service of the poor is most important.

> Their principal employment being to serve the poor sick, they shall acquit themselves of it with all possible care and attention, considering that it is not so much to them as to Jesus Christ that they render service; on this account, they shall carry them food and remedies themselves; treating them with compassion, mildness, cordiality, respect and devotion.[115]

In addition to the three virtues he gave to the sisters, Vincent exhorted his priests and brothers to cultivate and practise the virtues of meekness, mortification and zeal. For him, the virtue of meekness entails being approachable and affable towards those with whom one comes in contact.[116] It combines gentleness and firmness.[117] It is based on respect for the human person.[118]

> Meekness makes us not only excuse the affronts and injustices we receive but even inclines us to treat with gentleness those from whom we receive them, by means of kind words and should they go so far as to abuse us and even strike us on the face, it makes us endure all for God.[119]

Vincent said people are won over more by gentleness and forgiveness than by argument. 'If a man is not won over by meekness and patience, it will be difficult to win him over in any other way.'[120] Mortification of which Jesus is the exemplar aims at indifference and detachment and features prominently in his conferences.[121] Zeal for spreading the kingdom of God, expressed through practical love enflamed the hearts of Vincent and

---

[115] D. C. Common Rules (1866), 11.1.
[116] Cf. Coste, XII, p. 189.
[117] Ibid.,VII, p. 226.
[118] Ibid., IX, p. 269.
[119] Ibid., XII, p. 192.
[120] Ibid., VII, p. 226.
[121] Cf. Coste, X, p. 282; XII, p. 20; Cf. also IX, p. 170; X, pp. 61, 398.

Louise. 'If the love of God is the fire, zeal is the flame. If love is the sun, then zeal is its ray.'[122] Although he challenges his followers to be zealous in their service of God's chosen ones, Vincent also counsels against indiscreet zeal.[123] He enumerates motivations for and means of practising all these virtues.

The vocation of a Daughter of Charity is to replicate the vocation of Christ the Servant. The service the sisters offer must be imbued with and characterised by the virtues of their state as outlined above. It is the *why* and the *how* a sister carries out her service of the poor which is the expression of her total gift to God that is important. The Daughters of Charity, 'servants of the poor', must accomplish this service with a 'servant' attitude which springs from and is nourished by contemplating Christ, the Servant, who came not to be served but to serve and Mary, the Handmaid, 'teacher of the spiritual life'. 'Whatever their particular type of work and level of professional competence, the sisters maintain towards persons who are poor an attitude of servant, which implies the practice of the virtues of their state: humility, simplicity and charity.'[124]

The mission of the Church calls the Daughters of Charity to reveal to the poor the preferential love God has for them. That is why they must serve them as they would serve Christ himself. 'This service nourishes their contemplation and gives meaning to their community life.'[125] The spirit of the Company colours in a specific way the following of Christ and comes from the contemplation of Christ as the compassionate face of God. This is the Christ who is the foundation, the centre, the rule and the *raison d'être* of the members of the Vincentian family. Central to the spirit of the Vincentian family is the dignity of the individual who is a member of the Mystical Body of Christ. This truth must never be forgotten as it is the touchstone of the Vincentian mission of service to the poor.

---

[122] Coste, XII, pp. 262, 307–8.
[123] Cf. Coste, I, 84, 96; II, 140; X, 671.
[124] D.C. Con., 24d; Cf. Con., 50, 51b also.
[125] Ibid., 16b.

Be very gentle and courteous towards your poor. We must love them tenderly and respect them deeply. It is not enough for these maxims to be in our minds; we must bear witness to them by our gentle and charitable care.[126]

Vincentian Marian Devotion

Devotion to Mary is a very distinctive strand woven throughout the multicoloured tapestry which expresses the many facets of Vincentian spirituality and is an integral part of it. For Vincent and Louise finding in Mary the inspiration to follow Christ was the motive for their devotional practices in her honour.[127] For both of them the central focus of their spiritual lives is found in the mysteries of the Blessed Trinity and the Incarnation. It is within this framework that they integrate their Marian devotion. The writings and correspondence of Louise are replete with references to Mary. She records the fruits of her meditations and reflections on the eminent dignity of Mary and presents her as God's collaborator in the Incarnation, participating in the mystery of God in Jesus. The mystery which she liked most to contemplate was Mary's Immaculate Conception. She gives thanks and praise to the Trinity 'for choosing the Blessed Virgin to be so closely united to the Godhead'.[128] Her reflection on the Immaculate Conception captures perfectly what the Church would later teach about this mystery.[129] Louise presents Mary to the sisters as teacher and exemplar of the spiritual life in several of her writings and letters and in some passages which deal with different Marian mysteries, especially her Immaculate Conception, her Virginity, her divine Motherhood and her collaboration in the work of Redemption.[130] The sisters are to contemplate Mary in order to learn from her how to be humble servants, faithful to the

---

[126] SWLM, L. 284b, p. 320.

[127] St Vincent used to go barefoot to the Marian Shrine of Buglose, near Pouy, his place of birth near Dax, in the Landes area in the southwest of France and he went on a Marian pilgrimage to Chartres in 1629; he used to fast on the vigil of some of the feasts of Our Lady and prayed the rosary and the angelus daily.

[128] SWLM, p. 819.

[129] Ibid., p. 830. A. 31B; The Dogma of the Immaculate Conception defined by Pope Pius IX in *Ineffabilis Deus:* papal bull (8 Dec. 1854).

[130] Ibid. Cf. pp. 693, 730, 805, 819.

Father's designs. The angelus reminds them of the mystery of the Incarnation and of Mary's readiness to listen to and welcome the Word Incarnate. 'The Founders inculcated in the Daughters of Charity the love and imitation of the Virgin Mary, inviting them to contemplate her as the humble, faithful Servant of the Father's plan, and model of the poor in spirit.'[131]

It was Louise's firm belief in the effective intercession of Mary that led her to go on pilgrimage to Chartres in October 1644. Here she confided to Mary two things she was most concerned about: her own son and the Company of the Daughters of Charity. She begged Our Lady whom she had named the guardian and only Mother of the Company to obtain for its members the grace of purity and fidelity and mutual love for one another.[132] On her deathbed, in the closing words of her Spiritual Testament, Louise strongly urged the sisters to 'pray earnestly to the Blessed Virgin that she may be your only Mother'.[133] The most dynamic act of fidelity for the Daughters of Charity is the annual renovation of their vows which they renew on the feast of the Annunciation. Louise made this renovation on that day and the custom was introduced in 1642. The devotion to Mary of the members of the Vincentian family must be inspired by and based on the mysteries of Mary's life. This devotion is expressed as filial love, trusting prayer, praise and gratitude in the spirit of Mary's Magnificat.[134] The traditional practices of saying the rosary and the angelus were something which the founders cherished.[135] The current Constitutions

---

[131] D. C. Con., 15b.

[132] To this day, the Daughters of Charity continue to go on pilgrimage to Chartres to honour Mary and seek her intercession. From 1658 onwards and on the initiative of Louise, the Company has kept up the practice of renewing the consecration of the Company to Mary on the feast of the Immaculate Conception. Added later was the Act of Consecration of 1 January, feast of Mary, Mother of God, bringing together the two Marian mysteries closest to the heart of Louise.

[133] SWLM, p. 823.

[134] Mary's apparitions to St Catherine Labouré in 1830, have had a decisive influence on the life of all groups belonging to the Vincentian family and on the direction that their Marian spirituality has taken. Several groups belonging to this family have their origins in these apparitions.

[135] Cf. Coste, IX, p. 220; X, pp. 620–3. In her Rule of Life before the foundation of the Daughters of Charity, Louise lists several devotional practices in honour of Mary – the Office of the Blessed Virgin; a quarter of an hour's prayer at midday to honour the moment when the Word took flesh in Mary's womb; saying five decades of the rosary each day and meditating on one of its mysteries; renewing her vows and good resolutions every first Saturday of each month and fasting on the eve of all feasts of Our Lady.

of the Daughters of Charity that relate to Mary express the Company's fidelity to the thinking of the Founders and also are enriched by recent Church teachings on Our Lady.[136]

In Vincent's conferences and letters we find many references to Mary and to her virtues which he exhorts the sisters to emulate. 'The Blessed Virgin must be your example.'[137] He concentrates mainly on three mysteries in the life of Mary: the Immaculate Conception, the Annunciation and the Visitation. 'Let us pray to the Blessed Virgin who, better than anyone else, has penetrated to the heart of the gospel maxims and put them into practice.'[138]

Conclusion

The concept of the Vincentian charism is not linked exclusively to the times in which Vincent and Louise lived. It is a dynamic reality, recreated in each era; continually rediscovered and enriched by the vitality of the faithful responses that each person, each community and each organisation makes to the Holy Spirit. For almost four hundred years, the Vincentian spiritual heritage has been treasured by religious and lay organisations, its unifying dynamic being the love and service of the poor. Vincentian spirituality is distinctive but not separate from mainstream gospel and Church teachings. A spirituality of service, punctuated by concrete, practical charity, it continues to have a wide-ranging appeal for both lay and religious organisations. Rooted in the Gospels and in the teaching of Vincent de Paul and Louise de Marillac and drawing its vitality and energy from the wisdom and holiness of their lived experience and from the values and principles which they prized so highly and passed on so faithfully to their followers, it has stood the test of time and is as valid and relevant today as it was in the seventeenth century.[139] Its unassuming, simple and humble

---

[136] Cf. Pope Paul VI, *Marialis Cultus* (1974), nos. 17, 21.

[137] Coste, IX, p. 87.

[138] Ibid., XII, p. 129.

[139] Cf. Catherine Prendergast DC, 'Deus Caritas Est and the Daughters of Charity: Looking anew at the Vincentian Charism' in Eoin G. Cassidy, ed., *Who is my Neighbour? Deus Caritas Est: An Encyclical for Our Times?* (Dublin: Veritas, 2009), pp. 41–55. Here, we see that much of the teaching and key themes of Vincent and Louise are reflected in *Deus Caritas Est:* Encyclical letter of Pope Benedict XVI (2005).

character continues to have a remarkable freshness and appeal. It is a visible, tangible testimony to Christ, 'the way, the truth and the life' and to the presence of the kingdom of God among us.[140]

'When God established the Company of the Daughters of Charity, He gave them a spirit of their own. It is the spirit that animates the body.'[141] The four Daughters of Charity who were the first to set foot on Irish soil in 1855 and whose story will be recounted in this volume, having braved the choppy November waters of the English Channel and the Irish Sea as they journeyed to Drogheda, embodied and were animated and energised by this same spirit of Vincent and Louise. This was the driving force of all their endeavours to alleviate human suffering in its myriad forms and to reveal the tenderness of a God of compassion as they constantly took Christ as their model of charity par excellence. They began the weaving and interweaving of yet another panel in the constantly unfolding Vincentian tapestry – the Irish panel, woven of Celtic threads: French, Irish and Welsh, of varying colours and textures. The many dark threads of the poverty, destitution, despair and hunger of so many of our people in post-Famine Ireland were interwoven and embellished with many threads of brighter hues – threads of the generosity, welcome, warm-heartedness and gratitude of the people of Drogheda and beyond.

Today, each Daughter of Charity and each member of the wider Vincentian family throughout the world, continues the weaving. Each one's thread is only a snippet of an eternal spool with which the divine weaver is weaving a multicoloured design – God's dream for us. Just one small snippet but a unique, unrepeatable and essential snippet without which the tapestry cannot be complete or whole. Vincent loved to remind us that God is 'the Author of your Company'.[142] In response to this divine call, and nourished and sustained by our Vincentian spirit, we strive today to rediscover and revitalise the inspiration and intuitions of our founders so that we may dynamically and creatively give shape to the new as we embrace the ever-changing and challenging context of our times in

---

[140] Jn 14:6
[141] Coste, IX, p. 582.
[142] Coste, IX, p. 113.

proclaiming anew the perennial truth of the gospel while trusting in the unfolding of the divine design.

> And that, Sisters, was the beginning of your Company. As it was not then what it is now, there is reason to believe that it is still not what it will be when God has perfected it as He wants it.[143]

From small, humble, mustard-seed beginnings, the Company has grown into a mighty tree of Charity, spreading its branches to ninety-five countries. May the current of the 'mysticism of Christ in the poor' continue to flow, nourishing, energising and sustaining us as we drink from our own wells, the wells of our Vincentian heritage, whose source and destiny is the ocean of God's abundant love.

---

[143] Coste, IX, p. 245.

Introduction

This collection of essays aims to reconstruct the events surrounding the introduction of the Daughters of Charity to Ireland in the nineteenth century and the subsequent development of their ministries. The charism of their founders, Vincent de Paul and Louise de Marillac, enabled the Daughters of Charity to commit to serving the weakest and most marginalised in society.

The prologue introduces Vincentian spirituality. This spirituality permeates the life of a Daughter of Charity, 'given to God in community for the service of the poor'. The sisters take four vows: chastity, poverty, obedience and service of the poor and they strive to live the virtues of humility, simplicity and charity.

The arrival of the first four Daughters of Charity to Drogheda, Ireland in November 1855 is recounted in Chapter One. Each subsequent foundation had its own unique story, which is explored by the authors in the various chapters. Beginnings were invariably small, usually without public fanfare and in most cases could be described as brave if not foolhardy undertakings.

The Ladies' Association of Charity of St Vincent de Paul as outlined in Chapter Two, worked among the people who lived in abject poverty in the post-Famine era in the slums of inner-city Dublin.

The foundation story of St Vincent's, North William Street, Dublin, with its ministries of parish mission, education and pastoral work, began in 1857, as described in Chapter Three. The devotional practices including Marian devotion are part of the fabric of life of the Daughters of Charity and are portrayed in Chapter Four.

The common thread which runs through the foundation stories are the role of local sponsors and benefactors, the active cooperation of authorities both church and state, the support of individual bishops and clergy and above all the welcome that was extended by the people to the Daughters of Charity. The works the sisters were invited to undertake were, in many cases, new to the district, such as the hospital for the mentally ill in Fairview, Dublin, which is the content of Chapter Five.

By contrast, Chapter Six illustrates how the Daughters of Charity undertook the administration of the North Infirmary Hospital in Cork, which had been in existence since 1751. Here the reader follows the story from 1867 to its becoming a teaching hospital in 1895 and on to its closure in 1987.

The sisters became involved in education in St Mary's Dunmanway, Co. Cork. They built a 'community house' and a parish primary school, the first building project undertaken by the sisters since their arrival in Ireland. This is the content of Chapter Seven.

While the term 'instruments of social change' was not yet in vogue, the pioneer sisters in each instance worked to effect real improvements in people's lives and Chapter Eight recounts the Daughters of Charity's cooperation with the state when they became employees in workhouse infirmaries. Their novel work for children with severe learning difficulties is explored in detail in Chapter Nine, describing the development of a workhouse for children into a centre specialising in education in St Vincent's Cabra, Dublin.

During their first fifty years in Ireland, the Daughters of Charity were represented in practically every arena of social work, education and health care. Chapter Ten gives a detailed account of the provision of accommodation for discharged female prisoners, which was based in Our Lady's, Henrietta Street, Dublin.

The foundation of the Daughters of Charity in Belfast provided opportunities for the sisters to serve in education, home visitation, hostel work and the care of migrant workers. Chapter Eleven provides an overview of these initiatives that were at the cutting edge of the provision of care for young people in the most industrialised city in Ireland at the end of the nineteenth century. This is illustrated effectively in the description of the education provided for the 'half-timers' in Belfast.

As members of an international community many of the early Daughters of Charity in Ireland had mission experience in France and further afield. Chapter Twelve gives a flavour of the large numbers of Irish-born sisters who served part of or all their lives overseas. Appendix I lists the names of many of these sisters and their places of mission.

In the decades before the 1850s, young Irish women joined the Daughters of Charity in France. Appendix II recounts their names and gives a glimpse of their lives serving wherever they were most needed across the continents. Appendix III lists the names and local communities of the sisters in the 1901 and 1911 censuses of population.

The Daughters of Charity worked with whatever was currently feasible and were open to new possibilities. This is evident from the comprehensive list of house openings and closures, compiled for this publication. Appendix IV gives an overall picture of the experimentation, reassessment, short- and long-term ventures; that were all part of the dynamic of being truly ready to serve wherever the sisters were most needed.

In some cases the period covered by a particular essay continues up to more recent years; in other cases the early years are the sole focus of the essay. Rather than aiming at an all-inclusive coverage (which could run to several volumes), this book aims to provide an introduction to the history of the Daughters of Charity in Ireland, their innovative work at national and local level and the spirit which has inspired them.

Chapter One

The Arrival of the Daughters of Charity of St Vincent de Paul to Drogheda, Ireland, November 1855

Olivia Sherlock DC, Carmel Casey DC, Jacinta Prunty CHF

In 1855 the Crimean War came to a conclusion with the seizure of the Malakoff Tower. Far more men were lost from disease and exposure than were lost in combat. In the same year the river Boyne was spanned by a magnificent engineering structure, the viaduct which carried the Dublin-Drogheda railway into the town. On 8 November of that year the first Irish foundation of the Daughters of Charity of St Vincent de Paul was made in the coastal town of Drogheda, County Louth in the diocese of Armagh.

Variously known as les Filles de la Charité, *les Sœurs Grises*, the French Sisters, the first Daughters of Charity to come to Ireland arrived in Drogheda on 8 November 1855. The leader of the little group of four was Sister Josephine de Virieu, age 37, a native of Crécey-sur-Tille, Côte-d'Or, France. She was accompanied by Sister Amelia Ellis, age 31, from Wales, Sister Gabrielle de la Moussaye, 28, Paris and Sister Jeanne Morris, 21, a native of Skryne, County Meath, Ireland.

Their journey began on 2 November 1855. After spending a night in Boulogne, they crossed the English channel by steamboat and on to London, where they stayed overnight in a hotel in Kensington. The following day they took the train for Holyhead, the newly-upgraded travel route for mail and passengers from London. When they arrived in Kingstown (Dún Laoghaire), Fr Philip Dowley CM and Fr Thomas McNamara CM welcomed them. That night they stayed in Kingstown with the Dominican Sisters. The following day they set out for Dublin. Fr Médard Salvayre, Secretary General of the Congregation of the Mission, who had travelled with them from Paris, reported back to Fr Jean-Baptiste Etienne, superior general in Paris:

> Our first visit was to the Archbishop of Dublin who was very affable, telling us, of his own accord, that he hoped he also might have Sisters in his Episcopal town. From there, we went to St Peter's (Phibsborough) where Fr McNamara welcomed us with unimaginable joy. On the

following day, Wednesday, the Sisters went to visit the Mother House of the Confrères at Castleknock, where the excellent Fr Dowley had organised a surprise which expressed all the cordiality he felt towards the Sisters.[1]

On Thursday 8 November, they set out for their new mission in Drogheda, having spent the night with the Sisters of Mercy in Baggot Street, Dublin. When they finally arrived in Drogheda they were met with a civic reception. The local newspaper, the *Drogheda Argus*, paints a word-picture of what the paper celebrated as 'an event which will be ever memorable in the history of our country – the introduction of the first branch of the French "Sisters of Charity" into Ireland'. The townspeople surpassed themselves, giving what the *Argus* describes as a reception 'worthy of Ireland, and eminently due to the dignity and importance of their mission'. All the ecclesiastics of note were present, the primate of all Ireland, Dr Joseph Dixon, archbishop of Armagh 1852–66, 'with all the Clergy of the Parish – secular and regular – and all the Clergy of the vicinity, assembled in the vestry of the Church (St Peter's) to meet them on their entrance to the town'.[2] The *Argus* goes on to say:

> His Grace addressed the vast assembly and thanked the Catholic people of Drogheda for attending in such numbers to testify their joy on the occasion. And after tracing the similarity of the Catholic spirit of the two countries – and passing a deserved eulogium on the labours of the 'Sisters of Charity' at the seat of war, and through the whole world – on his own behalf and in the name of the Clergy and people of the town and vicinity, he welcomed them to Ireland.[3]

Fr Salvayre penned his own personal account to Fr Etienne dated 9 November 1855:

> Here I am, having returned from Drogheda, to tell you that the installation of our first four Sisters in Ireland was done amid a combination of circumstances which permit one to hope that this second branch of the family of St Vincent will prosper as much as did the first. Yesterday, Thursday morning, we set out for Drogheda, where the Sisters were awaited with the greatest impatience. When they had left the train, an elegant barouche, drawn by two horses with liveried attendants carried them across the whole town as far as the Presentation convent, where they took some rest. At eleven o'clock, the Cathedral

---

[1] Fr Salvayre to Fr Etienne, 9 November 1855, PA:CM/Raheny (Provincial Archives, Congregation of the Mission, Raheny, Dublin, here abbreviated as PA:CM/Raheny).
[2] *The Drogheda Argus*, 10 November 1855.
[3] Ibid.

bell announced the beginning of the ceremony. The Church was packed. His Excellency, the Monsignor Primate, in pontifical robes, led them into the chancel in the middle of the clergy, of the town and its environs, together with the Superiors of religious orders while the *Laudate* was sung with organ accompaniment. After this singing, the Primate gave an admirable and most appropriate sermon, of feeling and sensitivity. The poor Sisters dissolved into tears as did Fr Dowley, who was beside them. Then Solemn Benediction of the Blessed Sacrament was given and the Te Deum was sung with a fervour and enthusiasm difficult to describe. At the Church door, a crowd of people surrounded the Sisters to bring them to their house. The Primate was at their head. At one moment, I thought we could no longer move forward since the crowd grew larger at each street corner. O how your heart would have rejoiced had you been able to see such expression of kindness in the midst of these people who are so good.[4]

The house to which the people of Drogheda accompanied the sisters was located in William Street. According to the official account of the foundation:

'The Sisters remained in this house until 1866 when they moved to the "Primate's House" in Fair Street,' when the residence of Archbishop Michael Kieran was transferred from Drogheda to Dundalk. The new parish priest of Drogheda, Canon Tierney, and the parochial clergy, made the house in William Street, on the sisters vacating it, 'then and for years afterwards their home.'[5]

The arrival of the sisters in Drogheda was a landmark for the people of Drogheda, who took pride in having the first house of the Daughters of Charity in their town and who were the immediate beneficiaries of their mission, both spiritual and temporal. It was an occasion for rejoicing for the Daughters of Charity who had made the long journey from Paris and for the Vincentian fathers who had given them such a warm welcome. It was an important boost for Irish Catholics who saw the arrival of the sisters as placing Ireland on the Catholic map internationally.

The plan for this new mission was a long time in gestation, as can be gleaned from a letter of Fr Etienne to Fr Dowley, on 17 October 1855:

For a long time I have wished to see [the Daughters of Charity] established in a country which was so dear to St Vincent and which,

---

[4] Fr Salvayre to Fr Etienne, 9 November 1855, PA:CM/Raheny.
[5] A. Hughes, *History of Drogheda* (Drogheda, 1893), p. 151.

through this very fact, is also so dear to my heart. I am happy to see this new link forming between it and the children of St Vincent. It augurs well for a very good future for our two families.[6]

Fr José Maria Román CM records in his biography of Vincent de Paul the following:

Vincent has been interested in Ireland for a long time. After the 1641 rebellion he asked Richelieu to help the Irish in their struggle. The Cardinal said he regretted that they could not help because at that time the king of France had to shoulder some very heavy burdens, so they could not possibly embark on any new ventures. ... If it was not in Vincent's power to provide military aid, he certainly could help them spiritually.[7]

In 1645, the Sacred Congregation for the Propagation of the Faith asked Vincent de Paul to send missioners to Ireland. He was happy to obey the order from Rome. Six men were chosen. They arrived in Ireland early in 1647. After six years, they were forced to withdraw because of the danger to their lives. Thaddeus Lee, a native of Limerick, who chose to remain, became the first Vincentian martyr. The Vincentian congregation, which was very involved in bringing the Daughters of Charity to Drogheda, did not re-establish itself in Ireland until well into the nineteenth century.

The background negotiations to the first Daughters of Charity foundation in Ireland were protracted and complicated. Appeals were underway from late 1850, led by Miss Margaret Aylward (later foundress of the Sisters of the Holy Faith), who had established a branch of the Ladies' Association of Charity in Dublin in the confident hope that Daughters of Charity would soon be sent from Paris, and would 'attend our meetings, work with us amongst the Poor, and give us the advantage of their experience and advice'.[8] Extensive correspondence survives between the key people involved: Miss Aylward in Dublin, Fr Etienne and Fr Salvayre in Paris, Fr Dowley in Castleknock and Fr MacNamara in Phibsborough.

Dr Jospeh Dixon, archbishop of Armagh and Dr Paul Cullen, archbishop of Dublin were in constant communication with each other and with Miss Aylward. Fr Etienne was entirely in support of an Irish foundation but did not

---

[6] Fr Etienne to Fr Dowley, 17 October 1855, PA:CM/Raheny.
[7] J. M., Román, *St Vincent de Paul: A Biography*, tr. Joyce Howard DC (London, 1999), p. 394.
[8] Draft notes by Margaret Aylward, Glasnevin Archives: Margaret Aylward/GC/no. 9, undated but statistics as in 1855 Ladies of Charity fourth annual report. (Holy Faith Archives Glasnevin, Dublin, here abbreviated as GA.)

have any great preference for Dublin over Drogheda or vice versa.[9] For him, the fact that Vincent de Paul himself had sent missionaries to Ireland in its hour of greatest need, in the likelihood of their being driven out or martyred, made the country very special to him.

Despite pressure from Miss Aylward, Fr Dowley was nervous about pressing the case for a foundation of the Daughters of Charity in Ireland because the Congregation of the Mission was still quite new to the country. In January 1851, Dr Cullen, bishop of Armagh, 1849–52, stayed overnight in Castle-knock but Fr Dowley did not discuss the matter of the Daughters of Charity with him:

> I have found him so entirely engaged with public projects of the highest importance to the interests of religion and the country, and dwelling very directly indeed upon the depressed local resources, that I have not ventured to reopen our question with him under the circumstances I thought he would have taken it as rather a troublesome intrusion, having so lately decided against it so strongly.[10]

Undaunted, Miss Aylward continued with her lobbying to bring the Daughters of Charity to Ireland. Plans had advanced to such a degree that she expected a community to move into the house she had negotiated for them in North William Street, Dublin on 8 October 1855. The timidity of the archbishop of Dublin delayed everything, and the Drogheda foundation was well established by the time the first houses were opened in Dublin in 1857.[11]

The simultaneous negotiations for a house in Drogheda continued apace under Dr Dixon and on 15 October 1855, Fr Etienne confirmed to Fr Dowley that all was now signed and sealed with Dr Dixon, for the opening of a house in his diocese.[12] Dr Dixon had provided a house for the Daughters of Charity and the necessary approbation. He had assured Paris of the financial solidity

---

[9] Fr Etienne to Margaret Aylward, 18 October 1851 (in French), acknowledging recent letter and assuring that he will send sisters as soon as the house she intends for them is ready, GA:MA/CH/02 no. 50. See also Fr Etienne to Fr Dowley, 17 October 1855, 'For a long time I have wished to see them established in a country which was so dear to St Vincent and which, through this very fact, is also so dear to my heart. I am happy to see this new link forming between it and the children of St Vincent. It augurs well for a very good future for our two families.' PA:CM/Raheny.

[10] Fr Dowley to Margaret Aylward, 15 January 1851, GA:MA/CH/02 no. 40.

[11] See for example the plans to buy 'two fine houses, quite detached' in Eccles Street, Dublin, directly opposite the archbishop's house. 'The sisters would become known here, they would be in the way of getting good subjects with fortunes.' Margaret Aylward to Fr Etienne, 19 August 1855, GA:MA/CH/02 no. 56. Reply from Fr Etienne, 22 August 1855 (in French), stating that the project still awaits the complete approval and permission of the archbishop of Dublin. GA:MA/CH/02 no. 44.

[12] Fr Etienne to Fr Dowley, 15 October 1855, PA:CM/Raheny.

of the venture despite the parish's inability to pay for the maintenance of the sisters. He had thus cleared the remaining obstacles to the coming of the Daughters of Charity to Drogheda.

Funding for the mission came from many sources. The Deputy Lord Mayor of Drogheda, James McCann, brother of Fr John McCann CM, undertook the funding for four years. Fr Hanratty from Drogheda who was very enthusiastic about the venture set out for Dublin to buy many of the things necessary to furnish the house for the sisters. Funds were also forthcoming through voluntary subscriptions, legacies and an annual church collection. Among the legacies was a substantial gift in 1866 from relatives of a Franciscan priest, Fr Dardis. It was not by any stretch a well-endowed foundation, but there was sufficient backing to get it started and it was self-evident that the people of Drogheda supported the sisters most generously.

The town of Drogheda, from the early nineteenth century onwards was in decline; the streets were 'ill kept' and the 'fine old family mansions' in the town were 'now inhabited by a somewhat different class from those by whom they were first occupied'.[13] As with most Irish towns of the period, 'Drogheda has extensive suburbs, composed of miserable cabins, which greatly disfigure the approaches ... and stretching for more than a mile out of town'.[14]

The post-Famine census of 1851 returned a population of 21,348, and it continued to decrease over the next decades: to 18,250 by 1861; to 16,098 by 1871. Its economic fortunes were based on the threatened industries of flax and cotton spinning, on brewing, tanning, ironworking, the manufacture of steam engines, shipbuilding, and the handling of imports and exports for the city and its prosperous hinterland. Competing firms throughout the United Kingdom were investing heavily in the latest technological advances, overtaking local firms such as those in Drogheda. More sophisticated distribution networks linking steamships and the new railways opened up Irish markets to industrialists throughout the United Kingdom and the huge British market to any Irish manufacturers that could adapt to the new realities. It was a time of profound transition economically, socially and culturally, with many, especially those who crowded into hovels along the edges of the town, getting left behind.

The town of Drogheda fitted criteria set out by Vincent de Paul and Louise de Marillac for a foundation. There were many poor people and many openings for the classic charitable works of the Daughters of Charity, including visiting the sick poor in their homes and teaching children that the established schools did not reach. Commentators remarked on the visibility of the sisters on the streets and on their warm-hearted charity echoing the popular acclamation of

---

[13] *The Imperial Gazetteer*, 1868.
[14] H. D. Inglis, *A Journey Through Ireland* (London, 1838), p. 386.

the people of France in the seventeenth century who gave the first sisters the title 'Daughters of Charity'.

Observers noted that the sisters cheerfully undertook the service of the most neglected, responding to differing needs in flexible ways. They began by visiting the poor of the town and opened a night school for girls working in factories. This school is celebrated in Anne Hughes' *History of Drogheda* where she records that

> hundreds of the poorer class of females, who would otherwise grow up in ignorance of even the merest rudiments of book learning, received at the hands of the Sisters a solid and perfect education in their night school, by which they were fitted, as many of them afterwards became, useful members of the community … They were literary and religiously instructed as well as taught sewing in plain and fancy work.[15]

In 1870, the sisters opened an industrial school, approved by the Chief Secretary of Ireland. It was intended for the care and training of vagrant and abandoned children for whom the adult gaol was the inevitable outcome if there was no intervention. The establishment of the industrial schools was heralded publicly as a great breakthrough in child care. The sisters also opened St Vincent's National School. Other local Drogheda initiatives in the early decades included St Vincent's orphanage for girls (1890) and a new national school for 300 boys (1894).

A small domestic economy school for girls working in factories was opened in 1931. In 1934, a piece of land by the sea – 2 acres, 2 roods, 2 perches – in Termonfeckin near Drogheda was given to the Daughters of Charity by Mrs Lentayne as a holiday home for the children. Second-hand army huts were purchased and erected. Each year the children spent the summer months there, where they greatly benefited from the fresh air and freedom that such a facility afforded. They returned to Fair Street, Drogheda, at the end of the summer to return to school. The boys attended the parish national school from 1939, to help them integrate with other boys of their own age. Anne Hughes writes in her *History of Drogheda*:

> The labours of the Sisters of Charity are most comprehensive. Wherever temporal suffering can be assuaged or spiritual destitution relieved, there is the chosen scene of their heaven directed labours. They visited the sick, instructed the ignorant, they fed the hungry and clothed the naked, with necessary funds coming from charitable donations.[16]

---

[15] A. Hughes, *History of Drogheda* (Drogheda, 1893), p. 151.
[16] Ibid., p. 151.

Hughes also noted how several local girls, 'the children of poor but honest parents taught by the sisters, afterwards embraced the Order of Charity; and by their bravery and devotion in attending the wounded and dying in the Franco-Prussian war, were decorated with the Legion of Honour.' The records show that a number of sisters left Drogheda for distant missions, among them Sister Alice O'Sullivan, missioned to China and martyred in Tianjin in 1870, and Sister Catherine McGuire sent to begin the foundation of the Daughters of Charity in Australia in 1926.

But all of this did not happen without considerable cost. During the first three decades that the sisters served in Drogheda, eight of them died at a young age: Frances Carroll, 25; Clare Golden, 30; Anne O'Shea, 34; Mary O'Shea, 35; Teresa Lucy Roice, 39; Joseph Ginnety, 39; Teresa Duffy, 40 and Clare Anne Boylan, 44. The remains of these sisters, originally interred in Cord Cemetery, Drogheda were reinterred in St Peter's Cemetery, Cross Lanes on 8 August 1980.

The Daughters of Charity arrived in Drogheda at a providential moment in Irish history, in time to witness the blossoming of Catholic charities. The good they were to accomplish in Ireland would not be limited to Drogheda. Within two years, on 14 May 1857, Sister Josephine de Virieu and seven other sisters set out for Dublin to begin two new ministries on the same day: St Vincent's, North William Street and St Vincent's Hospital, Fairview. On that day the words of Vincent de Paul in 1646 regarding the Company of the Daughters of Charity were beginning to take form in Ireland, 'As it wasn't then what it is now, there's reason to believe that it's still not what it will be when God has perfected it as He wants it.'[17]

---

[17] P. Coste CM, *Saint Vincent de Paul: Correspondence, Conferences, Documents,* vol. 9, ed. and tr. Marie Poole DC (New York: New City Press), p. 194.

Chapter Two

Ladies' Association of Charity of St Vincent de Paul: Laying the Groundwork for the Daughters of Charity

Breege Keenan DC

The Ladies' Association of Charity of St Vincent de Paul, initially known as a Confraternity of Charity, was founded in 1617 in Châtillon-les-Dombes, now named Châtillon-sur-Charlaronne, France. The story of the origins of the Ladies of Charity has been told and retold. Its beginning was not planned but rather Vincent de Paul took up the challenge of responding to a need.

One Sunday morning, as Vincent de Paul was vesting for mass, he was told of a family in bad circumstances with no food or medicine, 'The good priest's heart ached at the news. He gave a very moving homily to the parishioners about this distressed family.'[1] The women of the parish sprang into practical action. Later that day as Vincent went to visit the family he met the women returning from the farmhouse. Vincent saw the family's dire poverty but quickly realised that they now had more food than they needed and that it would be wasted. He recognised that this charitable work needed to be organised. Three days later, on 23 August 1617, Vincent organised a meeting of pious ladies from the town. He urged them to begin an association to help the sick poor of the area and they immediately agreed. Three months later the association was formally approved by the Vicar General of Lyons and was established as a confraternity. The constitutions were given to the eighteen members on the 8 December 1617.

The main objective of the confraternity was to care for the sick poor. The Ladies were to be 'servants of the poor', the title later used to describe the Daughters of Charity.[2] They had everything worked out in detail, from the spirit and aims of the Association to the procedures for electing officers; from the spirituality that animated its members to the manner in which they were to serve the sick. The Ladies were to attend to the spiritual and material needs

[1] J. M., Román, *St Vincent de Paul: A Biography*, tr. Joyce Howard DC (London, 1999), p. 123.
[2] Ibid., p. 124.

of the poor: to distribute food, clothes and medicine and to invite them to go
to Confession and Holy Communion. They were advised that, 'when they
visited anyone for the first time they were to take them a white shift and, if
necessary, some sheets. They would also take a crucifix ... and provide any
basic furniture.'[3] The rule dealt with how to greet the sick on entering their
homes and sample menus were given, for example:

> Each sick person will have all the bread they need, together with a
> quarter of a pound of cooked veal for the midday meal and the same
> quantity roasted for supper, except on Sundays and feast days when they
> can have chicken. Two or three times a week they will have mince for
> supper.[4]

As the Association developed, the Ladies did not confine themselves to
preparing meals and home visitation, but began working with galley slaves,
foundlings, foreign missions, in disaster areas and anywhere there was poverty
and need. A number of confraternities also included men but these were
disbanded and Vincent de Paul noted:

> When you have men and women working together they cannot agree
> on matters of administration; the men want to be in charge of
> everything and the ladies do not like this. In the beginning the Charities
> of Joigny and Montmirail had mixed membership; the men took charge
> of the able-bodied poor while the ladies cared for the sick, but as their
> funds were held in common we found it necessary to withdraw the men.
> As for the ladies, I can only speak highly of them; nobody could fault
> their administration for they were very careful and most trustworthy.[5]

The Confraternities of Charity gave some women of France an opportunity
to be involved in philanthropy. The Confraternity was approved by Pope
Innocent XII in 1695 and spread quickly throughout France. Like other
organisations, it disappeared during the French Revolution but was re-
established in 1840 with the approval of the archbishop of Paris. Since then it
has continued to grow and establish itself in many countries.

The early members of the Association came from the upper classes; well-
off families had the means to aid the poor materially, providing food, medicine,
furniture and clothes on a regular basis. It gave them a sense of purpose,
allowed them a chance to organise and manage, while providing an outlet for
them to socialise and interact with other women from their own social class.
It fulfilled a religious and charitable duty. These women had servants in their

---

[3] J. M., Román, *St Vincent de Paul: A Biography*, tr. Joyce Howard DC (London, 1999), 124.
[4] Ibid., p. 125.
[5] Ibid., p. 139.

households and difficulties arose in the Paris Charities when the Ladies began sending their servants in their stead to care for the sick in their homes. In 1630, a young peasant girl, Marguerite Naseau from Suresnes, came to Vincent de Paul and said she wanted to devote her life to looking after the sick. Other young women came to join her and Vincent sent them to Louise de Marillac to be trained. Louise saw the need of gathering these young women into a community. Hence, the Daughters of Charity were founded in 1633 to carry on the work of the Ladies of Charity and both organisations continue to work together throughout the world.

When the Ladies of Charity regrouped after the French revolution, they became one of the most important philanthropic groups in Paris. The Ladies of Charity in particular, 'whether viewed from the perspective of church or state, lay not on the margins of the poor relief mission in nineteenth-century Paris but at its heart'.[6] In mid-nineteenth-century Paris, there were two epidemics of cholera that killed over eighteen thousand inhabitants. In addition many people were migrating from the countryside to the city and hence forcing 'the elite to consider the problem of the poor seriously and this helped to shape attitudes towards social class and poor relief'.[7] From a Catholic perspective, there were an insufficient number of priests to meet the needs of the migrants in Paris and many women turned to philanthropy as a means to bridge the gap between the rich and poor. During this time the Ladies of Charity were the most successful and the least specialised of the thirty-nine charitable associations visiting in Paris and they attracted the largest number of volunteers.

The first branch of the Ladies' Association of Charity in Ireland was formed in Kingstown (Dún Laoghaire) in 1843, the result of a mission preached by the Vincentian Fathers. In Ireland the Ladies were mainly middle-class women including the founder of the Metropolitan branch, Miss Margaret Aylward. There were few outlets for women so philanthropy gave them an 'opportunity to meet and collaborate with like-minded women, to reinforce their own faith and values, to manage money, and learn administrative skills, to venture into the neighbourhoods and the homes of the poor and to create relationships across class lines'.[8] Their goal was not to empower but to care for the sick and expansion to the city quickly followed:

The people of Dublin hearing of the great good done by the Ladies in Kingstown longed to have a branch in the city. Their longing was

---

[6] Sarah A. Curtis, 'Charitable Ladies: Gender, Class and Religion in Mid-Nineteenth-Century Paris', *Past and Present*, 177:1 (2002), p. 125.

[7] Ibid., p. 126.

[8] Ibid.

satisfied when a number of women interested in the project met in the Church of St Francis Xavier ... and founded the Metropolitan branch.[9]

The first meeting of the Metropolitan branch was held on the 6 June 1851 in St Francis Xavier Church on Gardiner Street. Miss Aylward had some contact with the branch of the Ladies of Charity in Waterford. Then she translated the rules of the Ladies' Association of Charity and published her own manual for visiting the poor. She encouraged the Ladies to read the life of Vincent de Paul so as to be imbued with the Vincentian spirit. Archbishop Daniel Murray of Dublin supported the Ladies of Charity:

We are happy to hail your Institute of Charity as a further work of St Vincent, which, beginning with you, will, we trust, extend by your good example amongst the faithful of other parishes, and secure extensive and lasting blessings for the humble objects of your zeal.[10]

From St Francis Xavier's Church, the Ladies visited in the parish of St Michan's, Anne's Street, and extended their good work beyond the Royal Canal. Their headquarters was at 20 Lower Dorset Street from 1851–4; in 1855 at 6 Middle Gardiner Street; in 1857 at 6 Berkeley Road, and finally in 1858 they moved to 42 Eccles Street. Miss Aylward chose to have their headquarters in inner-city Dublin where the Ladies of Charity could visit the hovels of the poor in the surrounding areas. It was a comfort for the Ladies to know that there were several Catholic churches nearby should they require a priest to administer the sacraments of Confession and of the sick. At this time, Miss Aylward was also negotiating with the Superior General of the Congregation of Mission to bring the Daughters of Charity to North William Street in Dublin, where she hoped for future collaboration in working for homeless children.

The Ladies of Charity was a female organisation consisting of active and honorary members. The honorary members contributed to the Association with their money, gifts and prayers for the active members. A priest was an honorary member of the Association and his main function was to chair their annual general meeting. The active members were expected to attend their monthly meetings and to visit, along with a companion, the sick in their homes. The active membership was drawn largely from these social groups: the wives and daughters of solicitors, barristers, doctors, and wine merchants, as well as women from manufacturing and business families. Membership was open to all women regardless of their status, and many of them were widows and single ladies. A large number of men, including spouses, the local clergy

---

[9] *The Irish Catholic*, 26 January 1918.
[10] *Ladies of Charity, First Report*, 1852, p. 7.

and business men were supporters of the Association. The Ladies of Charity were attached to a local parish and the clergy put them in contact with the poor of the area.

The management was confided to a superior and two assistants, one of whom acted as treasurer and the other as secretary. The Association was to meet once a month and the active members were to visit the sick poor once a week, always with a companion. Each member was requested to keep a register in which she noted: '(1) names of the sick visited; (2) the number of visits paid; (3) the kind and amount of relief given; (4) the subscriptions received; and (5) the results obtained, such as conversions, baptisms and the like.'[11]

The funds for the Association came from the honorary members and from the active members at their monthly meetings. Honorary members could pay quarterly, annually or biannually. Various methods of acquiring funds are mentioned in the annual reports, such as sermons, lotteries, raffles, wills and donations. The annual lottery was held in March and was their chief source of funds. Many of the Ladies donated jewellery: a gold bracelet when raffled realised £34. The annual report of 1861 states that the 'Charity Sermon realised for the Sick Poor the sum of £40 10 s.'[12] On the occasion of the tercentenary of the foundation, at a sermon preached by Fr John Carr CM, in St Mary's Pro-Cathedral, he urged the congregation, 'You might also look at your wills and see if you have mentioned the Ladies there.'[13]

Miss Aylward was a woman of vision and from the outset she published the annual reports of the Ladies of Charity. This gave her the opportunity to highlight the works carried out by the Association and to show the public what they did for the poor of the city. It was also a means to encourage the public to support the Ladies and to recruit new members to join them. The Ladies requested donations of 'old clothing, carpeting, sheets, rugs, blankets, shoes … '[14]

The primary aim of the Ladies of Charity was to visit the sick poor in their own homes and to give them corporal and spiritual assistance. For Vincent de Paul, the Ladies of Charity were to provide people with food, medicine, clothing and anything else that made life more comfortable for them, thus responding to their corporal needs. He knew many poor people had lost faith in God and he believed that it was important for the Ladies of Charity to assist those who were dying to die well, and those who were recovering to lead a better life. He believed that one must preach the gospel in word and in work

[11] P. Boyle, *St Vincent de Paul and The Vincentians* (London, 1909), p. 138.
[12] *Ladies of Charity, Ninth Report*, 1861, p. 5.
[13] *The Irish Catholic*, 26 January 1918.
[14] *Ladies of Charity, Second Report*, 1853, p. 24.

thus practising what Jesus did while on earth. Vincent saw charity as a Christian virtue and he contemplated God in his neighbour. The Ladies of Charity believed that they too were assisting Jesus Christ in the person of the sick poor. Miss Aylward urged the Ladies to become better every year by practising the virtues of humility, gentleness, patience and love. She organised days of retreat and conferences. The annual reports relate story after story of the abject poverty of north-inner-city Dublin where people lived in dreadful conditions:

> The bed was a hard palliasse; she had a straw bed, but the want of fire, of covering, and the excessive cold, obliged her to have this straw removed, in order that the ticken or cover in which the straw was might be put over her in place of a blanket. This wretched bed was obliged to accommodate, besides the dying woman, her two children, and her sister's two children. And on the bare ground beside her lay, at night, this fond and affectionate sister.[15]

The Ladies were able to assist this poor family and place one of the children in an orphanage. When they visited another family, they enquired where the woman slept and she pointed to a handful of straw and her husband's coat, which she used for a blanket. Again, the Ladies were able to bring her blankets to make her feel comfortable. The report added:

> The father and mother were seated near a few embers; another child, now struck by sickness, lay on a little straw in a corner; no earthly comfort was there; the entire furniture of that room consisted of two stools![16]

This couple were to experience the anguish and pain of the death of six of their children and yet the Ladies of Charity were concerned for the spiritual well-being of the father and encouraged him to go to Confession.

From the outset, the Ladies were concerned with resisting the efforts of proselytising, as they were informed of the energy the local bible-readers spent on visiting the very houses that the Ladies visited. Hence they organised a fact-finding mission throughout the city. They divided the city into districts and sent two members to each district to identify the children going to proselytising schools. They were relieved when they succeeded in getting the children into Catholic schools. Concern was also expressed for children attending Sunday schools. The Ladies believed this was 'equal to going to church' and that those who attended were 'virtually Protestant'. It is unclear how successful they were

---

[15] *Ladies of Charity, Second Report,* 1853, p. 11.
[16] *Ladies of Charity, First Report,* 1852, p. 10.

in their efforts to prevent proselytising but they were concerned enough to set up an Anti-Proselytising Fund. This fund was to provide children with clothing and school books, and in 1851 they published anti-proselytising pamphlets. Miss Aylward and the Ladies picketed Sunday schools where Catholics were lured by the offer of a cut of bread. The Ladies distributed crucifixes to the children despite Protestant missionaries accusing them of handing out idols. They made every effort to ensure that the sick poor attended the sacraments:

> Where persons were found neglecting their religious duties or ill-instructed in them, the visiting Ladies exerted influence to induce them to approach the sacraments; and, at the same time, spared no exertion to instruct such as needed it.[17]

One of the Ladies describes her visitation to a couple where the husband was dying. He was forty years of age and had never been to the sacraments and for 'seven long months she sought to bring back the prodigal to his Father's house'; eventually she succeeded; he went to Confession and died some days later.[18] The Ladies made every possible preparation in advance of death, encouraging the person to receive the last sacraments, arranging for a priest to visit, providing rosary beads and a crucifix and putting the room in order. Almost all of the annual reports give information on the poor people returning to the sacraments, especially Confession, after much persuasion by the Ladies. During the sermon for the tercentenary of the foundation of the Ladies of Charity, Fr John Carr CM commended the Ladies for their good works and 'their efforts to save the souls of the little ones of the faith'.[19]

The Ladies of Charity became involved in what was termed 'accessory or accidental work' such as the 'instruction of the ignorant'. Adult catechism classes were held on Tuesdays and Thursdays in St Francis Xavier Church, Gardiner Street, in the north-inner-city of Dublin, primarily to prepare adults for the sacraments. Few attended the classes so Miss Aylward decided that for those who never knew 'the mysteries of faith' it was necessary to take a different approach. The Ladies were 'to go to these poor people, to meet them after their work, and on Sunday evenings, in their courts and alleys, and waste houses, and teach them in batches'.[20] Others were instructing children for their First Communion in the parish schools of St Michan's.

Under the banner of the Ladies of Charity, St Mary's Industrial Institute was founded in 1853 to provide poor women with training and employment. They acquired an old coach factory in Dorset Street and employed a woman from the north of Ireland who 'understands the sewed-muslin-work or

---

[17] *Ladies of Charity, Fifth Report*, 1856, p. 8.
[18] *Ladies of Charity, Second Report*, 1853, p. 10.
[19] *The Irish Catholic*, 26 January 1918.
[20] *Ladies of Charity, Seventh Report*, 1858, p. 9.

embroidery in all its branches, to teach the same gratuitously to all who may wish to learn'.[21] The Society of St Vincent de Paul contributed a substantial sum of money to the Institute and donors presented various items to be raffled including 'a valuable pair of earrings', 'a pair of rare Turkish cushions' and 'a silver snuff-box'.[22] St Mary's would admit 'only such persons as will be free to devote to it their whole time, and to follow it up as a regular pursuit of industry' and after three or four months would earn between 2 s. 6 d. to 4 s. a week.[23] The setting up of a pre-school would give mothers skilled at needlework the opportunity to work in St Mary's. It endeavoured to 'avail itself, according to opportunity, of every prudent speculation that shall present itself for the advantage of the workers in every kind of employment suitable to females'.[24] The Ladies of Charity anticipated that orders would come for all kinds of plain work, muslin embroidery, crochet, netting, quilting and repairs. They hoped this would enable the poor to become self-sufficient and decrease the numbers dependent on public charity.

In 1856, St Mary's Industrial Institute ceased operations for a number of reasons: attendance was irregular and unsatisfactory; women who applied were inexperienced; supply and demand for their goods was uncertain; they were unable to compete with foreign markets, especially Australia; and most important of all, it would never be self-supporting. For all involved it was a bitter disappointment, but they recognised that to expect mothers to 'sit down patiently to learn or to improve themselves, with scarcely any remuneration whilst so doing, and with no other means of support' was unreasonable.[25]

The second annual report demonstrates that the Ladies of Charity did not confine themselves to visiting the poor in Dublin. Fr Henry Leader, parish priest of Rath, Cape Clear and Sherkin Islands in Cork, contacted Fr Thomas McNamara, a member of the Congregation of the Mission in Phibsborough and requested relief for the poor of his parishes. The islands were ravaged by the Famine and emigration; families were in 'want of clothing, whole families were unable to leave their wretched homes'.[26] The Ladies organised the 'Cape Clear Clothing Fund' and sent 632 articles of clothing to the Islands; '150 great coats and 50 capes, and freight of five bales of goods.'[27] The Ladies of Charity were particularly active in Belfast, 'where the association is so extensive that it is divided into thirteen sections, and much good is accomplished by

---

[21] *Ladies of Charity, Second Report*, 1853, p. 15.
[22] Ibid., pp. 16–17.
[23] Ibid., p. 25.
[24] Ibid., p. 26.
[25] *Ladies of Charity, Third Report*, 1854, p. 19.
[26] *Ladies of Charity, Second Report*, 1853, p. 6.
[27] Ibid., p. 22.

means of visits to the sick in hospitals and in workhouses, and by the establishment of sewing classes'.[28]

The sixth annual report of the Ladies of Charity included a description of St Bridget's Orphanage, 'an accessory work which we undertook during the last year.'[29] Miss Aylward was the founder of St Bridget's Orphanage; its primary goal was to find foster homes for children.[30] A committee was set up with the Ladies of Charity and other influential women to oversee this new work. St Bridget's became separate from the Ladies of Charity though it maintained close ties, as the Ladies referred children to the orphanage.

Miss Aylward hoped the Daughters of Charity would come to work with the Ladies of Charity.[31] She believed that it would ease her workload, as these two organisations had the same founder, Vincent de Paul. To this end, she had written to Fr Jean-Baptiste Etienne, superior general of the Congregation of the Mission, over four long years, inviting the Daughters of Charity to Dublin. Finally, in 1857, the Daughters of Charity arrived in North William Street, Dublin.

---

[28] P. Boyle, *St Vincent de Paul and The Vincentians*, p. 139.

[29] *Ladies of Charity, Sixth Report*, 1857, p. 13.

[30] J. Prunty, *Margaret Aylward, 1810–1889: Lady of Charity, Sister of Faith* (Dublin, 1999).

[31] Miss Aylward later founded the Sisters of the Holy Faith in 1866.

Chapter Three

North William Street, Dublin:
Founding Parish Mission, Education and Pastoral Work

Anne Neylon DC

'An institution that forgets its own past will have difficulty finding and defining its special role with regard to the social, cultural and religious context of humanity.'[1] One cannot understand the arrival of the Daughters of Charity of St Vincent de Paul to North William Street, Dublin in 1857 without reference to the foundations that preceded them in the mission there. Dublin in the nineteenth century was a city of sharp contrasts between rich and poor. Life moved at a slow pace. The famine of 1845–7 left a trail of destruction in terms of the people it left destitute and the flow of emigration that followed. A mood of bitterness and despair prevailed. Roads were bad and throngs of beggars were a familiar sight. The gentry travelled in private carriages and stage coaches while most people travelled on foot. Social and housing conditions for the majority of the population were far from adequate. Gradually, rich and powerful people withdrew from the narrow streets of the old walled city and districts like North William Street in Dublin's inner city degenerated into slum land.

North William Street Pre-1857
The Trinitarian Orphan Charity was one of the oldest in Dublin (1815) and the only one of its kind within the extensive union of the parishes of St Mary, St Thomas and St George comprising a Catholic population of upwards of 40,000. The guardians and the governesses of this institution met on the first Friday in every month in the Orphan House at 1.00 p.m. Donations were sought, received and acknowledged by His Grace the Archbishop, by the Rev Guardians or by any of the Revd Gentlemen.[2]

---

[1] Echoes of the Company (Introduction), no. 1 January/February, 2007.
[2] Indenture made between Christopher Elliott and the Most Reverend Daniel Murray, (1812), DDA:Dublin Reference 30/1/90 (Dublin Diocesan Archives, Dublin, here abbreviated as DDA:Dublin).

The beginnings of the convent in North William Street, with buildings and small burial ground can be traced to the Trinitarian Confraternity – a body of laity who established an orphanage there.[3] There were fourteen orphans resident in the premises at North William Street until the arrival of the Sisters of Charity in 1815.[4] Archbishop Daniel Murray was looking for accommodation for these sisters and the President of the Confraternity offered to hand over the convent to Sister Mary Augustine Aikenhead and her sisters, provided they took care of the orphans.[5] On 22 August 1815, Sister Mary Augustine Aikenhead and Sister Mary Catherine Walsh initiated their first foundation in North William Street.[6] They arrived from Micklegate Bar, York and settled there, sharing the premises with the Ladies of the Confraternity, until such time as they assumed full responsibility for the orphanage.[7]

In September 1815, Sister Mary Aikenhead was appointed superioress general of the new congregation of the Irish Sisters of Charity and Sister Catherine Walsh was appointed Mistress of Novices.[8] The new community was placed under the special care of Fr Peter Kenney SJ, who stressed the importance of the sisters' dedication to the service of the poor. In his address to the sisters on the occasion of their first reception ceremony, he told them of the work of the Daughters of Charity of St Vincent de Paul, 'a congregation founded by St Vincent de Paul a century and a half earlier in France'.[9] Sisters Mary and Catherine made their first vows in the chapel in North William Street on 1 September 1815 and in 1816 they made their perpetual vows in this same chapel.[10]

Life was difficult and demanding for the sisters in North William Street and in 1818 two young sisters died, one from consumption and the other from fever.[11] This was a great blow to the community and as a result of increased poverty and poor diet Mother Mary Aikenhead's health broke down. Having

---

[3] S. J. Greene, 'The Building of St Agatha's Church' in *Saint Agatha's Church, North William Street: 75 Years Old* (Dublin, 1983), p. 6.
[4] Now known as Religious Sisters of Charity.
[5] In Admissions Register B, 1812–1940, Dublin, RSCG, no. 1, Aikenhead, Mary, (Sr Mary Augustine) (birth) 19 January 1787, (entrance) 6 June 1812, (reception) no date recorded, (profession) 1 September 1815, (death) 22 July 1858. RSCG:Dublin/no.1. (Religious Sisters of Charity Generalate, Dublin, here abbreviated as RSCG:Dublin.).
[6] In Admissions Register B, 1812–1840, Walsh, Alicia, (Sr Mary Catherine), (birth) 25 June 1773, (entrance) 6 June 1812, (reception) no date recorded, (profession) 1 September 1815, (death) 25 December 1854. RSCG:Dublin/no. 2.
[7] Bishop of Canea, *Short Histories of Dublin Parishes,* Part XII (Dublin, 1913), p. 94.
[8] Irish Sisters of Charity Annals, D. 2, RSCG:Dublin/vol.1, undated, pp. 55, 262.
[9] Sermon preached by Fr Peter Kenney SJ, on the occasion of the first reception ceremony of the Religious Sisters of Charity, 24 September 1817. RSCG:Dublin/5/6.
[10] North William Street, Chapter 7, p. 231, RSCG:Dublin.
[11] In Admissions Register B, 1812–1940, Chamberlain, Catherine, (Sr Mary Magdalen), (birth) 26 April 1777, (entrance) 24 November 1815, (reception) no date recorded, (profession by privilege) 12 August 1818, (death), 22 August 1818. RSCG:Dublin/no.6.

recuperated in Rahan, Co. Offaly she returned to North William Street.[12] She was then invited to transfer to Stanhope Street 'to accommodate the number of young women seeking to be admitted as postulants'.[13] On 29 January 1819, Mother Mary Aikenhead and Sister M. Joseph O'Reilly moved there and Mother Catherine Walsh was appointed superior of North William Street.[14]

From 1816, the Irish Sisters of Charity visited the sick poor in their homes in the neighbourhood of North William Street.[15] The nuns were a familiar sight in the streets, lanes and alleys. They brought much practical support and consolation to the sick and the poor as they cared for, talked and prayed with them on their visits. They helped many people as they faced death through suffering and sickness. For twelve years, the sisters persevered with this demanding work and they were encouraged by the faith of the people.

Two months after their arrival, the Irish Sisters of Charity opened a day school (October 1815) for the poor children of the neighbourhood. With the increase in the number of sisters, Mother Aikenhead desired to set about the work of the schools, a work she had envisaged from the outset. The first apostolate for the sisters in education was in North William Street. In 1827, the parochial returns for the Orphan and Day School record an increased pupil attendance. The school catered for 126 Roman Catholic pupils, 26 of whom were orphans living in the orphanage.

In 1827, some Poor Clare nuns from Dunabeen, Co. Dublin, under the leadership of Mother Michael Treacy, offered to undertake responsibility for North William Street convent and orphanage. Mother Mary Aikenhead gladly accepted their offer and the Irish Sisters of Charity moved to rented accommodation until their convent was opened in Gardiner Street in January 1830, where they established free schools on a large scale.[16] On 31 May 1830, the Poor Clare Sisters left North William Street to establish a foundation in Newry, Co. Down, where they were invited to open a school.[17]

On 14 August 1830, some members of the Carmelite Convent in Warrenmount, Dublin went to North William Street and undertook the care of the orphans until 1856, when they moved to Lakelands, Sandymount.[18] They brought eleven orphans with them and once again it fell to the

---

[12] Annals, D. 2 RSCG:Dublin/vol.1, undated, pp. 113, 262.

[13] Stanhope Street, Chapter 8, p. 264, RSCG:Dublin.

[14] In Admissions Register B, 1812–1940, Dublin, O'Reilly, Bridget Mary, (Sr Mary Joseph), (birth) 30 April 1793, (entrance) 13 April 1817, (reception) 24 September 1817, (profession) 15 October 1819, (death) 20 December 1872. RSCG:Dublin/no.9.

[15] RSCG:Dublin (v. Doc. 3).

[16] Annals, D. 2, vol. 1, undated, pp. 270–1, RSCG:Dublin.

[17] Celebrating at a civic reception, 175 years of service in Newry, Co. Down as well as 800th anniversary of the Poor Clare Order, 26 November 2012. <www.cinews.ie> accessed 3-03-2013.

[18] Ibid.

Archbishop of Dublin to find an order of sisters who would carry on the work at North William Street.

The invitation to North William Street

In 1855, the Daughters of Charity were established in Drogheda having been invited by the Most Revd Dr Joseph Dixon, archbishop of Armagh and primate of all Ireland. On 14 May 1857, they were established in North William Street. There are two accounts of this establishment: the first gives priority to the role of Archbishop Cullen; the second emphasises the role of Miss Margaret Aylward.

One account records a personal appeal to the superiors in Paris, made by Dr Paul Cullen (1852–78), archbishop of Dublin, for sisters to take charge of the House of Charity, North William Street.[19] The Archbishop's invitation is linked to a bequest to his predecessor, Dr Murray, of a large sum of money from a Catholic lady for the establishment of a Visitation Convent in the Archdiocese. When Archbishop Murray died, the money was bequeathed to Dr Cullen, who decided to use the funds to encourage another congregation to establish a foundation in Dublin. Dr Cullen remembered the links between the Visitation Order and Vincent de Paul. In view of these connections, Dr Cullen made a personal appeal to the superiors in Paris to establish the Company of the Daughters of Charity in Ireland.[20] In this request the Vincentians and the Daughters of Charity in Paris were made aware of the great distress and poverty in Ireland. They learned that the famine which devastated the country during the previous decade had impoverished the working class and left countless children orphaned. The outcome of the request led to the arrival of the Daughters of Charity in North William Street on 14 May 1857.

The second account of the arrival of the Daughters of Charity to North William Street gives the initiative to Margaret Aylward. Born in 1810, in Co. Waterford, Miss Aylward was a lay woman with heart and mind set on improving the plight of the poor when she came to Dublin in the 1840s.[21] She was highly educated and she joined, in turn, the Irish Sisters of Charity and the Ursuline Sisters. She left both, though she still hankered after the ideal of community life. She involved herself with the Ladies' Association of Charity of St Vincent de Paul for the Spiritual and Temporal Relief of the Sick Poor.[22]

---

[19] PA:DC/Dunardagh/North WIlliam Street (Provincial Archives, Daughters of Charity, Dunardagh, here abbreviated as PA:DC/Dunardagh/North WIlliam Street).

[20] PA:DC/Dunardagh/North William Street.

[21] J. Prunty, *Margaret Aylward, 1810–1889: Lady of Charity, Sister of Faith* (Dublin, 1999), pp. 13–19.

[22] Ibid., p. 22.

Through her involvement in this association, Miss Aylward became steeped in the Vincentian charism and by 1851 she founded her own branch of the Association in the parish of St Mary's, Marlborough Street. Her work with the poor was conducted efficiently and effectively.

Miss Aylward was well attuned to the work of the *Sœurs Grises* and she knew they would be a great asset to the work of the Association. She had a plan. Knowing it was common practice in the Archdiocese of Dublin in the nineteenth century for Catholic lay charities to be transferred to religious congregations, Miss Aylward hoped the lay charity would come under the direction and guidance of the Daughters of Charity.[23] In this way there would be an assurance of effective organisation, adequate funding, continuity in the work and the Vincentian charism would be sustained. From 1851, Miss Aylward began her negotiations with the relevant authorities to have the Daughters of Charity come to Dublin and she worked unceasingly in the background to promote the establishment of the Daughters of Charity in North William Street. Those she directly involved were the priests of the Congregation of the Mission: Fathers Philip Dowley, provincial; Jean-Baptiste Etienne, superior general; Thomas McNamara, Thomas Kelly and John Lynch, Dublin. The result of the negotiations led to the arrival of the Daughters of Charity to North William Street on 14 May 1857.[24]

Sister Josephine (Charlotte Clementine) de Virieu (1818–90) was the first Daughter of Charity to come as sister servant[25] to North William Street.[26] Charlotte de Virieu was born in the Côte-d'Or France. Her father held a distinguished position in the court of Charles X. She lived in an aristocratic society. While she was growing up she was very aware that life was given for a higher purpose than the pursuit of pleasure. She realised that God was calling her to bring compassion, love and practical assistance to people suffering injustice and poverty. Charlotte announced to her family her intention of joining the community of the Daughters of Charity. Her family protested in vain.[27]

In May 1850, Sister de Virieu began the first phase of her spiritual journey as a postulant in the parish of St Médard, Paris. Her sister servant was Sister Rosalie Rendu (1786–1856).[28] In many respects, Sister de Virieu's life with her sisters in community and her service of those most in need mirrored the life of Sister Rosalie, who sought to respond to the ever-growing needs of the people

---

[23] J. Prunty, *Margaret Aylward, 1810–1889: Lady of Charity, Sister of Faith* (Dublin, 1999), p. 79.
[24] Ibid., pp. 79–91.
[25] See Glossary.
[26] PA:DC/Dunardagh/North William Street.
[27] *Pioneer Sisters of Charity of Saint Vincent de Paul in Great Britan and Ireland* (London, 1955), p. 1.
[28] Sr Rosalie Rendu was beatified in 2006.

of the Mouffetard district in Paris. Sister Rosalie worked tirelessly and creatively in expanding the works of education and health care to alleviate the poverty that oppressed human life and dignity, especially evident in the lives of women and children. Frédéric Ozanam (1813–53) and his companions were influenced by Sister Rosalie in the foundation of the Society of St Vincent de Paul. Sister Rosalie was often heard to say that 'a Daughter of Charity must be like a milestone on a street corner where all those who pass by can rest and lay down their heavy burdens'.[29] Having finished her novitiate in 1851, Sister de Virieu was sent to the Charity of Arras. She was employed in the day school and felt totally fulfilled in her first years as a Daughter of Charity. During this time she prepared to make vows, which she did on 8 September 1855.

Fr Etienne thought Sister de Virieu would be the ideal person to pioneer the mission to Drogheda, Ireland, in 1855.[30] She had the essential qualities to set up this new foundation. Fr Etienne perceived Ireland as a country that had suffered for its faith. Recognising Ireland as a profoundly religious country, he foresaw that the life of the Daughters of Charity would awaken vocations among the people. Sister de Virieu was fluent in English and she lived her vocation as a servant of the poor with single-mindedness, commitment and love. On 5 November 1855, Sister de Virieu arrived in Ireland with three sisters as her companions.[31]

Sister de Virieu had gained a wealth of experience in Drogheda and it was no accident that after eighteen months she was appointed to open the mission in North William Street. Very quickly, she saw the dire poverty and with her companions she searched for new ways to combat the poverty through the provision of services in education and health care. The sisters who formed this first community with Sister Josephine de Virieu were sisters Elizabeth Crawford, Vincent Behan, Monica Roice and Jeanne Morris. They were installed there on 14 May 1857 by Fr Médard Salvayre, Secretary General to Fr Etienne.[32] Sister Jeanne Morris was born in 1834, in Skryne, Co. Meath and celebrated her twenty-first birthday on Christmas Day, 1855. She was missioned to Dublin in 1857 and to Sheffield, England in 1859, after which she was sent to the pharmacy in the motherhouse, Paris. In 1861, Sister Jeanne was sent to Ardennes, Sedan. She died on 29 June 1899 and is buried there. Sister Marie (Vincent) Behan, born in Dublin in 1827, entered the Daughters of Charity on 5 May 1854 and was missioned to Boulogne when she had

---

[29] L. Sullivan DC, *Sister Rosalie Rendu: A Daughter of Charity on Fire with Love for the Poor* (Chicago, 2006), p. 37.

[30] Fr Jean Baptiste Etienne to Fr Philip Dowley, 19 October 1855, PA:CM/Raheny (Provincial Archives, Congregation of the Mission, Raheny, here abbreviated as PA:CM/Raheny).

[31] See Chapter 1, 'The Arrival of the Daughters of Charity of St Vincent de Paul to Drogheda, Ireland, November 1855'.

[32] PA:DC/Dunardagh/North William Street.

completed the seminary. She was then missioned to North William Street when it opened in 1857 and here she made her vows for the first time. She died in Dublin on 13 April 1883. Sister Elizabeth Crawford, born 7 July 1827 in Ireland entered the community on 21 June 1850 and was missioned to Aversa in Italy in 1851. She was sent to North William Street in 1857 and later that year was appointed the sister servant of St Vincent's Hospital, Fairview. In 1859, she was missioned to Gros Caillou, Paris and later to Sheffield as sister servant, where she died in 1897.[33] Sister Roice was one of the pioneer sisters to North William Street in May 1857, where she died a few months later on 28 July, aged 26 years.

Two agreements were set in place on 15 April 1857.[34] These agreements were drawn up in Paris.[35] One was between the Superioress of the Daughters of Charity, and Archbishop Cullen;[36] the other was between the Daughters of Charity and the administrators of the City of Dublin Health Centre.[37] Sister de Virieu received copies of the agreed documents as the superioress of the establishment.[38] Both legal documents set out in a professional, clear, concise format the provision for accommodation, finance, pastoral situation and broad working conditions for the sisters. There were similarities in terms and conditions laid down with distinctive rules and regulations listed, safeguarding the ethos and charism of the Daughters of Charity. The two agreements safeguarded the accountability of and transparency in dealing with finance. Provision was also made for the protection of the rules and constitutions and for the needs of the sisters living in community.

Article 1 of the agreement with the Archbishop stated that the number of sisters in community should be five, though Article 2 states the number could be increased 'according to the development of the services'. Dr Cullen agreed to pay the sum of £120 per annum for the salary of five sisters (Article 5). This sum covered a small portion of the expenses. The sisters had to feed and clothe the poorest of the children and give relief to the poor in their homes. In addition to maintaining the school they had to pay the assistant teachers. Article 6 stated that the Ladies of Charity would donate 'a yearly sum of £50'

---

[33] *Pioneer Sisters of Charity of Saint Vincent de Paul* (London, 1955), p. 88.

[34] PA:DC/Dunardagh/North William Street.

[35] Preliminary Observations on the Agreements Negotiated, tr. Tom Davitt CM, 20 November 2004. PA:DC/Dunardagh/North William Street.

[36] Agreement negotiated between Archbishop Cullen of Dublin and the Superioress General of the Daughters of Charity of St Vincent de Paul, 15 April 1857, PA:/DC/Dunardagh/North William Street.

[37] Agreement negotiated between the administrators of the City of Dublin Health Centre and the Superioress General of the Daughters of Charity of St Vincent de Paul, 15 April 1857, PA:DC/Dunardagh/North William Street.

[38] Agreement One and Two, 15 April 1857, PA:DC/Dunardagh/North William Street.

to the sisters on condition that 'they take charge of a small orphanage founded by the ladies'. Furthermore, the agreement stated that the Ladies would provide finance for their established orphanage. The agreement also outlined the responsibilities of the sisters. They would visit the 'sick poor' in their homes and those sisters involved with the orphanage would collaborate with the Ladies and they would teach 'gratuitously the small needy girls of the city of Dublin' (Article 10). The Daughters of Charity would be obliged as parishioners to attend mass and vespers in the parish, though they would not attend devotions which would take them away from the service of the poor (article 11).

The second agreement drawn up with the administrators of the City of Dublin Health Centre does not refer to the Ladies of Charity. Each article focuses entirely on the day-to-day work of the sisters and their terms of employment (articles 1–15). It specifically includes the provision for a chaplain (article 12). The agreement also stated 'when a sister shall die' that 'one high Mass and three low Masses will be celebrated for the repose of her soul' (article 13).

The sisters were distressed by the misery and poverty they encountered but they believed it was a privilege to be at the service of a people who experienced so much suffering. The sisters began the mission in North William Street by visiting those who were sick and poor in their homes. They also took a Sunday class for adult women. According to their means they provided families with soup, meat and coal. The works gradually developed. Education soon became a priority.

Correspondence shows that Miss Aylward, the Ladies of Charity and Sister Josephine de Virieu initially worked together. As time passed, differences emerged regarding the method of working and Miss Aylward and the Daughters of Charity decided to work independently of each other.[39] With the congregation Miss Aylward founded, the Sisters of the Holy Faith, she played a pioneering role in the Irish society of the nineteenth century.

Education

On arrival to North William Street a school had been put in the sisters' care. The building was in urgent need of enlargement and there were no funds. However, Sister de Virieu found herself surrounded by generous benefactors and on one occasion a missionary gave her the sum of ten thousand francs.[40] From 1857–84 three school rooms were built and all expenses were paid by the sisters.[41] In 1879, Sister de Virieu had the building enlarged. She had four

---

[39] J. Prunty, *Margaret Aylward, 1810–1889*, p. 88.
[40] Remarks about Sister Josephine (Charlotte) de Virieu, PA:DC/Dunardagh/North William Street.
[41] Acquisition Book of North William Street, May 1857, PA:DC/Dunardagh/North William Street.

big classrooms built and many children who came to school received free books, clothes and meals. Assistance was also provided to families.[42] Sister de Virieu recognised the importance of a good education and ensured that all pupils studied a variety of subjects. She was insistent that the religious instruction of the children would be solid and enlightened and that it would be strong enough to enable them to cope with the trials they would experience as adults. She gave catechism classes to past pupils on Sundays, thus ensuring a continuation of what they learned in school.

Sister de Virieu had a holistic view of education including life skills so she had the children instructed in needlework, flower-making and household duties. She kept close ties with her French roots and she employed a French woman who bore an Irish name, Mlle Emma Donovan, to help with the craft work.[43]

The sisters also had the care of an infant school of girls and boys under seven with an attendance of 100 children.[44] On arrival to North William Street in 1857, the Daughters of Charity discovered that the school formerly run by the Carmelite community was under the National Board, which paid them an allowance and provided them with school requisites. The Archbishop requested that the sisters withdraw from the National Board, because the Board prohibited religious instruction. Thus they had to relinquish the government grant. From 1858, the Daughters of Charity administered the school without any aid from the government. The Archbishop paid £25 for each school sister. The sisters were thus enabled to reorganise and shape their school and include religious education.[45] In time, the sisters built three large schools, capable of holding 550 children. The school received no state support until 1897, when under the principalships of Sister Mary Cullen and Sister Agnes Barraud it again received grant aid.[46] Sister Mary Cullen, a niece of Cardinal Paul Cullen, conducted a catechism class on Sundays after the 10.00 a.m. mass. From this class developed the Holy Angels' Sodality, which later became the Association of the Children of Mary.[47] Sister Mary Cullen also organised classes for pupils who dropped out of school and for those whose attendance was poor. Her devotion to Our Lady prompted the establishment of the Virgo Potens office which is the main supplier of miraculous medals and scapulars. This office is

---

[42] PA:DC/Dunardagh/North William Street.

[43] J. Prunty, *Margaret Aylward, 1810–1889*, p. 89.

[44] Acquisition Book of North William Street, May 1857, PA:DC/Dunardagh/North William Street.

[45] S. J. Greene, 'The Convent in North William Street', p. 7.

[46] Ibid., p. 6.

[47] The Association of the Children of Mary was established on 2 February 1840 in Paris by Fr J. M. Aladel, see Chapter 4, 'Historical Marian Devotional Practices among the Daughters of Charity'.

now located in Henrietta Street, Dublin.[48] A periodical, entitled *Virgo Potens* was also published as a result of Sister Mary's desire to honour the Immaculate Heart of Mary in a particular way.[49] In 1916, during the week of the Rising in Dublin, Sister Mary Cullen was hit by a stray bullet. This necessitated the removal of her right eye and impaired her hearing.

Sister Agnes Barraud came to North William Street from Whitevale Refuge, Glasgow in 1898. She engaged in the work of extending the school buildings and also gave good practical instruction to the members of the Association of the Children of Mary. Sister Agnes was particularly noted for the support she offered to the sister servants in the Dublin houses. Her health declined through the years and she died in St Vincent's, North William Street on 7 February 1938. At the time of her death the Children of Mary recited the office of the Immaculate Conception and the rosary at her bedside.[50]

While there was an infant school in the parish of North William Street, there was no boys' school. In 1893, Sister Monica McCarthy established the boys' school catering for boys up to fourth class.[51] This school was located inside the uncompleted walls of the new church, which subsequently opened as St Agatha's Church in 1908.[52]

Orphanage

The original orphanage, St Mary's Parochial Female Orphan House, founded by the Trinitarian Confraternity, accommodated only a few children, the greater number being boarded out.[53] By 28 December 1858, Sister de Virieu, with the assistance of Revd James Dixon CM, opened the new St Vincent's Orphanage and a large classroom was also built.[54] The extension of the old orphanage was essential, as poverty and unemployment in the wake of the Famine had impoverished the working population of Dublin, and there were many applications for the admission of children. At first two little girls were received and later there was accommodation for two hundred girls. When establishing the orphanage, Sister de Virieu placed it under the patronage of the Ladies of Charity who gave it considerable support. The Ladies received applications for enrolling the children in the orphanage.

---

[48] Office of Virgo Potens, Henrietta Street, Dublin 1.

[49] Remarks on Sr Mary (Teresa) Cullen, PA:DC/Mill Hill/deceased sisters (Provincial Archives, Daughters of Charity, Mill Hill, London, here abbreviated as PA:DC/Mill Hill).

[50] Remarks on Sr Agnes (Mary Margaret) Barraud, PA:DC/Mill Hill/deceased sisters.

[51] S. J. Greene, 'The Convent in North William Street', p. 7.

[52] Ibid., p. 7.

[53] Notes of Sr Langdale, PA:DC/Dunardagh/North William Street.

[54] Ibid.

The orphanage received no state aid and was reliant on private funding raised through the Vincentian Fathers and the Dublin dockers. In the early days a committee of Ladies was formed to help the sisters in their work. They met on a weekly basis. Initially the Ladies came in great numbers to assist but as numbers declined the sisters continued their work unaided. From 1859 to 1930, the number of children received into the orphanage rose to 9,012.[55] Apart from the £25 the Archbishop paid for each school sister, other financial assistance was provided by the Association of the Holy Angels and from collections, known as the 'Penny Collection'. The contributors were the labourers and poor working men. They gave a penny or halfpenny from their weekly wage for the 'destitute and helpless orphans'. A considerable sum of money was collected between 1862 and 1930.[56]

A fundraising campaign was undertaken by the commercial men of Dublin in 1864 and another extension was made to the orphanage. In 1898, the oldest part of the building was falling into disrepair so a large wing was built to accommodate the orphanage. Further developments took place over the years. The Ladies visited the children's families and collected subscriptions. Religious from different orders visited the orphanage to see the work in progress and its organisation. Many were impressed with the collaborative measures that were in operation between the committee and the sisters. 'But', they would say to the sisters, 'how does your superior manage to get on with a committee of Ladies!?'[57] This was a two-way venture as Sister de Virieu respected the Ladies' rights and abilities, she always showed a spirit of gratitude for their dedication and generosity and she sought their advice.

In 1872, a property was bought in Mount Prospect Avenue, Clontarf near Dollymount Strand.[58] This provided holiday facilities for the children, with a large beach within walking distance. Many sisters travelled there to make their annual eight-day retreat.

Other parish ministries
The Pioneer Total Abstinence Movement was established in North William Street by Fr Cullen SJ who was much supported in the work by Sister Mary Cullen. While Fr Cullen held a temperance meeting in North William Street, the first Pioneer meeting was held in Gardiner Street with the assistance of four Ladies in the house of the Jesuits. Sister Mary Cullen was drafted in to do the clerical work and distribute the pins under the supervision of the Jesuits.[59]

---

[55] Notes of Sr Langdale, PA:DC/Dunardagh/North William Street.
[56] Ibid.
[57] Remarks about Sr Josephine (Charlotte) de Virieu, PA:DC/Dunardagh/North William Street.
[58] PA:DC/Dunardagh/North William Street.
[59] Ibid.

In the agreement negotiated in 1857 with the administrators of the City of Dublin Health Centre and the Superioress General of the Daughters of Charity and her officers, there was provision for a link to be made with the hospice with regard to financial aid for the sisters' quarters (Article 5).[60] In 1888, the administrators of one of the big hospices in Dublin requested sisters to work there.[61] The venture was immediately supported by Sister Eugénie Marcellus, provincial. Sister de Virieu was instructed to acquire furniture and everything necessary for the accommodation of the sisters there. In spite of her own fragile health, she oversaw everything for the new mission. Any effort to relieve the lot of those who suffered was carried out with energy and enthusiasm.[62]

When the Daughters of Charity arrived in North William Street, it was part of the parish of St Mary's Pro-Cathedral.[63] It was not until 1865 that St Agatha's became an independent parish. Its first parish priest, Fr Francis Doran (1865–77), was appointed on 4 September 1865.[64] As there had been no local parish church the sisters' chapel was opened to the public and served as a chapel of ease (along with St Joseph's, Portland Row). Many local people were baptised and confirmed there. St Agatha's new parish church was blessed by Archbishop Walsh on 25 October 1908. The sisters, in addition to their work in the parish, schools and orphanage, took charge of the altar-linen and the choir. The chapel was served by a parish priest and three curates, who, as the diocese expanded, were regularly changed. Sister de Virieu and the sisters managed with wisdom, tact and prudence to provide what was needed to contribute to the parish effectively, in spite of their very limited means.

The end of an era

Though Sister Josephine de Virieu was a dynamic and energetic person, she was prone to sickness and gradually her health failed. Initially she grew deaf. Then her sight failed as cataracts formed in both her eyes. She had eye surgery in 1883 which was successful, but reading and writing remained difficult for her. From time to time, she suffered from bronchitis. In spite of her illness and the opposition she encountered, the mission flourished. In her wisdom, Sister de Virieu worked in such a way that the sister who would replace her could

---

[60] Agreement negotiated between the administrators of the city of Dublin Health Centre and the Superioress General of the Daughters of Charity of St Vincent de Paul, 15 April 1857. In the Preliminary Observation by Tom Davitt CM he explains 'there is no other reference to this hospice', 20 November 2004, PA:DC/Dunardagh/North William Street.

[61] Remarks about Sr Josephine (Charlotte) de Virieu, PA:DC/Dunardagh/North William Street.

[62] Ibid.

[63] S. J. Greene, 'The Convent in North William Street', p. 6.

[64] Ibid.

continue the work without difficulty or anxiety. In 1890, Sister de Virieu was succeeded by Sister Agnes Robinson, who also made many improvements in reorganising the whole establishment.[65] In 1896, Sister Barraud became sister servant and remarked that 'all the works of this dear house have been firmly established: the orphanage, the four day-school classes, the reception of the poor all are in excellent condition and no trouble to run. I found everything in perfect order.'[66] Development of the works was consistent and thorough and called for much energy and self-sacrifice from all involved.

The reflections of the sisters at the time of the death of Sister Josephine de Virieu indicate aspects of her personality. She encouraged them to be ever vigilant in the care of poor persons, saying, 'You must understand sisters how the thought of being forgotten can be so hurtful to them.'[67] The sisters spoke of her kindness and generosity to the people she served. They recounted her many gifts and skills. One sister said of her, 'She taught us less by word than example what devotion, activity and love of work should mean to a servant of the poor.'[68] They also recalled her great grief when four young sisters died of tuberculosis and typhoid, brought on by poor nutrition and hardship. While they experienced her hastiness and impetuosity at times, they also experienced her love, her readiness to apologise and to seek forgiveness. The sisters loved and reverenced this woman who gave so unstintingly of herself to the people and to them. They knew more than anyone that the plight of the suffering people was her burden and sorrow. For them, Sister Josephine's work for justice was boundless. Because of them she was happy to live in exile from her own family and her beloved country.

Sister Josephine's last illness caused her great suffering. True to character, she responded with a great spirit of patience and calm. Faced with death, she experienced a deep peace, and on 12 December 1890, she died, surrounded by her companions.

On hearing of the death of Sister Josephine, the archbishop of Dublin, Dr Cullen came to pay his respects. He expressed his regrets to the sisters that he could not attend the funeral. He promised: 'I shall make up for this at the month's mind.' Seeing the sisters' surprise that the month's mind, which was reserved for priests only, was going to be offered for Sister de Virieu, the

---

[65] PA:DC/Dunardagh/North William Street.
[66] Ibid.
[67] Remarks about Sr Josephine (Charlotte) de Virieu, PA:DC/Dunardagh/North William Street.
[68] Ibid.

Archbishop continued: 'Oh! You must have it for her and I will come and preside. For your Foundress in Ireland, we cannot do enough; she deserves everything.'[69] Sister Josephine de Virieu is buried in the sisters' graveyard in North William Street, alongside the younger sisters who predeceased her as listed in Figure 3:1.

Figure 3:1 Daughters of Charity interred in the graveyard of St Vincent's North William Street

Name	Date of Death	Age
Sister Anne Carroll	13-10-1858	23
Sister Monica Roice	28-07-1857	26
Sister Rosalie Reilly	15-05-1873	28
Sister Cecelia Cliffe	07-07-1863	29
Sister Monica Vasey	07-06-1880	33
Sister Pauline Penney	06-12-1870	33
Sister Theresa Doyle	21-11-1864	34
Sister Louise Rohrer	27-10-1885	40
Sister Vincent Behan	13-04-1883	55
Sister Cecelia Robinson	08-12-1896	60
Sister Agnes Ward	15-01-1892	62
Sister Josephine de Virieu	12-12-1890	73

The Daughters of Charity came to North William Street in 1857 because they were profoundly moved by the suffering and deprivation of so many people in Dublin. Their motto, 'The Charity of Jesus crucified urges us' inspired them to make their home among the people in North William Street.[70]

---

[69] Remarks about Sr Josephine (Charlotte) de Virieu, PA:DC/Dunardagh/North William Street.
[70] Ibid.

Chapter Four

Historical Marian Devotional Practices among the Daughters of Charity

Anne Neylon DC

Devotional practices are a particular means of nurturing the spiritual life. Roman Catholic devotions are 'expressions of piety' that 'extend the liturgical life of the church, but do not replace it'.[1] Devotions to saints, with the Virgin Mary as the most prominent example, are a central characteristic of Roman Catholicism. Catholic devotions have various forms, ranging from formalised multi-day prayers, such as novenas, to activities which do not involve any prayers – the wearing of scapulars, the veneration of the saints and even horticultural practices, for instance, maintaining a Mary garden.[2] When the Daughters of Charity came to Ireland in 1855, they brought with them the devotional practices in which they were formed during their seminary training in Paris, practices regularly recited, from the beginning of the Company in 1633.

Louise de Marillac and devotion to Mary
The Blessed Virgin Mary is central in the story of the Redemption in the early Church.[3] Louise de Marillac, co-foundress of the Daughters of Charity had a remarkable devotion to Mary. There were essentially five points on which Louise's devotion to Our Lady hinged: Mary as the Mother of God; celebration of the feasts of Our Lady; Mary as the model of all the virtues and therefore an example and inspiration for all Daughters of Charity; praying each day the

---

[1] *Catechism of the Catholic Church* (Dublin, 1994), p. 374.
[2] A. Ball, *Encyclopaedia of Catholic Devotions and Practices* (Indiana, USA, 2003), p. 341b.
[3] L. Sullivan DC, ed. and tr., *Spiritual Writings of Louise de Marillac: Correspondence and Thoughts* (Brooklyn: New City Press, 1991), p. 830.

angelus and rosary; other personal and local devotional practices. In her writings Louise states:

> Let us celebrate, in a special way, the Church feasts honouring Mary and meditate, during the day, on the mystery proposed … We should faithfully recite, each day, those prayers which we have chosen to honour her. These should include acts of love as well as of joyful praise for the glory that is hers in heaven.[4]

Louise considered the Blessed Virgin Mary as 'Protectress', even before the foundation of the Company of the Daughters of Charity.[5] From its foundation in 1633, Louise prayed that Our Blessed Lady would be the only Mother of the Company and that it would always be under her protection.[6] The first draft of the Rule of the Company of the Daughters of Charity, preceding the common rules, expresses the desire of Louise to place the Company under the protection of the Blessed Mother. The text of this rule states that:

> the Confraternity of widows and village girls [referring to the first Daughters of Charity] has been instituted to honour Our Lord, its patron, and the Blessed Virgin, and to imitate, in some way, the women and young girls of the Gospel who followed and ministered to Our Lord and His Apostles.[7]

It is evident from Louise's writings that she endeavoured to inculcate the same devotion in her sisters. Her keen sense of the liturgical life of the Church is evident in her prayer journal, writing her thoughts frequently on feast days, such as Saint Fiacre and prominent times through the Church year.[8] On 15 August 1659, feast of the Assumption of Mary, Louise reflected on the greatness of Mary as she participated in the great mysteries of the life of her Son, Jesus.[9] Louise believed that the feast days set by the Church in honour of Mary should be celebrated by the Daughters of Charity and that they remain faithful to the daily prayers and devotional practices in honour of the Blessed Virgin. These still form part of the order of day in the life of the Daughters of Charity as outlined in the constitutions.[10]

---

[4] L. Sullivan DC, ed. and tr., *Spiritual Writings of Louise de Marillac*, p. 786.
[5] Ibid., p. 695.
[6] Company of the Daughters of Charity of St Vincent de Paul, Constitutions, p. 37.
[7] L. Sullivan DC, ed. and tr., *Spiritual Writings of Louise de Marillac*, p. 727.
[8] Ibid., p. 776.
[9] Ibid., p. 831.
[10] Company of the Daughters of Charity of St Vincent de Paul, Statute 7, p. 53.

Louise de Marillac's focus on the Immaculate Conception

Writing in c.1626, Louise expressed her desire to give herself to God to 'glorify' Him for the choice He made of 'Mary to be Mother of His Son'.[11] Mary's conception was immaculate because of this divine action.[12] Louise writes emphatically on the subject of the Immaculate Conception leading 'us to realise and to adore the omnipotence of God because grace totally vanquished nature in her'.[13] Between 1647 and 1660, Louise's writings explain that the Immaculate Conception was the subject of her Marian devotion. She is clear that in contemplating the Immaculate Conception she is called to adore God's omnipotence for what He has done in and through Mary, choosing her to be the Mother of His Son. Louise expresses gratitude to the Blessed Trinity for the choice of Mary.[14] Louise shared her thoughts on the Immaculate Conception with the Daughters of Charity long before it was declared a dogma of faith by Pope Pius IX in 1854.

The Cathedral of Chartres was a place of pilgrimage in seventeenth-century France and was regularly visited by Louise. On 14 October 1644, she consecrated the Company to the Virgin Mary of Chartres.[15] At the time of consecration, the Company had been in existence for eleven years. On the Solemnity of the Immaculate Conception, 8 December, the Daughters of Charity recite communally the Act of Consecration.[16] This act recalls that at Chartres Louise offered the infant Company to God through Mary. The Act of Consecration is part of the Company's tradition and in reciting it the Daughters of Charity reaffirm their total belonging to the Lord and to the Company. The Act is designated as 'the act of offering by which every year on the feast of the Immaculate Conception, the Daughters of Charity take the Blessed Virgin Mary as their Mother and Protectress'.[17] On 1 January another Act of Consecration is recited by the sisters to honour the Solemnity of Mary, Mother of God. The Daughters of Charity renew their vows annually on 25 March, feast of the Annunciation. This feast day was chosen by Louise for the renewal of vows in order to associate her own oblation and that of the Daughters of Charity with the fiat of the Blessed Virgin Mary. In renewing the vows of poverty, chastity, obedience and service of the poor, by reciting the vow formula individually and silently during the celebration of the Eucharist,

---

[11] L. Sullivan DC, ed. and tr., *Spiritual Writings of Louise de Marillac*, p. 695.

[12] 'The Immaculate Conception', *Catechism of the Catholic Church* (Dublin, 1994), p. 110.

[13] L. Sullivan DC, ed. and tr., *Spiritual Writings of Louise de Marillac*, p. 830.

[14] Ibid., p. 831.

[15] Ibid., p. 121.

[16] Daughters of Charity of the British Province, *Together Let Us Praise God's Name* (Cambridge, 2003), p. 265.

[17] 'Mary Immaculate and the Company of the Daughters of Charity, in the History of the Company', *Echoes of the Company*, no. 1, Jan/Feb 2005, p. 87.

each sister makes herself totally available to the Holy Spirit as she takes Christ the Servant as her model and thus she is united to His mission, the evangelisation of those living in poverty.[18] The devotion to Our Lady of the Miraculous Medal dates from the apparition of the Blessed Virgin to Catherine Labouré (1806–76) on 27 November 1830 where she entrusted Catherine with a mission to have a medal struck and distributed. Catherine explains that while at prayer she

> saw a picture representing the Blessed Virgin, in the way that she is customarily portrayed under the title of the Immaculate Conception, full length and holding out her arms. [She was] dressed in a white dress and a silvery blue mantle, with a veil the colour of the dawn. From her hands came rays of light, beautifully glittering, and as if in bundles.[19]

On seeing this picture Catherine heard a voice saying, 'These rays of light are a symbol of graces that Mary obtains for men.' On the surround of the picture Catherine read the following invocation in gold letters, *O Mary conceived without sin pray for us who have recourse to thee.* On the reverse side of the medal Catherine saw the letter M surrounded with a little cross and at its foot the hearts of Jesus and Mary. Then Mary spoke these words to Catherine: 'All who wear the medal with confidence and make this short prayer will enjoy the special protection of the Mother of God.'[20]

Catherine suffered greatly in trying to convince her confessor, Fr Jean Marie Aladel, that this mission had to be carried out. He was her spokesperson and she remained silent and anonymous in her mission almost until her death, as instructed by Our Lady at the time of the apparition. In June 1832, Fr Aladel and the superior general of the Congregation of the Mission, Fr Jean-Baptiste Etienne spoke to Archbishop of Paris Hyacinthe-Louis de Quélen about the apparitions and on 30 June 1832, the Archbishop gave permission for the medal to be struck. Devotion to the medal spread throughout Paris and the world. Stories of conversions to religious practice and cures of bodily ailments were so renowned that the people called the medal miraculous. The medal rapidly spread internationally, to the United States (1836), Poland (1837), China and Russia (1838). The story of the apparition of Our Lady to Catherine Labouré is told and retold so that the message of the medal may be more widely known. The wearing of the medal represents a sign of reverence for the Mother of God and confidence in her protection. Members of the Legion of Mary

---

[18] Daughters of Charity, *Together Let Us Praise God's Name*, p. 263.
[19] R. Laurentin, *The Life of Catherine Labouré, 1801–1876*, tr. Paul Ingwood (London, 1983), p. 79.
[20] Ibid., p. 80.

worldwide, in their apostolate of evangelisation are promoters of the miraculous medal.[21]

It is claimed that the conversion of a Jewish banker from Alsace, Alphonse Ratisbonne, in the Sant'Andrea delle Fratte Church, Rome in 1842 is due to the intervention of Mary through the miraculous medal.[22] Providentially, this conversion took place in Rome, the result being that there was an increased general revival in devotion to the Immaculate Conception of Mary. Numerous petitions poured into Rome beseeching the Pope to acknowledge Mary's Immaculate Conception. In 1894, Pope Leo XIII instituted the feast of Our Lady of the Miraculous Medal including its Proper Mass and Office and designated the feast for 27 November, celebrated annually by the Daughters of Charity.

Marian devotion in Ireland and the founding of the Virgo Potens
On their arrival to North William Street in 1857, Sister Josephine de Virieu and her companions brought the charism of Vincent de Paul and Louise de Marillac to Dublin.[23] The sisters introduced the Vincentian Marian devotional practices, in particular devotion to Our Lady of the Miraculous Medal and set up the Virgo Potens office. The title of *Virgo Potens* (Virgin most powerful) arose from the apparition of the Blessed Virgin to Catherine Labouré in rue du Bac, Paris on 27 November 1830. The Blessed Virgin was holding a globe, representing the world, in her hands and her eyes were raised to heaven, presenting it to her divine son.[24]

The establishment of the Virgo Potens Office, North William Street, Dublin, originated with Sister Mary Cullen (1866–1940). She conducted a catechism class on Sundays after the ten o'clock mass from which the Holy Angels' Sodality was established and out of which grew the Children of Mary.[25] The founding of the Children of Mary dated to an apparition on 18–19 July 1830 when Mary entrusted Catherine Labouré with a mission, one which she was to communicate to Fr Aladel, her confessor: 'The Blessed Virgin requires a mission of you … You will be its founder and director. It is an *Association of Children of Mary* to which the Blessed Virgin will grant many graces.'[26] Subsequently, on 8 December 1838, the first Confraternity of the Children of Mary was proposed. The Association was set up on 2 February 1840 and spread

---

[21] Legio Mariae, *The Official Handbook of the Legion of Mary,* (Dublin, 2005), p. 344.
[22] R. Laurentin, *The Life of Catherine Labouré*, p. 135.
[23] See Glossary.
[24] The Chapel Pamphlets, Chapel of Our Lady of the miraculous medal, July 2004, p. 4.
[25] S. J. Greene, 'The Convent in North William Street' in *Saint Agatha's Church, North William Street: 75 Years Old* (Dublin, 1983), p. 7.
[26] R. Laurentin, *The Life of Catherine Labouré*, p. 145.

throughout the provinces of France, receiving the approbation of Pius IX in 1847. Fr Aladel published a Manual of the Children of Mary (1848), and 25,000 copies were available within ten years.[27] This association grew in popularity and as part of its revitalisation in later years the Association took the name Marian Youth, a popular, international and currently vibrant youth movement.[28] Sister Louise O'Sullivan established the Association of the Children of Mary in April 1858 in the sisters' house in Drogheda. Sisters Mary Cullen and Agnes Barraud were among the first sisters involved. A periodical called *Virgo Potens* was published by the Daughters of Charity which enjoyed an international circulation. This was a means of promoting Marian devotion and the Vincentian charism and contained a remarkable treasure of story, illustration, poetry, song and prayer.[29] At a time when proselytising was rife in Ireland and Catholic doctrine was being undermined, publications such as the *Virgo Potens* upheld the Catholic faith and the Catholic ethos.[30] The subtitle of the publication was the Crusade of the Miraculous Medal.[31] Today the Virgo Potens office, located in Henrietta Street, Dublin, is the centre from which miraculous medals and scapulars are distributed nationally and internationally.[32]

The first edition of the *Virgo Potens* periodical was published on 8 December 1923 in Dublin and it was sold at two pence. It was the editor's hope that the title of this periodical would 'bring joy to every heart' and that it would be 'received with a warm burst of welcome in every Catholic home'.[33] The periodical was produced to honour Mary under the title of 'Mary conceived without sin'.[34] It was a means of revealing to the world the many favours obtained by wearing the medal. By 1923, the story of Catherine Labouré and the miraculous medal was well known, thus giving credibility to devotion to Mary inside and outside the Vincentian family. The editor saw the publication as a means to evangelise and to nourish the spirituality of its readers. The Crusade of the Miraculous Medal was established and advertised in the periodical to spread devotion to Our Lady through the propagation of the miraculous medal.[35] Devotion to Our Lady of the Miraculous Medal was encouraged by the appointment of standard bearers whose role it was to

---

[27] R. Laurentin, *The Life of Catherine Labouré*, p. 146.
[28] *A Light Shining on the Earth: The Message of the Miraculous Medal: The Fiftieth Anniversary of the Canonization of Saint Catherine Labouré (1947–1997)* (Strasbourg, 1997), pp. 46–7.
[29] PA:DC/Dublin/Virgo Potens, vol. 1&2.
[30] J. Prunty, *Margaret Aylward, 1810–1889: Lady of Charity, Sister of Faith* (Dublin, 1999), p. 40.
[31] PA:DC/Dublin/Virgo Potens, p. 1.
[32] Virgo Potens Office, 10 Henrietta Street, Dublin 1.
[33] PA:DC/Dublin/Virgo Potens, p. 1.
[34] L. Sullivan DC, ed. and tr., *Spiritual Writings of St Louise de Marillac*, p. 830.
[35] *The Sisters of Charity, Centenary Record, 1857–1957* (Dublin, 1957), p. 75.

distribute at least twelve copies of the *Virgo Potens* magazine per month and these people were rewarded for fidelity to devotion by receiving a badge.[36] James Donnelly writing on Marian devotion in Ireland, states that the Irish 'devotional revolution' established itself firmly in the period 1850–75 and it reached its climax between 1930 and 1960. He says that 'what propelled the extraordinary surge in Irish popular devotion to Mary was the deep ideological impact of the Spanish civil war, the perceived dangers of international communism and socialism and the battle to preserve 'moral purity' amidst the corrupting influences of changing social and sexual mores.'[37]

International Marian Devotion

The spirit of the Crusade of the Miraculous Medal exists today in the Association of the Miraculous Medal (AMM). Devotion to Mary is promoted through this association.[38] The principal objective of the AMM is to honour the most Blessed Virgin Mary in the mystery of the Immaculate Conception. It is a public association of the Church with ecclesial, missionary, Marian and Vincentian characteristics. The conditions of membership are to wear a miraculous medal and to recite the prayer, 'O Mary conceived without sin, pray for us who have recourse to thee.'[39] Pope Pius X approved the Association of the Miraculous Medal, on 3 June 1905.[40]

In 1854, 210 years after the dedication of the Daughters of Charity by Louise de Marillac to Our Lady at Chartres and twenty-four years after the apparition of Our Lady to Catherine Labouré in the motherhouse at rue du Bac, Paris, Pope Pius IX defined the Dogma of the Immaculate Conception in an Apostolic Constitution. On that day, he said, 'We declare and define that the Blessed Virgin Mary, in the first moment of her conception, by a singular privilege of Almighty God, was preserved Immaculate from the stain of original sin.'[41] Thus the Immaculate Conception, which was a subject of Louise's writings in the 1600s was made a dogma of faith. The dogma of the Immaculate Conception was again confirmed by the appearance of Our Lady to St Bernadette Soubirous in Lourdes on 11 February 1858, where she proclaimed to the child Bernadette, 'I am the Immaculate Conception.'[42]

---

[36] *The Sisters of Charity, Centenary Record, 1857–1957* (Dublin, 1957), p. 27.
[37] J. Donnelly, 'The Peak of Marianism in Ireland, 1930–1960' in S. J. Brown and D. W. Miller, *Piety and Power in Ireland 1760–1960: Essays in Honour of Emmet Larkin* (Belfast, 2000), pp. 252–83.
[38] *The Message of the Miraculous Medal*, pp. 69–71.
[39] Prayer inscribed on the miraculous medal.
[40] The Association of the Miraculous Medal <www.famvin.org> accessed 1-5-2014.
[41] Pius IX, *Ineffabilis Deus:* Apostolic Constitution (1854).
[42] R. Laurentin, *The Life of Catherine Labouré*, p. 163.

In 1880, the Chapel of Our Lady of the Miraculous Medal, Paris was opened to pilgrims.[43] It was renovated in 1980 for the centenary of the apparitions.[44] The incorrupt body of Catherine Labouré lies under a side altar, on display in a glass casket. The walls are decorated with mosaics and murals. A marble statue of Mary with the globe was installed in the chapel and this statue was replaced in 1930. It is known as the statue of the Virgin with the globe.[45]

A further devotion to Our Lady, the Novena in Honour of Our Lady of the Miraculous Medal, has grown in popularity through the years.[46] Fr Joseph Kelly CM introduced the novena in Philadelphia, USA, on 8 December 1930. This perpetual novena was brought to Sunday's Well, Cork in 1940. Fr James Bennett CM sought permission from Archbishop McQuaid (1940–72) for the novena to be recited in St Peter's Church, Phibsborough, Dublin, and it began there in 1941. It is currently prayed on a weekly basis in many churches in Ireland, particularly in the Archdiocese of Dublin.[47]

After the manifestation of the miraculous medal in 1830, another event occurred to promote devotion to the Immaculate Heart of Mary. On 18 January 1840, the Blessed Virgin Mary singled out a Daughter of Charity, Sister Justine Bisqueyburu (1817–1903), to reveal to her in a series of apparitions 'The Badge of the Immaculate Heart of Mary', popularly called the green scapular. This scapular was approved by Pope Pius IX in 1863 and again in 1870. The prayer to be recited daily is printed around the heart on the reverse side of the scapular: 'Immaculate Heart of Mary, pray for us now and at the hour of our death.' This prayer can be recited either by the donor or the recipient of the scapular.[48]

Daily devotion to Mary is practised as the Daughters of Charity strive to be faithful to the Marian character of the Company.[49] Catherine Labouré's urgings to have Mary's requests fulfilled are as pertinent today as they were in her lifetime. Though her identity had never been revealed as the sister to whom

[43] R. Laurentin, *The Life of Catherine Labouré*, p. 245.

[44] Ibid., p. 323.

[45] Ibid., p. 253.

[46] Daughters of Charity, *The Novena in Honour of Our Lady of the Miraculous Medal* (Elo Press, Dublin), pp. 3–5.

[47] Archdiocese of Dublin, The Diocesan Directory 2014.

[48] Daughters of Charity, *Among Mary's Gifts: The Green Scapular* (Dublin, 1985), pp. 3–5.

[49] Company of the Daughters of Charity of St Vincent de Paul, Constitutions, p. 63.

Mary had appeared in 1830, on her deathbed (1875) she left a parting message
for the members of the Company:

> make sure everyone prays properly. May the Good Lord inspire our
> Superiors to honour Mary Immaculate. She is the Community's
> treasure. The Rosary should be said often. Vocations will be plent-
> eous … if all these things are done and profited from.[50]

Louise de Marillac's thoughts on the Blessed Virgin Mary continue to
inspire devotion among those who trust her as the star of the new evangelisation:

> Reveal your conscience to her and ask her to obtain for you conversion
> of life, deliverance from your most urgent needs as well as a greater love
> for her Son and closer union with His divine humanity.[51]

---

[50] R. Laurentin, *The Life of Catherine Labouré*, p. 231.
[51] L. Sullivan DC, ed. and tr., *Spiritual Writings of St Louise de Marillac*, p. 735.

Chapter Five

St Vincent's Hospital, Fairview, Dublin: From Lunatic Asylum to Therapeutic Intervention

Jacinta Prunty CHF

In the summer of 1867 the English visitor Fanny Taylor walked out to the 'quiet suburb' of Richmond 'consisting of green fields and lanes, with detached houses and cottages next them'. Behind high wooden gates, unlocked by a porter, she made her way up a short avenue to 'a small neat villa' with a garden on one side and large grounds at the rear:

> At the extreme end of these grounds, on rising ground, stood a large newly-built house, with windows from which it would not have been easy for anyone to make their exit and this, we were told, was the asylum, containing sixty lunatics under the charge of the Sisters of St Vincent de Paul.[1]

Her initial reaction was surprise. As the leading authority in the British Isles on the work of religious congregations, author of numerous histories and guides and well-travelled throughout Europe,[2] Fanny Taylor was 'accustomed to see the white cornette surrounded by little children, or bending over the sick bed of the poor'. Sister Louise de Missey, the sister in charge understood her bemusement and admitted that 'at the present moment she believed that there was only one other establishment of the kind among their many thousand houses'. Despite being an unusual work, Sister de Missey believed 'there was nothing foreign to their spirit in doing so, for their holy founder had an especial compassion for the insane and would have rejoiced to see his daughters called to their service'.[3]

Negotiations for the establishment of St Vincent's Lunatic Asylum, Fairview, opened early in 1857. The sisters took possession of the building on

---

[1] F. Taylor, *Irish Homes and Irish Hearts* (London, 1867), p. 79.
[2] Frances Magdalen Taylor was foundress of the Poor Servants of the Mother of God and was a prolific Catholic author.
[3] F. Taylor, *Irish Homes and Irish Hearts*, p. 79.

the 14 May, the same day as North William Street. The first sisters missioned were sisters de Missey, Doyle, Hinkson, Wallace and King. By November of that same year the hospital was ready to admit its first patients.

A generous legacy had been entrusted to three persons jointly, 'to dispose of how we think proper in support of any public institution', and a lunatic asylum for middle-class patients was determined upon.[4] Dr Connolly, one of the principal legatees gave evidence of his involvement to the Lunatic Asylums Commissioners in 1858 but it was a certain Dr Thomas Fitzpatrick of 31 Lower Baggot Street who was most active among the 'seven or nine gentlemen of position' who made up the governing body.[5] He set about selecting a suitable site, with room for expansion; simultaneously he sought experienced sisters to staff the institution which would allow the committee 'to work it at a much cheaper rate than other asylums in this country'.[6] By April 1857 the signed deed of foundation had gone to the Vincentian superior general, Jean-Baptiste Etienne, in Paris for his approval and minor amendments were communicated back to Dublin through the Vincentian provincial superior in Ireland, Fr Thomas MacNamara.[7] A sum of money had been forwarded to Paris, presumably to cover the travel expenses of the four sisters whom Fr Etienne said were ready to come; he intended to delay their departure until May so that he might accompany the little group himself once the good sponsors in Dublin raised no objection.[8]

The geographical location and site selected for St Vincent's were both ideal for the purposes of an asylum or hospital. Richmond House was on the northern fringes of the city, an area which enjoyed healthy sea breezes but was within easy reach of the city centre. The house itself, a gentleman's villa, was unprepossessing but set back from the road in its own gardens and reached by a lengthy avenue. Deeds, leases and conveyance documents dating from 1775, enable the previous gentlemen occupiers and changes in ownership to be tracked.[9] There were two meadows in connection with the house; these were surveyed in June 1857 and their content returned as just over 3 Irish acres (4¼ statute acres).[10] Richmond House was chosen for the project because of this extra land.

---

4 *The Freeman's Journal*, 13 October 1858.

5 Ibid.

6 Ibid.

7 Fr Salvayre, Paris to Fr MacNamara, Dublin, 6 April 1857 (Archives of St Vincent's Hospital, Fairview).

8 Ibid.

9 These documents are held in the archives of St Vincent's Hospital, Fairview.

10 In acres, roods and perches the survey returned the larger field at 2.0.37 Ir. (3.2.19 statute) and the smaller field at 0.3.7 Ir. (statute 1.1.6), giving a total of 3.0.4 Irish (4.3.25 statute); Thomas J. Gaffney to Dr Fitzpatrick, 30 June 1857 (Archives of St Vincent's Hospital, Fairview).

Dr Fitzpatrick established this private but not-for-profit 'lunatic asylum' because of his great concern for the lunatic and insane. It was important for a doctor's career to be associated with a reputable hospital and the position of visiting physician, with access to inpatient facilities, could enhance one's private practice. Access to significant numbers of mentally ill patients in a clinical setting, where they could be closely observed, was key to the development of what was to become psychiatry.[11] However, few medical practitioners in Ireland used the opportunities thus afforded to undertake professional research, or at least, to publish their findings, unlike colleagues in Britain and on the continent and no evidence has yet been found of doctors associated with St Vincent's up to 1900 developing novel treatments or sharing their insights in the medical press.[12] It should be noted that as a specialist field of medicine, few doctors in the nineteenth century were prepared to devote themselves to the treatment of those with mental afflictions, 'though many are ready and quick to theorise about the many hypotheses respecting mental alienation'.[13] The doctors associated with St Vincent's from its early decades were without doubt motivated by real concern for the mentally ill and the fact that they were noted for their kindly concern rather than for innovative clinical approaches is not surprising given the undeveloped state of psychiatry in Ireland at the time.

The term 'lunacy', though offensive today, was not considered derogatory in the nineteenth century.[14] It was only gradually replaced (from the 1920s onwards) with terms such as 'mental illness' and 'mental disorder' in line with movements internationally. The office of the 'Inspector for Lunacy' gave way to the 'Inspector of Mental Hospitals' in 1924 but it was not until 1949 that he changed the opening section of his annual report from 'Number and distribution of the insane' to 'Number of patients under care'. Similarly, the term 'asylum' had not the negative connotations it now holds, but was used to convey a place of safety and refuge, where specialised care and humane treatment would prevail as opposed to the harshness of prison or the strict discipline of the workhouse.[15]

---

[11] Jean-Etienne Dominique Esquirol's influential theories were derived from his own extensive case experience of mental illness through work in a number of French asylums which provided the large quantity of data necessary to the building up of profiles of psychiatric diseases capable of being identified by their symptoms, see Roy Porter, *Madness: A Brief History* (Oxford, 2002), pp. 134–5.

[12] For a critique of Irish research, see Henry C. Burdett, *Hospitals and Asylums of the World: Their Origin, History, Construction, Administration and Legislation*, 3 vols, ii (London, 1891), pp. 263–6.

[13] E. Esquirol, *Mental Maladies: A Treatise on Insanity* (Philadelphia, 1845), p. 72.

[14] 'Lunacy' in *The Oxford Companion to the Mind*, ed. Richard L. Gregory, (Oxford, 1987).

[15] 'Asylum' in *The Oxford Companion to the Mind*.

In the early and mid-nineteenth century the promotion of institutionalised care was prompted by public outrage at the discovery of the revolting and inhuman conditions in which the mentally ill were frequently kept especially in private boarding houses and prisons and partly by the new-found faith in the possibility of 'cure' for at least some of those afflicted.[16] Compassion for the 'destitute lunatic' motivated the members of the 1817 committee to promote the development of district asylums throughout the country, but there was also concern around the confinement of sane people or those 'temporarily mad' by unscrupulous relatives, particularly where inheritance was at stake.[17] Popular novels, such as Charlotte Brontë's *Jane Eyre*, regularly featured 'mysterious confinements'; with little state regulation, the fear that an uncooperative female, or indeed male, relative could be effectively imprisoned was not without foundation. Running a private boarding house for the insane, commonly known as a 'madhouse', could be a very profitable enterprise indeed for unscrupulous operators.

Under the Private Lunatic Asylums (Ireland) Act 1842 it was enacted that no person could keep a house for the reception of insane persons unless it was licensed and to secure such a licence the proprietors needed to apply to the quarter sessions for the county wherein the house was situated.[18] This act also stipulated that private asylums were to be inspected every six months by one of the two inspectors of lunatics in Ireland appointed by the lord lieutenant with offices in Dublin Castle.[19] The Act was designed to end the outrageous business of unregulated private 'madhouses' and did introduce some welcome reforms. However, as the mandate of the inspectors covered all the institutions which held insane persons in Ireland, listed by 1891 as twenty-two district asylums, a criminal asylum, twenty-four private asylums and 161 workhouses containing insane inmates, it is not surprising that visits to the private asylums were reported, if at all, in 'meagre and rosy-tinted generalities'.[20] There was also a loophole that allowed private institutions that were not a commercial or for-profit venture to seek derogation from being licensed.[21]

For the setting up of St Vincent's a full, official on-site investigation was conducted and all the requirements for being licensed were met. The inspection

---

[16] 'Asylum' in *The Oxford Companion to the Mind.*

[17] 'Report from the select committee appointed to inquire into the expediency of making provision for the relief of the lunatic poor in Ireland, 1817', House of Commons, (1817) (430), viii.

[18] Private Lunatic Asylums (Ireland) Act, 1842, 5 & 6 Vic. C. 123.

[19] H. C. Burdett, *Hospitals and Asylums of the World,* ii (London, 1891), p. 577.

[20] Ibid., pp. 247, 263.

[21] Burdett condemned the thirty laws relating to lunacy in Ireland passed between 1820 and 1890 as 'chaotic and confused', framed in 'an extraordinarily careless and confused manner', and badly needing to be codified 'in the interests of the insane and those who have the care and custody of them'. H. C. Burdett, *Hospitals and Asylums of the World,* i, p. 575.

of Richmond House, which 'is proposed to be opened as an institution for the insane, under the name of "St Vincent's Lunatic Asylum"', was carried out by Mr John Ingram on 25 November 1857.[22] He was entirely happy with the physical arrangements, 'The apartments are in good order, clean and comfortably furnished and there is ample accommodation for seven female patients, the number proposed to be at present received.'[23]

A copy of the deed establishing the hospital was also forwarded to the Office of Lunatic Asylums, requesting an exemption from the licence fee; the official noted that it was indeed exempt under the Act, 'being *in part* at least supported by voluntary contributions and *not kept for profit* by any individual' (emphasis in original).[24] However, in all other respects St Vincent's Lunatic Asylum was 'in a similar category as private licensed houses' and subject to inspection. The most important regulation was that all patients admitted 'shall have the certificates required by the Act'.[25] This was expressly designed to stamp out, in so far as that was possible, imprisonment without independent medical assessment, probably the most notorious feature of the private 'madhouses'. The certificate was issued on 25 November 1857, from which date the governors were entitled to receive patients.[26]

At the time of its foundation and indeed for much of its history, St Vincent's Fairview occupied a position somewhere between 'charitable' and 'private'. Among the very poor in 1850s Ireland, those suffering from mental illness could be cared for in admittedly overcrowded public asylums, while the rich had ample resources to make whatever arrangements they or their families judged best, as given in evidence to the Lunatic Asylums Commission of 1858:

> The rich, if insanity falls upon them, are surrounded with all the care that wealth can command or sympathy suggest; the poor can apply to the parish and be relieved into a county asylum; but the class between the rich and the poor suffer without resources and often long unknown, till the prolonged pains and griefs of concealed poverty beset and torture them and no relief presents itself until they have wholly fallen into the ranks of paupers.[27]

St Vincent's therefore was to provide for afflicted persons belonging to the 'middle class of society', the professional and mercantile educated class, having

---

[22] Memorandum signed John Ingram, Office of Lunatic Asylums, Dublin Castle, 21 November 1857 (Archives of St Vincent's Hospital, Fairview).

[23] Ibid.

[24] Ibid.

[25] Ibid.

[26] A letter from the Office of Lunatic Asylums to Messrs Kernan and Treacy, 55 Lower Dominick Street, 25 November 1857 (Archives of St Vincent's Hospital, Fairview).

[27] Lunatic Asylums Commission of Inquiry 1858, as reported in *The Freeman's Journal*, 13 October 1858.

only 'small means'. As one doctor testified, the 'educated portion' of the middle classes when affected with even 'temporary mental disorder' quickly descend 'from comfort to ruin', dragging their families into hopeless poverty and want.[28] From the perspective of Vincentian teaching, there was no contradiction in running a private hospital or asylum; this was truly a class of persons in need, shunned by many medical practitioners and feared by society at large. That this was clearly understood is evident from the first version of the contract with the Daughters of Charity where the word 'poor' is employed; however, for its final version it was stipulated that 'the word *poor* in the deed shall be substituted by the word "patients," as the good founders [the medical men] desire'.[29]

It was vital to the financial standing and long-term viability of the hospital that it was perceived by the public as an eminently respectable, middle-class institution; to that end any taint of 'charity asylum' or mention of 'pauper inmates' was vigorously suppressed. As a non-profit establishment 'the payment of each patient will be merely sufficient for his [her] support'. In terms of the class of those cared for, St Vincent's aimed to model itself on Charenton, the renowned mental hospital near Paris, where all the patients ('with very few exceptions') paid their way.[30] The chief difference between Fairview and Charenton was to be in the social classification of patients; in Charenton, there were three divisions depending on how much was paid per annum, but in Fairview 'it is not proposed to have either a first or second class, we shall confine ourselves to the third'.[31] The classification system employed at Charenton was reflected in the quality of food served, with the patients who paid most enjoying the highest culinary standards; the sponsors of the new hospital dispensed with this as unworkable, on the basis that Irish people would not tolerate any difference in diet, though the accommodation could reflect differences in the pension paid.

While the foundation of the asylum was made possible by a generous bequest, the running costs were to be met by the income from patients and, hopefully, from the generosity of the public through donations and bequests. By placing the asylum in the hands of religious sisters, its promoters sought to ensure economy and financial probity over the long term; in evidence before the Lunatic Asylums Commission in 1858, Dr Fitzgerald boasted:

> we shall be able to work it at a much cheaper rate than other asylums in
> this country, for we intend to employ Sisters of Charity in the

---

[28] Lunatic Asylums Commission of Inquiry 1858, as reported in *The Freeman's Journal*, 13 October 1858.

[29] Fr Salvayre, Paris to Fr MacNamara, Dublin, 6 April 1857 (Archives of St Vincent's Hospital, Fairview).

[30] *The Freeman's Journal*, 13 October 1858.

[31] 'The first class pay about 57 *l* a-year (about 1,425 francs); the second class pay 45 *l* a-year (about 1,125 francs); and the third class pay 33 *l* per year (about 825 francs).'

Institution. The expense of each of these will be little more than 20 guineas a year.[32]

There was little chance of finding 'respectable' staff in the open market at that salary. The intended staff–patient ratio was generous, for its time, at six sisters for twenty patients.[33]

The hospital's founders expected to control all aspects of its management according to the first draft of the foundation deed of 1857 which was criticised for containing restrictions that were 'all in favour of the administrators'.[34] The founders were prevailed upon to be more generous in spirit to the sisters who were going to run the asylum on a day-to-day basis: 'But if they will confide the whole establishment to the care of the sisters, they will take that very willingly. The deed is made for every position and circumstance.'[35] In practice the sisters saw to all aspects of the personal care and nursing of the patients along with the housekeeping; their role was to carry out the instructions of the medical officers. Their around-the-clock presence on site was essential and was written into the foundation documents: 'There is no difficulty to have some sisters helping in a room immediately connected with the bedrooms of the female patients. The sisters shall here have all the care of the patients.'[36]

Care and treatment regime

The interchangeable of the terms 'asylum' and 'hospital' in relation to St Vincent's, Fairview throughout the later nineteenth century reflect the ambiguity around the understanding and treatment of people with mental illness at the time. Shocking exposure of the barbaric treatment of those afflicted with mental disorders, often chained, unclothed and treated worse than animals, led several philanthropists, in the early part of the nineteenth century, to champion the 'moral management' of insanity. This advocated the abandonment of physical restraint and an appeal to the will of the patient. It aimed to restore the dignity of the patient and to enlist him or her as an ally in the treatment process. The two requirements of moral management were the early detection of insanity and the separation of the patient from the circumstances precipitating his or her attack, usually perceived as their home environment.

Treatment within an asylum, under skilled and compassionate medical supervision, met both these requirements, which also boasted high recovery

---

[32] *The Freeman's Journal*, 13 October 1858.
[33] Ibid.
[34] Fr Salvayre, Paris to Fr MacNamara, Dublin, 6 April 1857 (Archives of St Vincent's Hospital, Fairview).
[35] Ibid.
[36] Ibid.

rates.[37] A model lunatic asylum therefore was not to be perceived primarily as a home for the insane but a hospital, holding out hope, at least, of recovery: 'The restoration and discharge of a patient inspires confidence in the hearts of others.'[38] The fact that increasingly large numbers of the Irish poor were committed to public lunatic asylums from the mid-nineteenth century into the 1940s, to rid local communities of those deemed troubled or troublesome, tends to blot out the debate around the asylum which was conceived, in its ideal, as a therapeutic instrument, as a hospital where full recovery of some was expected and where all would be somewhat better or enjoy some degree of 'cure' or healing.

There is little detail in the founding documents on the medical treatment proposed for St Vincent's, which was of course largely entrusted to the medical professionals, the doctors. Anything reminiscent of a place of detention or repugnant to the 'genteel feelings' of the patients was to be avoided and the new asylum was to have 'all the requisites of a respectable establishment'.[39] Scrupulous care was to be taken against wrongful admission, while the ability of the patient or their family to pay was to be ascertained in advance: 'Forms (similar to those used at Charenton) for demanding admission and giving security for payment of pension to be adopted.'[40]

However, in so far as it can be reconstructed, the regimen of care at Fairview was firmly in the continental Pinel tradition, dating from 1792, which advocated 'moral treatment' and kindness, in a comfortable asylum setting, over physical restraint.[41] This approach advocated the close observation of asylum patients, leading to more precise differentiations in the theory and practice of mental illness.[42] Many of the principles are still valid, such as the recognition of the uniqueness of each individual and the resultant need for treatment to be designed for that person alone. From the perspective of the sisters, great store is placed in their rule of 1672 on kindly, faithful and scrupulously exact attendance on the sick and feeble, ensuring no one is overlooked and that each receives what he or she, as an individual, requires. The sisters appointed to St Vincent's hospital, therefore, were well grounded in the approach that was to be implemented in Fairview though they themselves were unlikely to have read the published work of Esquirol or other medical authorities of the time.

---

[37] 'Asylum' in *The Oxford Companion to the Mind*.
[38] E. Esquirol, *Mental Maladies*, p. 77.
[39] Fr Salvayre, Paris, to Fr MacNamara, Dublin, 6 April 1857 (Archives of St Vincent's Hospital, Fairview).
[40] Ibid.
[41] J. Robins, *Fools and Mad: A History of the Insane in Ireland* (Dublin, 1986), pp. 55–6.
[42] R. Porter, *Madness: A Brief History*, p. 135.

Although St Vincent's was not founded upon a single theory or treatment regime, from the constant references to Charenton, Paris, as a model, it is reasonable to assume that Fairview's first medical officer, Dr Fitzpatrick, drew many of his ideas from this celebrated institution. The authorities in Paris who appointed the sisters to Dublin were certainly familiar with Charenton, which was renowned as the earliest institution in France devoted entirely to mental cases.[43] Dr Fitzpatrick was surely familiar with the writings of its director the renowned Dr Esquirol, whose landmark study was published in English in 1845 under the title *Mental Maladies: A Treatise on Insanity* (Philadelphia, 1845) and who was one of the foremost advocates of the asylum as a therapeutic instrument.[44] In presenting the new hospital to the public in its first decade of operation, the involvement of experienced Daughters of Charity was one of its chief selling points, as was the fact that it was introducing enlightened continental practices in a familiar Dublin setting: 'All the requisites of the continental establishments under the care of the religious are to be found here without the discomforts attendant on a change to a foreign country.'[45]

The removal of the patient from the environment in which she had suffered from mental illness, the first principle underlying the asylum 'cure', was most effectively implemented at St Vincent's, where the sole access was through 'high green wooden gates' controlled by a porter.[46] Weighty arguments in favour of institutional treatment over treatment at one's private residence were advanced by medical practitioners, who admittedly often had a professional and financial interest in filling asylum places. A private house, no matter how large, was rarely able to contain a 'furious patient' who was then, for his own security 'bound and confined to his bed, a painful condition which augments the delirium and fury'.[47] In the dedicated institution physical restraint was rarely needed:

> In a suitable house, he could be indulged in his propensities with less danger to himself and his attendants. In a house of this kind, his wants are better understood and the domestics better instructed. The distribution of buildings permits the patient to be removed from one habitation to another, as his condition, his disposition to injure himself, or his progress towards recovery, may render expedient.[48]

The various rooms, spread over several premises and the extensive grounds to which the patients of St Vincent's had access was the aspect that first struck

[43] H. C. Burdett, *Hospitals and Asylums of the World*, i, p. 58.
[44] R. Porter, *Madness: A Brief History*, p. 134.
[45] *The Freeman's Journal*, 4 April 1862.
[46] F. Taylor, *Irish Homes and Irish Hearts*, p. 79.
[47] E. Esquirol, *Mental Maladies*, p. 76.
[48] Ibid.

Fanny Taylor on her visit to St Vincent's in 1867: 'Those who are tractable are allowed to be in the sisters' house and the grounds, the reception parlours only being shut off from them.'[49] Within the asylum building itself, behind a locked door, was 'the portion set aside for those who cannot be at all trusted alone', where she encountered the patients most to be pitied and most likely to self-harm.[50] At the back of the asylum was a piece of ground 'where the poor patients too much afflicted to mix with their peaceable companions were allowed to take the air' and at the time of her visit was occupied by two women 'leaping, dancing and howling exactly like wild beasts'.[51]

The institutional setting, well regulated in a tranquil setting and separate from the busy world, was proposed as a setting in which healing might happen:

> The quietude which the insane enjoy, far from tumult and noise, the moral repose which their withdrawal from their former habits, their business and their domestic cares procure, are very favourable to their restoration. Subjected to a regular life, to discipline and a well-ordered regimen, they are constrained to reflect upon the change in their situation. The necessity of restraining and composing themselves with strangers and the dwelling together with companions in misfortune, are powerful auxiliaries in restoring their lost reasons.[52]

Much attention was given in the international literature to the site and situation of establishments for the insane. It was stipulated that the site should preferably be exposed to the south-east or the south, to maximise the sunshine:

> The soil should be dry and light. The lodging rooms should be protected against humidity and cold; and favorably disposed for ventilation. It is a grave error to suppose that the insane are insensible to atmospheric influences. The great part of them avoid cold, and desire warmth.[53]

Within doors the environment should be such as to promote healing. The premises should be 'well lighted, cheerful and picturesque' especially for hyper-maniacs.[54] This requirement was fulfilled in the case of St Vincent's where 'the buildings, gardens and exercise grounds are bright and well kept'.[55] Warm clothing, fresh bedding, with a bed of quality horsehair, not straw, light

---

[49] E. Esquirol, *Mental Maladies*, p. 80.
[50] F. Taylor, *Irish Homes and Irish Hearts*, p. 81.
[51] Ibid., p. 83.
[52] E. Esquirol, *Mental Maladies*, p. 77.
[53] Ibid., p. 82.
[54] Ibid.
[55] *Annual Report of the Inspector of Mental Hospitals for the year, 1937*, Department of Local Government and Public Health (Dublin, 1939), p. 34.

covering or bedclothes and 'the head usually uncovered' were recommended by Esquirol, with lots of water freely available to all patients to quench thirst.

Despite the 'institutionalising' of the patient in a controlled environment, one of the beliefs driving the asylum movement was that of the individualised nature of insanity:

> As this malady is not identical in every case; as in every instance it depends upon different causes and presents varied characteristics and requires new combinations; a new problem is to be solved for every patient whom we are called to treat.[56]

There could be no single 'one size fits all' approach in the effort to 'restore man to himself', 'we must correct and restrain one; animate and sustain another; attract the attention of a third, touch the feelings of a fourth. One may be controlled by fear; another by mildness; all by hope.'[57]

For those suffering from 'melancholy' (depression) 'corporeal exercise' such as horse riding, tennis, fencing, swimming and travel were all recommended 'in aid of other means of treatment'.[58] Gardening or 'the culture of the earth' could be substituted 'with a certain class of the insane'.[59] The idle wealthy, both men and women, posed the greatest challenge as patients as they were deprived of the 'precious resource' of manual work in their treatment, 'An imperfect substitute is furnished in walks, in reading, assemblies, etc. The habit of idleness among the wealthy counterbalances all the other advantages which this class enjoy for obtaining a cure.'[60]

The dearth of information around the medical regime at St Vincent's through to the 1940s can be attributed, at least in part, to the fact that it was the asylum setting itself, safe, secure and calm, with its familiar rhythms and regular routines, that was regarded as curative. As Esquirol propounded, in a well-governed asylum, even the patient classed as 'maniac' finds himself 'attracted by the order, harmony and regularity of the house, defends himself better against his impulses and abandons himself less to his eccentric actions.'[61] He counselled against unnecessary medical interference on the basis that many patients, though undoubtedly subjects for admission to the asylum, needed only rest, quiet, good food and kindness to effect a recovery. Erring on the side of non-interference was undoubtedly wise, as the treatments that were commonly inflicted on the mentally ill in the nineteenth century included the

---

[56] E. Esquirol, *Mental Maladies*, p. 73.
[57] Ibid., p. 21.
[58] Ibid., p. 82.
[59] Ibid., p. 83.
[60] Ibid.
[61] Ibid., p. 76.

use of cold showers and water baths (where the patient was half drowned), evacuants and purges, electric shock treatment and the prescribing of narcotics. Esquirol counselled that 'a simple warm bath might very often be recommended in their stead'.[62] That little happened at St Vincent's in the line of progressive or experimental therapies up to the 1940s at least may be read as evidence of how thoroughly the institution embodied the Pinel/Esquirol asylum principles. It may have saved patients from being the subject of barbaric or ill-informed treatments in the era before drug therapies became relatively safe and effective.

A model asylum in the mid-nineteenth century was expected to be governed by regulations 'to which all must submit' and the lines of authority were to be very clearly drawn.[63] Esquirol laid down that there should be one single head:

> When there are several coordinate powers and the mind of the insane knows not upon whom to repose it wanders in doubt and confidence is not established. Now without confidence there is no cure. A spirit of independence evades obedience when authority is divided.[64]

But following orders was not sufficient. According to Esquirol, the mentally ill needed to know medical and nursing staff really cared about them, that they empathised with them in their suffering and truly wanted their recovery: 'It is not enough to say to the sick, courage, you will be better. A feeling heart must dictate these consoling words that they may reach the mind and heart of him who suffers.'[65]

As Daughters of Charity, principles of obedience had already been inculcated in them, while their Vincentian tradition emphasised above all the kindness and compassion with which the poor of Christ were to be served. The avoidance of 'restraint or seclusion' was, it appears from the reports of outsiders, the policy of the house, but this could also be an indicator that seriously disruptive and violent patients were not admitted to St Vincent's.[66] At the twice-yearly statutory inspections, the visitor had to testify to having access to all of the patients without exception; his memo for 1928 that 'all of them speak highly of their treatment by the Sisters in charge of them' is therefore worthy of note.[67] One trenchant critic of the private institutions for the insane run by religious orders in the 1890s expressly excluded the Daughters of Charity, noting that the institutions on the continent in which

---

[62] E. Esquirol, *Mental Maladies*, p. 87.

[63] Ibid., p. 76.

[64] Ibid.

[65] Ibid., p. 80.

[66] *Annual Report of the Inspector of Mental Hospitals for the year, 1930* (Dublin, 1931), p. 25.

[67] *Annual Report of the Inspector of Mental Hospitals for the year, 1928*, p. 34.

these sisters were involved 'were always famed for the kind and considerate treatment which the inmates received from their attendants'.[68]

Problems in the early decades

In 1857, its first year of operations, St Vincent's had an average of seven patients. It quickly expanded so that by April 1862 it had thirty patients and was able to advertise that it had recently returned two patients 'perfectly cured' to their families, with another four 'in a stage of mental improvement approaching recovery'.[69] The new building was praised for its 'ventilation, temperature and cheerful aspect' and once the new baths, then in progress, were completed St Vincent's committee would be able to boast that 'every requisite care and curative advantages of the afflicted will exist in the most perfect force in this institution'.[70] But it did face a number of serious challenges in its early decades both in financing the institution and in combating public ignorance and prejudice around those with mental illness.

There was undoubtedly a demand for the service provided by St Vincent's but the difficulty was to attract the kind of wealthy patient whose family could pay the full cost of her treatment and from whom a surplus could be generated to make up for the shortfall caused by the many middle-class but impecunious residents. The marketing challenge was to make the better-off aware that 'all the requisites of the continental establishments under the care of the religious are to be found here without the discomforts attendant on a change to a foreign country'.[71] If they could be further persuaded that keeping their custom in Ireland would be a form of charity, 'affording practical benefits to an afflicted class well worthy of sympathy', they might be tempted to favour St Vincent's over its competitors. But all efforts to generate custom at the upper end of the market would come to nought if the institution was to become in the least tainted by pauperism. Its income flow depended on the maintenance of its 'respectable' character but it had been founded on the presumption that charitable contributions would also accrue. Its early advertising tried to reconcile these contradictory positions by appealing for charitable support while underlining its middle-class credentials, 'All the inmates belong to the educated class and unfortunately, among the most respectable families deficiency of means is to be found, often aggravated by concealment.'[72]

---

[68] H. C. Burdett, *Hospitals and Asylums of the World*, i, p. 623.
[69] *The Freeman's Journal*, 4 April 1862.
[70] Ibid.
[71] Ibid.
[72] Ibid.

The other serious obstacle faced by St Vincent's was overcoming the prejudice against having an asylum for the mentally ill located anywhere near private or indeed public property. Several objections were voiced to the development of the asylum complex at Fairview. Lengthy and complex correspondence ensued between the hospital's promoter, Dr Fitzpatrick and their near neighbours, the Presentation Sisters, Richmond. It was only after several senior clergymen failed to find a solution to the problem that the Presentation Sisters decided to sell their house to the asylum, on the basis that 'such are the prejudices of people generally, that the immediate contiguity of the Asylum would be ruinous to the convent'.[73] The first complaint appears to have centred on the noise emanating from St Vincent's. Dr Fitzpatrick contacted his colleague Dr William Corbett, director of the Central Lunatic Asylum, Dundrum, in July 1859, for expert testimony on the noise level to be expected from an asylum.[74] Dundrum held 130 patients at that time and Dr Corbett stated categorically that only two men and one woman were reported as 'occasionally noisy' by night. In any case, the disturbance caused by these patients 'is confined to the chambers in which they are lodged, to those immediately near them, above and below, or to those who are on the same corridor'.[75] It could not be said that they upset the neighbourhood of Dundrum. He himself had resided in the hospital since he took up this post and had rarely been disturbed at night. It was, he claimed, the fear of the insane that was at the heart of such complaints:

> What I have stated will show that I do not think there need be any apprehension on this head [regarding noise]. There is in fact very little knowledge among the best informed classes of the insane, who are generally looked upon as something akin to wild beasts. But the vast majority of them have some degree of reason and it is only in some directions that they go wrong, or only at some particular seasons. And the extreme fear arising in many, from being anywise near the insane, becomes very little indeed by a practical knowledge and acquaintance with them.[76]

Despite what the director of the Central Lunatic Asylum claimed, the Presentation Sisters were troubled by the shrieking and screaming coming from St Vincent's over several years. The story was told to Fanny Taylor on her tour

---

[73] Bartholomew Woodlock to Dr Thomas Fitzpatrick, 10 August 1859 (Archives of St Vincent's Hospital, Fairview).
[74] William Corbett, Central Asylum to Dr Fitzpatrick, 21 July 1859 (Archives of St Vincent's Hospital, Fairview).
[75] Ibid.
[76] Ibid.

of convents and charitable institutions in Ireland in 1869, who recounted in poetic terms how:

> Solitude and silence fled from their pretty chapel, their quiet cells, their pleasant grounds. They could not even be at peace when they wandered to the little cemetery at the extremity of their enclosure where some of their dearly-loved companions reposed and where they had marked out their own graves. ... The Presentation nuns at Richmond soon found that novices would not venture within their walls for fear of their strange neighbours.[77]

From the windows of the former Presentation Convent she saw and heard for herself a number of 'wild, haggard-looking creatures with their grey hair streaming on their shoulders, talking incoherently to themselves, one keeping up a perpetual moaning' and sympathised with the nuns who had felt forced out of their beloved convent.[78]

The valuation of furniture and effects for fire insurance, dated 6 January 1919, gives a good idea of the internal disposition of rooms, how they were furnished and the overall complex of buildings which made up St Vincent's Asylum at that time.[79] By extension, something of the regime in place and the character of the institution, can be deduced, though the layout of the details, with 'ditto' used throughout, means that the following analysis may not be exactly correct in point of numbers of bed spaces.

The buildings consisted of a residence, which could sleep ten sisters (in a dormitory of five, two shared rooms and one single room); each had an iron canopy bedstead (with chair and toilet ware). The remainder of the accommodation consisted of a front sitting room, a back sitting room, hallway and community room, with a good selection of religious images throughout. The adornments were firstly typical of houses occupied by the Daughters of Charity – a statue of Vincent de Paul 'on Caen stone pedestel' in the hall, two photogravures of the 'Founders' and framed portraits of the current pope, Leo XIII and the archbishop of Dublin, Dr Walsh. But they were also more generally typical of any religious house, with the Sacred Heart, St Joseph, the Blessed Virgin, the Holy Family all featuring variously as photogravures, oil paintings, as oleographs and chromolithographs in the convent and throughout the asylum. The few secular illustrations actually named were some 'photoviews of Irish scenery', while three volumes of *Punch* and one volume of the *Illustrated*

---

[77] F. Taylor, *Irish Homes and Irish Hearts*, p. 81.

[78] Ibid.

[79] Valuation of furniture and effects for fire insurance, St Vincent's Asylum, 6 January 1919, 2 vols. Battersby and Company, Westmoreland Street, Dublin. The valuation totals £8586 17 s. 0 d.

London News were the only books in the convent worth recording for insurance purposes.

St Anne's Unit had fifteen bedrooms, one dormitory for ten persons and one servant's room. Each of the single bedrooms was furnished with a small birch bed, wire mattress, hair mattress, bolster and pillow and birch chairs; each had a gas light, a birch chest of drawers, small birch washstand and toilet ware. The dormitory for ten persons had a Dutch carpet, photogravures and statues, fireplaces; the servant's room had a painted chest of drawers, two pieces of wardrobe and two chairs. There was also a room with two beds and two further 'double rooms' variously furnished with strips of carpet and rugs, washstands, oak grained wardrobes, birch elbow chair, wall mirror, pier press, valances and blinds. These types of details, with small gradations in quality, are to be found for all the accommodation. What is most striking is the variation; the furnishings were more like those of a genteel home than of an institution, probably as much from the piecemeal development of the complex as from efforts to avoid being too institutional.

St Catherine's Unit had eleven bedrooms, of which the largest held seven persons and the two smallest were single rooms. The patients' sitting room had: hanging baskets and plants, mottled hearthrug, wicker armchairs, brass gasoliers, mahogany dining table and mahogany bookcase, a great mixture of armchairs, small tables and pictures.

St Teresa's Unit had ten bedrooms, St Joseph's had five 'very good' bedrooms, of which four were single occupancy; and St John's Unit had a further fourteen bedrooms, of which thirteen were single bedrooms with pitch pine bed and bedding and one was a two-bedded room. St Gabriel's Unit had nineteen bedrooms for patients and two rooms for servants, while St Vincent's Unit consisted solely of the dining room and scullery.

Richmond House, the former Presentation Convent, was devoted entirely to sleeping accommodation except for the oratory. It had a dormitory for six and nine bedrooms, consisting of two cubicles, a cubicle for one and a cubicle for two, four single bedrooms, all 'very good', a 'small room', an attic room and a servant's room, as well as the oratory.

St Mary's Unit had two dormitories for eight and for five persons and nine bedrooms of which six were single rooms. Here was to be found a good wool carpet, mahogany elbow chair, Axminster square-shaped mats. And all parts of the complex were amply decorated throughout with religious and other images. The disposition of the rooms, mostly single rooms but also some doubles and small dormitories and the grouping of patients into small units, each with its own patron saint certainly contributed to the 'homely' character of the institute so frequently commented on by outsiders and belied the numbers of persons held at any one point in time.

The published annual reports of the inspector of mental hospitals for the 1920s reveals that the total number of inmates was fairly steady, between 129 and 139 on the 31 December of any year in that decade; in the 1930s the numbers were a little higher reaching 151 persons in December 1937; but did not reach these figures again until the modern hospital was well established in the 1960s. Until 1945 St Vincent's was one of twelve private establishments for the insane in Ireland, of which eight were licensed under the Private Lunatic Asylums (Ireland)1842 and the remaining four, St Patrick's Hospital, Bloomfield Institution, St Vincent's Institution and Stewart Institution 'being charitable institutions supported wholly or in part by voluntary contributions and are not kept for profit or by any private individual' were exempt from licensing.[80] While the number of admissions, discharges and deaths fluctuated in any year, it is clear that in the 1920s and 1930s at least, the majority of the patients were long-term residents for whom St Vincent's was now their permanent and only home.

The inspector of mental hospitals generally limited his observations to the cleanliness of the institutions he visited, how the patients were physically cared for and the humanity exhibited by the carers towards the residents. His readiness to publicly expose and rebuke can be taken as evidence that he did take his inspection visits seriously, issuing a deeply critical report on the St John of God hospital in the same year (1924) that St Vincent's was commended for being well managed, 'and everything possible is done for the welfare of the patients'.[81] His visits to the private asylums were reported to both the minister for local government and public health and to the chief justice. It was the assistant registrar in lunacy who was responsible, under the lord chief justice, to protect the rights of those who might be committed to a private asylum by magistrate's licence. It was from this office that a certain Mrs Dobbins undertook a meticulous inspection of St Vincent's in May 1923. She had most certainly taken to heart the principle that an asylum for women of genteel birth should have all the refinements they had a right to expect and she brought to the duty of inspection a rather different perspective to that of her male medical colleague.

Mr Daniel Kelly, inspector of mental hospitals from at least 1924 until 1937, who took great care with his inspections of the private establishments, ensuring that 'every patient in residence was seen', repeatedly found that St Vincent's mental hospital 'continues to be managed in an excellent manner',[82] 'magnificently kept and is well equipped and furnished'[83] with ongoing

[80] *Annual Report of the Inspector of Mental Hospitals for the year, 1924*, p. 18.
[81] Ibid., p. 20.
[82] *Annual Report of the inspector of Mental Hospitals for the year, 1927*, p. 27.
[83] *Annual Report of the Inspector of Mental Hospitals for the year, 1935*, p. 33.

improvements such as the introduction of electric light in April 1923 and the opening of the new concert hall in 1932. The patients 'are well cared for and spoke highly of their treatment'.[84] The well-maintained grounds 'in which the patients spend most of their time especially in summer' were a distinguishing feature of St Vincent's; while from 1929 onwards 'a large number of patients go for motor drives and walks outside the institution'.[85] Spiritual needs were well catered for, with either daily visits from a clergyman or the note that 'Mass is celebrated daily' featuring in most reports.[86] Mrs Dobbins, however, focused all of her attentions on the dining room with which she was not at all satisfied. Although the table linen was clean it was not laundered to the high standard she felt these ladies would be used to and the meals were not served as one might expect in a hotel, 'Altogether in the dining room the dinner was not served as a gentlewoman would be accustomed to.' From their conversation and their demeanour (some 'spoke very nicely and remarkably intelligently') she felt the patients were conscious of the 'want of refinement at their meals', such as the failure to remove the dishes for the first course before dessert was served and the 'wretched fern' that was the only table decoration. Little fault was found with the food: the roast meat and cabbage seemed 'nicely cooked' but the potatoes, being served in their jackets, 'looked most unappetising'. However, she thought the upper class patients 'could easily have things made more comfortable and the meals served with refinement and not so rough and ready' and her official report resulted in follow-up visits to see for herself that dining room standards had been raised.[87]

There is very little information on the medical or therapeutic regime of the 1920s and the 1930s and the inspectors, men or women, gave surprisingly little attention to this aspect of the institution despite its being, nominally, a hospital. There is merely the general observation that 'the visiting medical officers are painstaking and earnest in their work'.[88] There was no requirement to have a resident medical superintendent, as there was in the district mental hospitals; in place of the medical superintendent's name, the private mental hospitals were required only to return the name of the proprietor or superintendent, who in the case of St Vincent's is given as 'the Sisters of Charity' until 1949, when it is amended in the annual reports to the Sisters of Charity of St Vincent de Paul. There was no recognised system of nurse

---

[84] *Annual Report of the Inspector of Mental Hospitals for the year, 1929*, p. 29.
[85] Ibid.
[86] *Annual Report of the Inspector of Mental Hospitals for the year, 1933*, p. 30.
[87] Report of Mrs C. E. A. Dobbin, 15 May 1923; J. E. Perry, assistant registrar in lunacy, to Reverend Madam, 22 May 1923; Reverend Mother to J. E. Perry, 25 May 1923 (Archives of St Vincent's Hospital, Fairview).
[88] *Annual Report of the Inspector of Mental Hospitals for the year, 1926*, p. 19.

training, no course of lectures delivered in-house, with merely the comment that the sisters followed the directions of the visiting physicians in relation to the management of patients. However, the sudden death of a female patient on 4 September 1928, immediately after forcible feeding, was the subject of a formal inquiry which provides a rare glimpse into the treatment that could be prescribed for individual patients and the responsibility carried by the visiting medical officers. The cause of death was given as heart failure but this was 'accelerated by the shock of feeding, the low physical condition of the patient through want of sufficient food, constant excitement and loss of sleep'.[89] Although the forcible feeding was ordered by a medical officer, 'the doctor in charge of the operation seems to have taken all possible precautions and no blame could be attached to him'. The Inspector of Mental Hospitals issued no directive or further comment, presumably because forcible feeding, where judged necessary, was standard practice throughout the sector and the publication of his report was regarded as sufficient warning to all involved to take the utmost care.

The transformation of St Vincent's from a nineteenth-century 'lunatic asylum' into a mental hospital with its own school of nursing in 1941 was part of the new thinking internationally around the treatment of those with mental health problems and the need for specialised nurse training. The treatment of shell-shocked soldiers from the 1914–18 war opened up new understandings of trauma-induced mental illness, while the work of the Royal Commission on Lunacy and Mental Disorder, 1926, though a United Kingdom body, also promoted a new public view of mental illness, taking a more humane and positive stance around treatment. The shift can be tracked in Dalhousie University, Halifax, Nova Scotia, for example. In the 1870s the very few hours of instruction that the students received on what was termed 'insanity' was dominated by lists of signs and symptoms.[90] In 1900, the term 'insanity' in the lecturer's job description gave way to 'mental diseases' and by 1910 the first Professor of Nervous and Mental Diseases was listed in the college calendar and students undertook a full programme of study under this heading which included an introduction at least to the 'newer methods' of psychotherapy which had developed under Sigmund Freud and his followers.[91]

The programme of the 1940s had shifted from the identifying of psychoses to what Patrick Flynn, a psychiatrist and historian, has described as 'a coordinated and relevant program of lectures and case presentations' intended to impart to the students, in stages, over four years, 'the accrued knowledge

---

[89] *Annual Report of the Inspector of Mental Hospitals for the year, 1928*, p. 25.
[90] P. Flynn, 'The Department's Roots and the Jones Years' in Patrick Flynn, ed., *Dalhousie's Department of Psychiatry, A Historical Retrospective* (Halifax, 1999), pp. 3–4.
[91] Ibid., pp. 5–7.

from scientific and objective studies as well as to foster a sincere interest in the functioning of the person as a whole'.[92] This new approach led to what Flynn calls 'a dynamic, psycho-bio-social understanding of people and patients,' an understanding of wellness and sickness that is the basis of modern psychiatry and its range of therapies.[93] The transformation of lunatic asylums into mental hospitals and eventually into psychiatric hospitals with outpatient departments; the integration of mental illness across the curriculum in medical education; specialist training for nurses and doctors; the certification of medical and nursing services; lessening the use of compulsion and locking up; seeking voluntary cooperation over legal formalities; and offering patients 'the same standard of domestic comfort as in an ordinary hotel' were part of this larger international story which (it must be admitted) did not advance at the same speed throughout all the counties of Ireland nor was it as complete a transformation as its advocates hoped.[94]

In the case of St Vincent's, there was considerable and long-standing pressure from the inspector of mental hospitals, on private and public institutes alike, to employ qualified personnel. A report for 1939, issued by the new inspector, Joseph Kearney, found that 'the nursing staff is adequate, but I consider that a greater number of the nurses should be in possession of certificates of proficiency in mental nursing'.[95] Registration under the Mental Treatment Act of 1945 imposed new regulations on the conduct of private asylums. It was in preparation for at least two decades and any observer could expect that it would force private asylums to employ at least some personnel with nursing qualifications. The decision by St Vincent's to apply for registration as a school of nurse training was to meet these pressures and ensure its future. Its graduates would have equal standing with those of Grangegorman and Portrane hospitals which were already recognised nursing schools. Following a formal inspection by M.M. Culhane, the Registrar and Mr Mullins of the General Nursing Council for Ireland, St Vincent's was approved, on 21 April 1941, as a 'training school for mental nurses'. An account of the inspection visit was published in the *Irish Nursing News* in May 1941, opening with the wholehearted endorsement of the application: 'It gave us great pleasure to see that everything was "for" and nothing was "against" Recognition.'[96]

---

[92] P. Flynn, 'The Department's Roots and the Jones Years' in Patrick Flynn, ed., *Dalhousie's Department of Psychiatry, A Historical Retrospective* (Halifax, 1999), p. 23.
[93] Ibid.
[94] E. H. Hare, *On the History of Lunacy: The Nineteenth Century and After* (London, 1998), p. 10.
[95] *Annual Report of the Inspector of Mental Hospitals for the year, 1939*, Department of Local Government and Public Health (Dublin, 1941), p. 29; Joseph Kearney noted that it had been recognised, *Annual Report of the Inspector of Mental Hospitals for the year, 1943*, Department of Health (Dublin, 1949), p. 30.
[96] *Irish Nursing News*, vol. xix, no. 8 (May 1941), p. 6.

In the discourse around the treatment of mental illness during the 1930s and 1940s and what should characterise a 'good' institution, one which the General Nursing Council for Ireland would be proud to certify as a teaching hospital, several strands can be teased out. The first was official recognition of the power of occupational therapy. The second was the adoption of modern treatments, most notably electroconvulsive therapy, which it was hoped would produce a greater proportion of recoveries to admissions and encourage more people to avail voluntarily of treatment at an earlier point, when recovery was more likely. St Vincent's, Fairview, led in the first but lagged badly behind in the second. The third strand was the desire to have as homely, comfortable and stimulating an environment as possible, in which field St Vincent's set standards that no other mental hospital of 1930s and 1940s Ireland came close to meeting.

A variety of 'recreations', 'occupations' and 'suitable employments' had been offered to patients at St Vincent's since its establishment, as well as the enjoyment of the 'artistically laid out' gardens.[97] The therapeutic value of such occupations was long recognised, with the sisters expressly commended in 1935 for their 'very keen interest in this side of the mental treatment with the result that the recovery rate is high'.[98] All patients were coaxed to engage in some occupation.[99] The existence of a department of occupational therapy was noted in 1940, while the inspection of 1943 noted that 'employment at rug-making, knitting, needlework, painting, music and in the kitchen and laundry was provided for those capable of benefiting therefrom'.[100] Few if any of the district mental hospitals had made advances on this front, despite the urging of the Inspector for whom an occupational therapy department was 'essential in any modern mental hospital': 'experience has proved the therapeutic value of congenial employment in the treatment of mental disease.'[101]

In the inspection leading to its recognition for nurse training in 1941 by the General Nursing Council, the 'Amusement Hall', which also served as a workroom, particularly impressed the visitors, one of whom confessed to being 'lost in admiration of the electric light fittings in this Hall. I have never seen such beauties'. On that occasion those patients who liked 'to pass the time doing needlework' were engrossed in work, with 'three or four Sisters giving a helping hand'. The hall was fitted out to an uncommonly high standard: 'The stage of this Hall is magnificent, with lighting-effects as good as any city theatre and Dressing-rooms superior to any, I am positive.' Drama therapy (though

[97] *Annual Report of the Inspector of Mental Hospitals for the year, 1926*, p. 19.
[98] *Annual Report of the Inspector of Mental Hospitals for the year, 1935*, p. 33.
[99] *Annual Report of the Inspector of Mental Hospitals for the year, 1936*, p. 31.
[100] *Annual Report of the Inspector of Mental Hospitals for the year, 1943*, p. 36.
[101] *Annual Report of the Inspector of Mental Hospitals for the year, 1940*, p. 16.

the term was not yet current) was in place as early as 1934 (and most likely earlier), with the Inspector of Mental Hospitals noting approvingly that 'concerts in which the patients themselves appear, are frequently arranged'.[102] No other mental hospital in Ireland had a comparable facility as early as St Vincent's. The concert hall allowed live 'entertainments', both by outside groups and prepared by the patients and it also allowed films to be shown: 'They are very much appreciated and of course help greatly in the treatment.'[103] In the report for 1951 the variety of therapies is impressive and most made possible by the existence of the aforementioned hall:

> Excellent facilities for occupation and recreation; Patients played tennis, croquet and went for walks and drives. Table tennis, bridge, badminton, chess, dancing, concerts, plays and films provided indoor entertainment. Handicrafts received special attention and patients were encouraged to find useful occupations in rug-making, upholstery, needlework, knitting, typing, cooking and light domestic work. There was also physical drill for any who wished to take part.[104]

Other occupations which featured sporadically were flower-making[105] and 'clock golf',[106] while the institute's unflagging efforts to cater for a genteel class of patient may be discerned in reports that 'pianos, gramophones and wireless sets are supplied to all the dayrooms'[107] and 'a liberal supply of reading matter is available'.[108]

In terms of 'treatment on modern lines', however, St Vincent's lagged well behind both private and public mental institutions during the 1930s and 1940s. Its proportion of recoveries to admissions, an admittedly crude measure of the effectiveness of individual hospitals, calculated by the inspector of mental hospitals, ranged from a record 55 per cent in 1926 to 0 per cent in 1942.[109] The very small numbers either entering or leaving each year strip these figures of real meaning, but there is a marked rise in the proportion of recoveries to admissions from the time the school of nursing is underway, as might be expected.

---

[102] *Annual Report of the Inspector of Mental Hospitals for the year, 1934*, p. 29; *Annual Report of the Inspector of Mental Hospitals for the year, 1937*, p. 31.

[103] *Irish Nursing News*, vol. xix, no. 8 (May 1941), pp. 6–7.

[104] *Annual Report of the Inspector of Mental Hospitals for the year, 1951*, p. 42.

[105] *Annual Report of the Inspector of Mental Hospitals for the year, 1937*, p. 34.

[106] *Annual Report of the Inspector of Mental Hospitals for the year, 1932*, p. 27.

[107] *Annual Report of the Inspector of Mental Hospitals for the year, 1933*, p. 30.

[108] *Annual Report of the Inspector of Mental Hospitals for the year, 1931*, p. 28.

[109] Up until 1947 the inspector of mental hospitals calculated each year the 'proportion of recoveries to admissions' across all twelve private hospitals, presumably as a benchmark against which the performance of any one of the institutions could be checked. Between 1924 and 1947 this average 'rate of success' fluctuated between 28.7% and 41.5%.

The leading mental hospital for 'all forms of modern treatment' was St Patrick's hospital, so much so that the report of 1938 listed medical, massage, electrical as well as recreational and occupational treatments, 'in fact, any treatment known to have a curative effect is tried'.[110] 'Electrical shock therapy' was used on suitable patients in St Patrick's in 1942 and possibly earlier,[111] and its high number of voluntary receptions and departures set an example for other hospitals.[112] Treatment, not incarceration, was its aim. Most if not all of the district mental hospitals also embraced electroconvulsive therapies with enthusiasm. Among the smaller private hospitals, Hampstead and Highfield, owned and run by the Eustace medical family, 'cardiazol treatment' was being tried in 1938[113] and by 1942, 'the Cerletti-Electrical treatment' had been instituted, while 'occupational therapy was practised with satisfactory results.'[114] At the two small private mental hospitals in Finglas, Farnham House and Maryville, 'medical treatment on general lines, as well as shock therapy, with Phrenazol' were carried out in 1942,[115] and by 1947 'modified insulin therapy' was available as was electroconvulsive therapy.[116] At the same time the sole therapies available to patients at St Vincent's were 'needlework, cookery, rug-making, flower-making, typing, painting, knitting, gardening'.[117]

Of the many mental institutions inspected up to 1949 the only ones which were returned as not offering 'modern treatments' were Palmerston House 'mostly chronic or senile patients' and St Vincent's Fairview.[118] The latter did manage to return a greater proportion of its patients as voluntary, that is, not admitted under certificate, which was in line with the trend to encourage people to voluntarily seek treatment for mental illness. The inspection which led to the certification of St Vincent's for nursing training in 1941 makes no mention of a treatment regime outside the occupational therapy, drama and pastimes supervised by the sisters. The only medical person named as associated with St Vincent's on that occasion was Dr Freeman and none of the 'kind sisters' are named, let alone their nursing qualifications or experience mentioned.[119] However, by the end of the decade the changes wrought by

[110] *Annual Report of the Inspector of Mental Hospitals for the year, 1938*, p. 34.

[111] *Annual Report of the Inspector of Mental Hospitals for the year, 1942*, p. 33.

[112] *Report of the Inspector of Mental Hospitals for the year, 1950*, Department of Health (Dublin), p. 37.

[113] *Annual Report of the Inspector of Mental Hospitals for the year, 1938*, p. 33.

[114] *Annual Report of the Inspector of Mental Hospitals for the year, 1942*, p. 33.

[115] Ibid.

[116] *Annual Report of the Inspector of Mental Hospitals for the years, 1947 and 1948*, p. 32.

[117] *Annual Report of the Inspector of Mental Hospitals for the year, 1942*, p. 33; see also reports for 1943–9 inclusive. Note that the report covering 1944, 1945 and 1946 was not published until 1950.

[118] *Report of the Inspector of Mental Hospitals for the year, 1950*, p. 36.

[119] *Irish Nursing News*, vol. xix, no. 8 (May 1941), pp. 6–7.

certification can be noted. In 1949 the Inspector was pleased to report that 'modern treatments' were given in St Vincent's 'and very good results were obtained'[120] while the following year 'a new treatment unit' was opened 'in which all recognised modern methods of treatment are given'.[121] By 1952 there was a resident medical officer 'and consultants visit regularly'.[122] 'Modern treatments', specified as electroshock and insulin therapy, had been introduced but without usurping the 'recreational and occupational therapy facilities' and outdoor exercise that had always been a feature of the house.[123]

It was in the arena of home comforts and attention to detail that St Vincent's stood in a class of its own. At the certification visit of 1941 the Inspector was quite overcome:

> The Dining-rooms were a revelation, the table-linen was truly perfect and the appointments equally so, with plenty of space between the tables. I was reminded of the Dining-rooms in one of the finest Hotels in Co. Kerry.[124]

It is interesting to speculate if this female inspector knew of the harsh verdict passed in 1923 on the dining room standards and was taking the opportunity to dispel any lingering doubts, but it is more likely that St Vincent's had made sure, in the intervening years, that such criticism could never again be levelled against it. What is certain is that high domestic standards were maintained throughout the 1930s, 1940s and 1950s with inspectors reporting on 'the various departments' of the hospital being 'well furnished and kept scrupulously clean'.[125] The laundry was 'so well equipped and so well machined', while the kitchen and isolation block were also ideally suited for their purposes.[126] The sitting rooms, bedrooms and dormitories were repeatedly judged to be 'neat, clean and tidy and most comfortably furnished',[127] so much so that the Inspector could refer to the 'usual high standard of order and cleanliness' being apparent on each visit. The 'kindly treatment' of the patients[128] and the fact that 'neither restraint nor seclusion were resorted to during the year' were highlighted repeatedly.[129] This may have

---

[120] *Report of the Inspector of Mental Hospitals for the year, 1949*, p. 35.
[121] *Report of the Inspector of Mental Hospitals for the year, 1950*, p. 37.
[122] *Report of the Inspector of Mental Hospitals for the year, 1952*, p. 37.
[123] Ibid.
[124] *Irish Nursing News*, vol. xix, no. 8 (May 1941), pp. 6–7.
[125] *Annual Report of the Inspector of Mental Hospitals for the year, 1940*, p. 29.
[126] *Irish Nursing News*, vol. xix, no. 8 (May 1941), pp. 6–7.
[127] *Annual Report of the Inspector of Mental Hospitals for the year, 1943*, p. 36.
[128] *Report of the Inspector of Mental Hospitals for the year, 1950*, p. 37.
[129] *Annual Reports of the Inspector of Mental Hospitals for the years, 1947 and 1948*, p. 33

been related, at least in part, to the demographics of the patient group; the conversion of a ward to an infirmary in 1949 was due to so many of the patients for whom this was and had been for many years their only home, entering their twilight years.[130] The principal fault noted by inspectors throughout the 1940s was the dearth of appropriate qualifications among the staff, a drawback which the new School of Mental Nursing would remedy but only in time.

An agreement drawn up in 1983 between the trustees of St Vincent's Hospital and the Daughters of Charity of St Vincent de Paul recalls the landmark meeting of 13 November 1857, chaired by the archbishop of Dublin, Dr Cullen, at which 'the institution was formally given in charge to the Sisters'.[131] It was confirmed that from that date onward

> the care of the said hospital has been entrusted to the Sisters who have accepted the responsibility and conduct thereof, subject to the rules and regulations provided by the Trustees and the Governors for the time being of the said hospital.[132]

In 1970, following on the enactment of the Public Health Act, St Vincent's became a privately-owned public voluntary hospital and cooperated with the Eastern Health Board Community Psychiatric Services for the Dublin northeast region. Men were accepted for the first time following on the health board involvement and a new unit, the Freeman Unit, was built. The new school of nursing was opened in 1983 and in 1996 nurse training went under the aegis of the Dublin City University School of Nursing Programme, which incorporates five north Dublin hospitals. Though always a small hospital, St Vincent's has seen the full range of approaches to the care and treatment of the mentally ill, from the humane asylum movement of the mid-nineteenth century to the modern community-based psychiatric services of the twentieth and twenty-first centuries.

---

[130] *Report of the Inspector of Mental Hospitals for the year, 1949,* p. 35.
[131] Agreement between the trustees of St Vincent's Hospital and the Daughters of Charity of St Vincent's, unsigned typescript, 1983 (Archives of St Vincent's Hospital, Fairview).
[132] Ibid.

Chapter Six

The North Infirmary Hospital, Cork:
From Charitable Infirmary to Teaching Hospital

Sheila Mathews DC, Carmel Ryan DC

On 15 January 1988, the last four sisters left the North Infirmary Hospital, Cork. The service of the Daughters of Charity in that mission had been completed. It was 120 years since the arrival there of the first four sisters from Paris.

The North Charitable Infirmary was Cork's first voluntary general hospital. At a meeting of that hospital's management committee in 1829, reference was made to 'this most ancient hospital of the Empire'.[1] According to some sources, the idea of an infirmary for the sick began in Cork, in 1719, due to the initiative of the Protestant clergy and parishioners of St Mary's Shandon, Cork.[2] For whatever reasons, however, no development took place at that time.

In 1744, the gentlemen of the Cork Musical Society were determined to give the proceeds of their performances to establishing an infirmary for the sick and poor in the parish of Shandon. Having secured a site where the old church of St Mary's had stood, they had a small house built to accommodate a few beds for the sick. This venture was successful and due to their generosity and funding, the number of sick being cared for continued to increase year by year.[3] The Infirmary was established under an Act of George II in 1751, the 25th year of his reign,

> to vest the house called the infirmary House and the back yard there
> unto belonging, which is built at the east end of the churchyard of St

---

[1] Report Hospital Management Committee, 1829, PA:DC/Dunardagh/North Infirmary (Provincial Archives, Daughters of Charity, Dunardagh, Blackrock, here abbreviated as PA:DC/Dunardagh/North Infirmary).

[2] St Mary's, Shandon, Cork was a Church of Ireland Parish in the northern suburbs of Cork city.

[3] Turkey's Cork Remembrances, 1835, PA:DC/Dunardagh/North Infirmary.

Mary Shandon, otherwise Saint Ann's in the liberties of the City of Cork.[4]

Although the patients were mainly Catholic, the majority of the management committee and lay staff were Protestant until well into the nineteenth century. It was at this time, however, that the voice of the Catholic community began to be heard, and the Catholic members of the management committee expressed their concern about standards of care in the hospital. Inspired by accounts of the skill and devotion of the French sisters who had nursed the soldiers on the battlefields of the Crimean War, they proposed that they be invited to care for the sick in the Infirmary. These sisters were the Daughters of Charity of St Vincent de Paul, who had been nursing the sick from the time of their foundation by Louise de Marillac and Vincent de Paul in France in 1633. They were known for their large white bonnets, 'cornettes', and grey habits which was why they were familiarly called the *Sœurs Grises*.

It was not until 1866 that the members of the hospital management committee agreed to this proposal, some of them grudgingly. Dr Stephen O'Sullivan, a member of the medical staff, travelled to Paris to earnestly request Father Jean-Baptiste Etienne, superior general of the Priests of the Mission and the Daughters of Charity, to send sisters to manage the Infirmary and nurse the sick. Prior to the arrival of the first group of sisters to the hospital, a contract was negotiated, agreed and signed between the trustees of the North Infirmary Hospital and the Company of the Daughters of Charity. This practice of having a contract, clearly outlining the duties and obligations of the sisters and the trustees of the hospital went back to the time of Louise de Marillac when she negotiated the sisters' involvement in the hospital of Saint-Jean in Angers, France on 1 February 1640.[5] The trustees were to pay the travel expenses of the sisters who were setting out from Paris to Cork and upon their arrival, were to provide adequate accommodation and the necessary household materials for the sisters. A sum of £30 a year was to be paid to each sister for undertaking nursing duties in the hospital. The sisters were obligated to undertake the internal administration of the hospital. The contract had thirteen articles clearly stating the duties and responsibilities of each party.[6] This contract was signed on 19 June 1866.

The first four sisters came to the North Infirmary on 25 January 1867. They were Sister Teresa O'Callaghan, the sister servant, recalled from the Military Hospital in Sedan, France, and her three young companions, sisters Josephine Murphy, Mary O'Connor and Vincent Guérin.

---

[4] Act of George II, City of Cork Archival Institute, Great William O'Brien Street, Cork.

[5] L. Sullivan DC, ed. and tr., *Spiritual Writings of Louise de Marillac: Correspondence and Thoughts* (Brooklyn: New City Press, 1991), p. 21.

[6] PA:DC/Dunardagh/ North Infirmary.

Sister Teresa O'Callaghan was born in Finglas, Dublin and educated by the Sisters of the Institute of the Blessed Virgin Mary [Sisters of Loreto]; it was her brother's entrance to the Lazarist seminary in Paris that introduced her to the Daughters of Charity.[7] On completing her seminary in the rue du Bac, Paris she volunteered for the foreign missions and before she arrived in the North Infirmary Cork she had experience of Constantinople, Smyrna and in the military hospital of Algiers. She was missioned in military hospitals in Lyons and Sedan in France.[8]

Sister Josephine Murphy was born in Dublin in 1843 and joined the Daughters of Charity in 1864. She worked in Liverpool for three years before her arrival in Cork. She served in the North Infirmary Hospital until her death in 1919. Sister Mary O'Connor was born in 1835 and joined the Daughters of Charity in 1859. She worked in the North Infirmary for three years and was missioned in 1870 to Liverpool. Sister Vincent Guérin was just nineteen years of age when she arrived in the North Infirmary Hospital. She was missioned in 1869 to London.

At the Infirmary, the sisters found sixty poorly fed patients in a run-down building, without ordinary essential equipment and an unwelcoming staff who resented their arrival. Having taken possession of the small, cramped quarters allotted to them, the sisters committed themselves to the care of the sick and the day-to-day management of the hospital. This was not easy. They were constantly watched by the Protestant employees and suffered many annoyances. The management committee members were grudging and unhelpful and constantly refused funds for improvements within the hospital. As time passed, however, the dedication and devoted care of the sisters for their patients, gradually gained for them the esteem and confidence of those who had opposed them, including most members of the hospital committee.

An excerpt from the *Cork Examiner* of Friday 25 January 1867 gives an account of the sermon and collection to take place in the Catholic Cathedral of St Mary and St Anne on Sunday 27 January 1867, on the occasion of the sisters' arrival in Cork:

> *The North Infirmary – The Sermon on Sunday*
> As this appeal will be in some respects exceptional it is desirable that the response to it should be even exceptionally generous. We are convinced it will be so if the public clearly apprehend the precise grounds on which it is made. They are simply these. The Directors of this great public institution, feeling deeply the primary importance of proper nurse-tending, wisely resolved to adopt the reform which has

---

[7] See Glossary.
[8] Sisters of Charity of St Vincent de Paul, *Pioneer sisters of Charity of St Vincent de Paul in Great Britain and Ireland* (London, 1955), p. 73.

produced such salutary results in other hospitals viz.: the substitution for untrained and hireling nurses for the members of a sisterhood thoroughly experienced in such matters and animated by those higher motives which Miss Nightingale considers almost essential for the due performance of their arduous, responsible, and repulsive duties. With this view, the Directors were so fortunate as to secure the services of the celebrated 'dames des Hopeteaus' – the Sisters of Charity of St Vincent de Paul, – whose skill and devotion in this very work is a matter of European and historical notoriety. As, however, this fortunate and beneficent change involves expenses which the ordinary funds of the hospital would be insufficient to meet, a special appeal became necessary. It is this appeal which Canon O'Sullivan will make on Sunday next, at the Cathedral. That it will be responded to with even more than ordinary liberality we cannot doubt. These ladies come to Cork at the invitation of some of the leading citizens of various denominations to perform a great public service; Cork will promptly supply whatever is requisite for them. The support of hospitals is the first and most urgent of public charities; no support can really much avail without good nurse-tending. Thus the honour of the city, the welfare of a great public institution, and the dearest interests of humanity and charity, are all concerned in its success. The music before and after the sermon will be of a specially interesting character. In addition to the presence of a splendid chorus and orchestra, the band of the 60th Rifles will be in attendance and perform selections from Moses in Egypt. The choral selection will be from Elijah, the Creation and Messiah.[9]

The same daily newspaper reported on Monday 28 January that 'the sermon and collection realised £245'.

The correspondence between the sister servant in Cork and the mother house at the rue du Bac opens with a letter from Sister O'Callaghan on 12 February 1871; she continues as the correspondent until 1907, when the role is taken up in turn by her successors sisters Josephine Murphy and Angela Mullally.[10] Sister O'Callaghan was to prove a remarkable woman; she was for Cork what sisters de Virieu and O'Grady were for Dublin. The official report of the hospital committee for the year 1869 states:

The Sisters of Charity have not only realised our expectations of their efficiency, but have surprised us by exceeding our greatest hopes. We foresee that the work they have already done gives fair promise for the

---

[9] *The Cork Examiner*, 25 January 1867.
[10] International Archives, Daughters of Charity, 140 rue du Bac, Paris.

future. It would appear that their desire is constantly to increase their sphere of usefulness without any consideration for their own temporal interests which they value only in so far as they can be devoted to the service of the poor.[11]

The sisters were responsible for the nursing duties of the hospital and were never represented on the hospital Board of Trustees. The trustees held an annual general meeting at which a Board of Management was formed for the general management of the hospital during the ensuing year. Two members of this board took responsibility each month for visiting the hospital and reporting to the board meetings. The Matron made requests to the board for any materials, equipment or finance that she deemed necessary for the good management of the hospital. All the details of hospital administration including the hiring and firing of household staff, porters and kitchen staff was the responsibility of the Board of Trustees. Tenders for the provision of all food stuffs and fuel were discussed at the meetings, and tenders were assigned by the Board of Trustees.[12] There was a special arrangement between the Board of Trustees and the Royal Irish Constabulary for the nursing care of its members. This is referred to on many occasions at the board meetings. The County Inspector of the RIC wrote to the trustees, '[We are] greatly pleased at the condition of the hospital, at the conditions afforded to the Constabulary patients.' He further said that he would never withdraw the constabulary patients from the Infirmary; and a section of the letter was read into the minutes on 10 May 1869.[13]

In the minutes of the meetings of the Board of Trustees there are fleeting references to the Daughters of Charity. The matron is referred to by name on some occasions but usually she is called the superior. The sister matron never attended the meetings. She communicated requests for equipment or funds in writing. The matron requested funds to purchase Christmas gifts for the patients and in particular the children in the hospital.[14]

The Disestablishment of the Church of Ireland Act was passed through the Westminster Parliament in 1870. This act removed the special status of the Church of Ireland from most aspects of Irish life. The local Protestant clergymen held the view that they could attend the annual general meeting of the board of the hospital. However, in May 1871, this situation began to

[11] Report, Hospital Management Committee, 1869, PA:DC/Dunardagh/North Infirmary.
[12] Minutes of the Board of Trustee Meetings of the North Infirmary, Archival Institute of Cork, Collection/H2.
[13] Ibid.
[14] Ibid.

change. At a meeting of the Board of Trustees on 1 May 1871 the following resolution was passed by those present:

> [W]e give credit to the retiring committee for the conciliatory spirit shown in dealing with the claims of the four officer members, we cannot consent to the perpetuation in this constitution of religious privileges which have been abolished by the law of the country. Resolve and therefore that acting upon the reply of the Church Secretary to the Lord Lieutenant founded upon the opinion of the Law Officers of the Crown, this meeting directs the Committee it is about to elect not to admit to its meeting any persons claiming to act then on by right of their position of Bishop or Rector of certain sees or parishes of the late established church.[15]

The resolution was proposed by Patrick Kennedy who was a subscriber, and seconded by Alderman Daniel O'Sullivan and adopted unanimously. The 'conciliatory spirit' was put to the test with the demands that this resolution be placed before the board. The Protestant members began to lose control of the board and therefore of the hospital. It was the Catholic members who began to have the overall majority on the board and this, with the presence of the sisters on the wards, meant that the Catholic patients experienced an ethos more familiar to them.

The hospital increased from a small badly equipped infirmary for the sick poor of the north side of Cork city with some sixty beds, to a hospital of one hundred and twenty beds. As the number of patients increased, so did the need for more sisters to care for them. In 1875, a doctor who had been a student at the Infirmary, realising the need for better accommodation for the sisters, published appeal in the Cork newspapers. As a result of this, Archdeacon John Murphy of Cork came to the Infirmary, that same day, to see for himself the sisters' cramped living quarters and poor little chapel. Subscriptions and collections were made and in 1875 a new building was erected for the community, which included a chapel. A stone plaque on the wall on the lower corridor testified to the generosity of Archdeacon Murphy and the citizens of Cork. Archdeacon Murphy, from his personal resources, supported the cost of two more sisters to join the staff of the hospital. This private source of funding for two sister nurses continued for some years.[16] New facilities were provided in the operating theatres and accident room. The funding from Archdeacon Murphy provided for one sister to take responsibility for the Accident Room (Accident and Emergency Department) and a second sister to undertake the

---

[15] Minutes of the Board of Trustee Meetings of the North Infirmary, Archival Institute of Cork, Collection/H2.
[16] A. J. Reilly, *Father John Murphy: Famine Priest* (Dublin, 1963), Ch. 11.

management and good running of the hospital kitchen. A sister was appointed as night superintendent in 1896, taking overall responsibility for the good running of the hospital at night.

By the end of the century, there were further developments in the building structure of the hospital. In 1893, the large yellow-brick building was completed and was known thereafter as the Gibbings Memorial Wing. At one time, Dr Robert Gibbings was a very devoted member of the medical staff. To perpetuate his memory, his daughter, Lady Combermere, made a very generous bequest to the hospital. This new building provided an additional forty beds for surgical patients as well as additional space on the ground floor for other facilities. A white marble bust of Dr Gibbings on a marble plinth on the corridor leading to the male surgical ward became a familiar sight to generations of doctors, nurses and medical students who passed it daily. This bust is held in the Crawford Art Gallery, Cork. A new operating theatre and annexes were built in 1905, through the generosity of Miss Honan.

According to an internal report of the community of the Daughters of Charity dated 15 August 1905, there were nine sisters working in the hospital. The sisters held the posts of: matron; night superintendent; operation department; accident room; three posts of ward sisters; kitchen sister; and laundry sister. This last position was at the expense of the community as the trustees refused to sanction a sister for that position or to pay her when she was appointed.

It was in the latter half of the nineteenth century, that the need for educating and training young women to care for the sick was recognised. Although there were already some nurses with diplomas in various hospitals in Cork, it was felt that a nursing school attached to a hospital was now essential. In 1895, a meeting was held in the presbytery of the Church of Saints Peter and Paul, presided over by the Reverend Dr Alphonsus O'Callaghan, bishop of Cork, at which the leading Catholic families of the city and suburbs were present. The object of the meeting was to devise a plan for supplying Catholic nurses for the sick. Dr Stephen O'Sullivan explained during the meeting the need to connect any future nursing school with an existing hospital. Some people present at the meeting explained that such nursing schools in the United States were attached to hospitals which were staffed and managed by the Daughters of Charity. After a full discussion, it was resolved to entrust this plan to the Daughters of Charity at the North Infirmary. The trustees wanted nothing to do with the school but would 'allow the school to be annexed to the infirmary under the care and control of the Sisters of Charity'.[17] The Daughters of Charity, at the wish of the Bishop and with the

---

[17] PA:DC/Dunardagh/North Infirmary.

consent of the Board of Trustees, agreed to accept the responsibility of supplying 'trained nurses for the North Infirmary, who would help the sisters in caring for the sick in the Hospital, and also a number of nurses with certificates to care for the sick in houses in the city and elsewhere'.[18]

The trustees of the North Infirmary refused to be financially involved with the enterprise and so the staffing and the finance necessary to open and manage the School of Nursing had to be sourced by the Daughters of Charity. Sister Teresa O'Callaghan, matron, set to work immediately to establish the Nursing School and it opened in June 1895. The nurses attended lectures given by the matron, her assistants and the medical staff, who cooperated fully and generously. The number of nurses increased steadily, necessitating the erection of additional buildings to accommodate them in 1903. Communications improved for the hospital in August 1894 when the first telephone was installed.

The establishment of the Nursing School was Sister Teresa's final under-taking. She died in 1909, having completed her mission as a humble, hard-working Daughter of Charity, Servant of the Poor. Sister Josephine Murphy, one of the pioneer sisters of 1867 succeeded her as matron until 1918. At that time there were twelve sisters serving in the hospital, which was developing and expanding its services throughout the city and county of Cork. Sister Louise Lane, who came to the hospital in 1890, nursed the sick in the Female Surgical Ward up to 1934. Sister Angela Mullally, who was a nursing sister in the North Infirmary from the early years of the twentieth century, succeeded Sister Josephine Murphy as matron in 1918 and held this post until 1944.

Constant developments took place in the hospital, including a new laundry in 1892. One of the most significant improvements took place in 1913, when the Dental Hospital and School was opened. The Dental Hospital was a joint venture between the North Infirmary Hospital and University College Cork. It was here that the students studying dentistry in the university undertook their practical experience. During the period between the two world wars; 1920–1939, the hospital continued to serve the people of the north side of Cork city and county. 'D' Infirmary or 'North Cha' was their refuge and haven in all kinds of ills and misfortunes. Its facilities were developed as far as limited finances would allow. Previous to the 1933, 'Hospital Sweepstakes' benefits, subscriptions and bequests were of the utmost importance in meeting expenses, even for essentials. As the need for nursing sisters increased, many Daughters of Charity received their nursing experience and tuition at the North Infirmary and became state-registered nurses from the mid-1920s to the time of the hospital's closure in 1987, a period of sixty years.

---

[18] Daughters of Charity, Narrative, PA:DC/Dunardagh/North Infirmary.

The medical staff and visiting consultants in the North Infirmary, both physicians and surgeons, generously continued to give their services to the hospital during all these years, caring for and treating the sick, and passing on their skills and knowledge to large classes of medical students in the wards and to the nurses in the nursing school.

The Daughters of Charity received two requests from Dr Daniel Cohalan, bishop of Cork and Ross in October 1923. The first was to establish a convalescent home for men discharged from hospital. The second request was to open a hostel for young workers in the city. Negotiations went on for many months but neither of the projects was undertaken by the Daughters of Charity.

Changes were on their way. The large housing schemes of Gurranabraher and Farranree were completed in the late 1950s. The increase in population meant an increase in patient numbers, putting a strain on bed accommodation in the wards, in the casualty and out-patients departments. Additional nursing staff was required as well as extra staff in other areas. Rumours began to circulate of the need for a new large regional hospital. Advances in the student nurse educational system during these years required that the nurses spend more time in the study and theory of nursing in the classroom, taught by qualified nurse tutors. A nursing sister from the North Infirmary community was successful in the inaugural course for nurse tutors in University College Dublin in 1962.

St Vincent's Nursing School commenced a new chapter of its history since its foundation by Sister Teresa O'Callaghan when a new Nursing School building with lecture rooms and annexes was completed at the rear of the hospital, near to Shandon Church and its famous bells, in the late 1960s. It was some years later that new living quarters for the student nurses were completed on the site of the old 'green-coat school' beside St Ann's Church of Shandon. This site had been purchased by the trustees of the hospital in 1956.

In 1967, the Daughters of Charity celebrated the centenary of their arrival in the North Infirmary. Many changes took place during those one hundred years, culminating in the change of their distinctive dress a few years earlier. This was commented upon by the Reverend Canon James Bastible who preached at the thanksgiving centenary mass on 7 June 1966, 'The familiar cornette is gone, the sign of the Sister of Charity in the homes of the poor, in the corridors of prisons, with the aged, and in the wards of hospitals, let us pray that their spirit of compassion will live on.'[19] The Board of Trustees and the Committee of Management at their annual meeting in 1967, paid tribute to the Daughters of Charity for their outstanding service to the North Infirmary during the previous one hundred years.

---

[19] Centenary Celebration Account 1966, PA:DC/Dunardagh/North Infirmary.

In 1969, a sister living in the North Infirmary community began to work with children who were deaf and their families. She was involved in establishing an effective education service for them and put structures in place for best practice. Another new ministry began in 1972 in Gurranabraher. This was the 'Before 5' nursery and family resource centre – a joint venture between the diocese, the Daughters of Charity and the city council. Its goal was to provide care for very young children and prepare them for entering primary school and to support young families in this newly developed area. In 1977 at the invitation of Bishop Cornelius Lucey, the sisters were to become involved in social and parish work in the newly developing area of Hollyhill/ Knocknaheeny.

In 1979, the Cork Regional Hospital, now known as the Cork University Hospital was finally completed and opened. The North Infirmary continued to function, but there were many visits from health board officials during the following years. In April 1987, with the arrival of a drastically reduced financial allocation from the government, its fate was sealed. The rumours of the previous years, which had been dismissed as gossip, were a reality. Noisy protest meetings and marches began and continued throughout the summer days of May, June and July. They served only to boost morale and simply allowed expression to be given to the utter disbelief with which many regarded the threatened closure of the hospital. Daily press and media coverage highlighted the situation, followed by constant visits and telephone calls from journalists and photographers. Battles were fought on the pages of the Cork daily papers. Several interventions by Bishop Michael Murphy of the Diocese of Cork and Ross were welcomed and appreciated by the Daughters of Charity, the staff of the hospital and the north-side people, most of whom or whose families had at one time or another been cared for in the 'North Infer', or who had been employed there.

The final decision in August 1987 and its subsequent speedy implementation came as a shock to all staff. The loud, angry, if sometimes even cheerful campaign of the summer months to 'save our Hospital' was quickly forgotten as staff came to grips with the reality of redundancy, redeployment to another hospital, or a 'no-job' future. For many, it was a day they said would never come. A whole way of life was being taken from many of them. In the words of one man, 'This hospital is my life; how will I get a job when there are hundreds of unemployed who have qualifications as long as the Mardyke?'[20] In those days of the 1980s, he spoke for many of the staff, especially the lower income group. For the Daughters of Charity, it was a sad time, and 'the visits, messages and prayers of our sisters throughout the Province, and of our friends and neighbours were a source of tremendous support and encouragement to

---

[20] S. Mathews, Personal memories (Sheila Mathews was a co-author of this essay).

us during those sad and anxious days'.[21] In October 1987, eighty sisters who had served in the North Infirmary, gathered together to bid farewell to the familiar old wards and corridors, each one recalling her own memories of past years. The departure of the student nurses during November left a void. It brought to a close a record of ninety-two years of teaching nursing skills to generations of young women at the School of Nursing, which had been established through courage and foresight. Without doubt, these nurses brought the Vincentian charism to the care of the sick wherever they continued their service.

The 'gloom and doom' of the weeks preceding the closure of the hospital, which had been set for the 27 November 1987, was greatly relieved by a succession of farewell get-togethers, exchange of gifts, speeches and tributes, laughter and tears. If there was an upsurge of emotions at that time, it was genuine and sincere. Barriers were down and all categories of personnel and staff joined together in lifting each other's spirits, despite the heart tugs many of them felt. This 'togetherness' was especially evident on the night of 24 November when nurses, doctors, household staff, porters, clerical and paramedical staff came together with the sisters, the hospital chaplains from the North Cathedral and the Reverend Canon George Salter, Church of Ireland clergyman and chairman of the hospital board, for a farewell celebration of mass in the hospital chapel. This was the last celebration in the chapel which had been donated by the people of Cork, through the intervention of Archdeacon Murphy, 112 years previously.[22] It was fitting that the last time the hospital staff was together was in the presence of the Lord, Healer of the Sick and Friend of the Poor. Later, all steps turned in the direction of one of the large empty wards, where a good time was had by all until the break of dawn. (Somewhat unexpected were the dancing partners on that night!) Finally, 'Auld Lang Syne' was sung with much feeling and emotion and the curtain came down.[23]

The North Charitable Infirmary had passed into history. For the Daughters of Charity who had served their Lord there, in the person of the sick, for 120 years, it was time to move on and answer other calls to mission.

---

[21] S. Mathews, Personal memories.
[22] A. J. Reilly, *Father John Murphy: Famine Priest*, Ch. 11.
[23] S. Mathews, Personal memories.

Chapter Seven

St Mary's, Dunmanway, Cork:
Initiatives in Education

Claire Sweeney DC

The second half of the nineteenth century was a time of great development in education in Ireland. Schools for girls under the direction of the Presentation Sisters, the Ursuline Sisters, the Loreto Sisters, the Irish Sisters of Charity, the Sisters of Mercy and the Holy Faith Sisters had been established in many of the towns throughout the country. By 1880, almost every town in West Cork had a convent school. One exception was Dunmanway.

Dunmanway had been established as a market town in the late seventeenth century by Sir Richard Cox. Cox obtained a grant from King William III to hold 'two fairs yearly on 23 April and 15 November and a weekly market every Tuesday'.[1] He made great efforts to make Dunmanway a thriving town – creating a fine entrance to the town with the building of the long bridge over the Bandon River, establishing woollen and cotton industries, and building a church. Over the years other industries were developed in the town – linen, leather, a brewery and flour mills.[2]

Like other towns in Ireland, however, Dunmanway was in the grip of poverty in the aftermath of the Famine. A letter from the women of Dunmanway to the 'Ladies of America' which was read at the 9 February 1847 post-famine meeting in Washington DC, tells something of the extent of the poverty and hardship. The letter speaks of men 'famished with hunger, with despair in their once cheerful faces, staggering at their work … of the dead father, mother and children lying coffin-less … and the agony of hunger.'[3]

The priests and some of the laity of the parish of Dunmanway believed that a convent would be a great asset for a town in such poor circumstances. The

---

[1] 'An Excerpt from the History of Drummanway [sic], County Cork' <http://www.kaweah.com/famtree/stories/donlin/Drummanway.html> accessed 21 March 2013.
[2] Ibid.
[3] C. Kinealy, *A Death-Dealing Famine: The Great Hunger in Ireland* (London, 1997), p. 115.

parish priest was given the incentive to begin his search for a congregation to set up a convent when

> a pious lady [the late Mrs Michael Collins] who resided in Cork, but whose family had long been connected with Dunmanway, bequeathed to the late Most Reverend William Delaney [Bishop of Cork] the sum of £1050.00 towards the erection of a convent in that town.[4]

It was the parish priest, Canon John Cotter, who began the negotiations with the Daughters of Charity in 1886, but it was left to his successor, Canon William Lane, to complete the project. In response to his invitation, Sister Juliette Minart, visitatrice of the province of Great Britain and Ireland, paid a visit to the town, accompanied by Sisters Mary Blundell, Gertrude Barraud and Teresa O'Callaghan, sister servant of the North Infirmary, Cork. The minutes of the council meeting of 27 June 1887, recount, 'Sr Visitatrice gave an account of her visit [to Dunmanway]. Msgr the Bishop asks for four Sisters. He will build parish schools and a house for twelve Sisters.'[5] No decision was reached at this stage, but negotiations continued between Canon Lane and Sister O'Callaghan. The minutes of the council meeting of 24 September 1887, show that these negotiations were successful, and Canon Lane's proposal accepted:

> The pastor paying for rent for the house; the bishop providing another priest so that the sisters may have mass in the house; about 100 children … for the Day School; we could not refuse such conditions.[6]

The council minutes go on to state that 'Sister Blundell has left [Mill Hill] with sisters Barraud, and Gray to establish the house'.[7] These Daughters of Charity set out for Dunmanway in the spirit of their founders: 'The Company makes every effort to be available and ready to respond creatively and courageously to the calls of the church and the urgent needs of the poor.'[8] (The Dunmanway notes, compiled by Sister Joseph Lavery, give the name of Sister Clare Harper, not Sister Gray, as one of the three founding members.)[9]

On 8 September 1887, the sisters took up residence in rented accommodation in Brook Park House on the outskirts of the town.[10] They were

---

[4] Eagle Supplement, Skibbereen, Co. Cork, Saturday 19 January 1889.
[5] Minutes of Council Meetings, 27 June 1887, PA:DC/Mill Hill/Dunmanway (Provincial Archives, Daughters of Charity, Mill Hill, London here abbreviated as PA:DC/Mill Hill/Dunmanway).
[6] Ibid., 24 September 1887.
[7] Ibid.
[8] Constitutions and Statutes of the Daughters of Charity, 2004, 12b, p. 35.
[9] Provincial Archives, Daughters of Charity, Dunardagh, Blackrock, Dublin (here abbreviated as PA:DC/Dunardagh/Dunmanway).
[10] Ibid.

primarily engaged to teach in the primary school, but true to their tradition, the sisters very quickly became involved in many other works. Their founders, Vincent de Paul and Louise de Marillac, had given the Daughters of Charity 'for cloister the streets of the city' and had intended that the sisters help people who were poor wherever they found them.[11] The sisters worked with the people, improving their lives in a holistic way: 'With constant concern for the promotion of the whole person, the Company does not separate corporal service from spiritual service, nor the work of humanisation from that of evangelisation.'[12]

The first little group of sisters quickly became established at the centre of the local community. There was no division in their minds between serving God and serving people in need. In listening to the Conferences of Vincent de Paul they regularly heard: 'A Sister will go ten times a day to visit the sick and ten times a day she'll find God there.'[13] They knew that people go together to God, in community. Their founders' challenge to the first sisters had been for them to spend their 'time visiting and healing the sick and instructing the ignorant for their salvation'.[14] The Daughters of Charity came to Dunmanway to be bearers of hope and to respond with creative charity to people living in poverty in the aftermath of the famine. They were conscious that people have a deep longing for God in their hearts, and a thirst for relationships that are life-giving. They wanted to help them to become aware, in their time of great need, of the great love of God for them, and of His desire to heal their wounds. The sisters wanted to help them to improve their situation in life, and they would do this particularly through education.

The leader of the little group, Sister Blundell, was a member of an aristocratic Lancashire Catholic family, the Blundells of Little Crosby, near Liverpool. Prior to coming to Dunmanway, she had been involved in running a boarding school for girls in Lanark, Scotland. She decided to use some of the accommodation in Brook Park House to start a small boarding school along the lines of the Lanark School, and so St Vincent's High School began. Some of her early pupils came from Lanark. She also brought a teacher, Ellen Bennett, a housekeeper, Mary Anne McGuinness, and a gardener.

Apart from teaching in the local primary school and starting the small boarding school in Brook Park House, the sisters visited the people in the workhouse,[15] brought food and medicines to the sick in their own homes,

---

[11] P. Coste CM, *Saint Vincent de Paul: Correspondence, Conferences, Documents*, vol. 10, ed. and tr. Marie Poole DC (New York: New City Press), p. 530.

[12] Constitutions and Statutes of the Daughters of Charity, 14, p. 36.

[13] P. Coste CM, *Saint Vincent de Paul: Correspondence, Conferences, Documents*, vol. 9, p. 199.

[14] Ibid., p. 14.

[15] PA: DC/Mill Hill/ Dunmanway. The Council Minutes, 19 February 1925 indicate that Canon O'Leary asked for a nursing sister for the workhouse, but this was refused.

organised the church choir, and taught catechism in the church on Sundays.[16] They were very warmly welcomed to the parish, and by 1888, the people were engaged in helping to build a new residence that was to be home to the sisters for over a hundred years. A piece of land, a little over seven acres, known locally as the 'Turret', was acquired for the 'convent' and for the schools which would later be built.[17] The Reverend Mother of the South Presentation Convent in Cork lent some money to the Bishop for the Dunmanway project. An agreement was reached between Canon Lane and the Daughters of Charity: the sisters would take on the repayment of the debt for the convent portion of the loan and it would then belong to them. Sister Mary wanted a written contract but Canon Lane said there was no need for this. Sister Mary was shown to have been astute in her judgement, for although the debt was cleared by 1913, there was a long delay in acquiring the deeds of the convent property. In 1941 the matter was taken over by Father Joseph Sheedy CM, provincial director of the Daughters of Charity, who put it into the hands of the Neville Family Solicitors, Macroom. It took a further two years for the deeds to be handed over.

The architectural plans for the convent in Dunmanway were copied from those of St Mary's, Lanark. They also included a little Gothic chapel, which was an exact replica of the one on the Blundell estates in Little Crosby, Sister Mary's home. The foundation stone of the new convent was laid on 21 June 1888, in the presence of Bishop Delaney, Mother Havard, superioress general, Sister Minart, visitatrice, and Sister O'Callaghan. Sisters Josephine Worthington, Mary Madden and Louise Devane had joined the original group of sisters as part of the Dunmanway community. A bottle with the names of the early sisters was buried in the foundation.[18]

If the sisters came to bring the benefits of community to Dunmanway, they certainly experienced it when they arrived. The building of the convent was a real community project in the way the people worked together to achieve it. The parish priest requested help from the pulpit one Sunday during mass. The initial response of the farmers was so generous that it was decided to set up a rota. Names of farmers were called out each week and those selected took responsibility for the carting of building materials for that week from the quarry. They brought their horses and carts free of charge. It was all done in a well-organised manner. With this help from the local people, it was possible to have the convent built by Messrs J. Sisk of Cork for £3,431 4 s. 11 d.[19] The

---

[16] PA:DC/Dunardagh/Dunmanway.

[17] Despite the Sisters' best efforts over the years to avoid using the terms 'convent' and 'nuns', St Mary's was never known by the people as anything other than the 'convent' and those living there were 'the nuns'.

[18] PA:DC/Dunardagh/Dunmanway.

[19] Ibid.

formal opening of St Mary's, the sisters' new home, took place on 11 July 1889.[20] This project draws attention to a number of factors: the warm way in which the sisters were welcomed in the town; the value the people placed on education and on the presence of 'nuns' in their midst; and above all, the great generosity and sense of community of the local people.

The new primary school building also officially opened on 11 July 1889. This new school, which consisted of two large classrooms linked by three smaller rooms and two cloakrooms, was built by a local builder, Mr Jones, and cost a total of £1,951 3 s. 11 d.[21] The Board of Education gave a grant of £825 19 s. 5 d.; Sister Mary organised a bazaar to make up the shortfall. The school replaced the smaller schoolhouse in the parish church grounds, and from this time on, the sisters assumed the administration of the school.[22]

From the beginning, the new school set high standards. The report of the 1890 school inspection by Mr Ross, district inspector, states:

> This school is in operation since 1889. The staff consists of three members of the community of the Sisters of Charity, four lay assistants paid by the community [of the Daughters of Charity], and four monitors, paid by the commissioners.[23]

The report also refers to:

> the handsome building ... the instruction ... discipline and tone ... distinct and intelligent reading ... superior penmanship ... tonic solfa ... drawing ... callisthenic exercises with musical accompaniment ... action songs and kindergarten games. The Kindergarten system has been introduced, a certificated teacher from England having been brought over for some months to instruct the staff in teaching the occupation.[24]

An 1891 report states:

> the proficiency of the Infants class in kindergarten was exceptionally good ... indeed the skill in the occupations throughout the school was decidedly creditable. The action songs and kindergarten games appeared to be greatly enjoyed by the children.[25]

Although teaching was not generally viewed as the primary ministry of the Daughters of Charity, it was the principal work undertaken by the community in Dunmanway. Louise de Marillac had always recognised the importance of

---

[20] PA:DC/Dunardagh/Dunmanway.
[21] Ibid.
[22] Ibid.
[23] Ibid.
[24] Ibid.
[25] Ibid.

education. She looked on it as a task of fundamental importance and central to life. Whenever Louise went on a visitation to one of the Confraternities of Charity,[26] if there was a school-mistress in the place she instructed her in her duties; if there was none, she tried to find a girl who could read and she showed her how to teach.[27] In seventeenth-century France, public instruction was not regarded as the responsibility of the state, thus it was undertaken by the Church. This is clear from the response Louise de Marillac received, in 1641, from the Rector of Notre-Dame-de-Paris to her request to open a school for poor little girls in the Saint-Denis district where the Motherhouse was located. The Rector stated: 'In consequence of our position as Rector of the above-named church of Paris, we are charged with the licensing and administration of the elementary schools operating within this city and in its suburbs and environs.'[28] When the early sisters were sent out to the parishes in France, one would look after the sick and another would 'teach the little girls … one of the two purposes for which you have given yourself to God.'[29] In 1642, Vincent de Paul spoke of Marguerite Naseau, whom he considered the first sister although she had died in February 1633, some nine months prior to the founding of the Daughters of Charity on 29 November 1633, saying, 'Sister Marguerite Naseau of Suresnes was the first to have had the happiness of pointing the way to others, both in the education of young girls and in nursing the sick, although she had no other teacher or school mistress but God.'[30]

While the focus of the Daughters of Charity in Dunmanway was primarily on education, they were always aware of the broader picture of the lives of the people. In this, they were true to their original spirit. Vincent de Paul had a deep sense of the importance of looking after the physical well-being of persons before trying to reach them spiritually. He believed that it was necessary to give people a sense of security prior to speaking to them about God. While the salvation of souls was his burning concern, he advised his priests of the Congregation of the Mission and the Daughters of Charity to bring food to those who were hungry and to treat them with compassion and respect before giving them spiritual nourishment.[31] It was clear from their actions that this was well ingrained in the minds and hearts of the Daughters of Charity who came to Dunmanway in 1887.

---

[26] In 1629, Louise de Marillac was invited by Vincent de Paul to visit the Confraternities of Charity that had been established in France.

[27] Gobillon, *The Life of Mademoiselle Le Gras* (London, 1984), p. 13.

[28] L. Sullivan DC, ed. and tr., *Spiritual Writings of Louise de Marillac: Correspondence and Thoughts* (Brooklyn: New City Press, 1991), p. 51.

[29] P. Coste CM, *Saint Vincent de Paul: Correspondence, Conferences, Documents*, vol. 9, p. 36.

[30] Ibid., p. 65.

[31] P. Coste CM, *Saint Vincent de Paul: Correspondence, Conferences, Documents*, vol. 9, p. 268.

Aware that the people had very little to live on in post-famine times, the sisters showed great creativity in their efforts to help them provide for their families. Sister Gabriel Carney taught in the primary school. She came up with the idea of starting a blackberry industry in her spare time. She contacted Ogilvie's of Cork, who had a jam factory, and made a contract with them to provide fresh berries during the blackberry season. Mr Ogilvie agreed to send casks to Dunmanway each day for the transport of the fruit to the factory. Sister Gabriel brought the local people together and they undertook to pick the blackberries for sale to Ogilvie's. The people involved in the project brought the berries they had collected each day to the sisters' kitchen (some in donkey carts) where Sister Gabriel, in coarse apron, sleeves rolled up and with stained black hands, weighed them while one of the other sisters recorded the amount. Every morning the full casks were taken to the railway station for transport to Ogilvie's. At the end of each week the people were paid in accordance with the amount of fruit they had gathered. Sister Gabriel also tried her hand at the shamrock industry. For a few weeks before 17 March, the people collected shamrock which Sister Gabriel had shipped to England and Scotland to fill the orders she had received. This too provided a little income for the local people.[32]

The sisters also created employment for people by reclaiming the convent land and laying out vegetable, fruit and flower gardens and a vinery, and erecting a forcing house and conservatory. When they moved to the convent in 1889, they had water pumped to a large reservoir at the top of the hill. The laying of the necessary pipes provided work for some of the men. Other workers built an engine house to provide lighting. Sister Mary obtained money from her friends in England, and during a very bad winter, when work was extremely scarce, she hired men to build the 'back walk' up behind the convent.[33]

Aware of the poverty around them and the needs of the people, the sisters gave out supplies of medicine, soup, meals and clothes to the poor sick people and to the children of the neighbourhood. In 1948, a former pupil of St Mary's, Michael J. Lynch, of Salem, Massachusetts, sent the sisters a donation of $5000 'to be spent on needy children' because he remembered how 'the Sisters had supplied the poor children in school with milk, bread and jam, under the supervision of little Sister Gabriel' when he was a pupil in the infant school in 1890.[34] Sister Mary Blundell helped the pupils of St Vincent's High School obtain situations as governesses with families in Paris, Manchester, Liverpool and other places. Sister Joseph Lavery, who spent over sixty-seven years in the

---

[32] PA:DC/Dunardagh/Dunmanway.
[33] Ibid.
[34] Ibid.

convent in Dunmanway, was noted for the great interest she took in her pupils and 'she continued to exert her beneficent authority for the furtherance of her pupils in life until her declining years'.[35]

While helping the people find a means of livelihood was very important for the sisters, at the same time they paid careful attention to their own spiritual life as well as that of the people. For the sisters, the day began and ended with prayer. Daily mass, which was celebrated in the convent chapel at 7.15 a.m., was the centre of their lives. The practice of the presence of God, as the clock struck the hour, meant that the day was punctuated with prayer. Vincent de Paul did not want the Daughters of Charity to be like cloistered religious but rather 'to have for chapel the parish church'.[36] Thus it was appropriate for them to join with the people of the parish in worshipping the Lord at Sunday mass and at devotions during Lent and October.

Of particular note was the contribution made by the Daughters of Charity to church music in Dunmanway. From the very beginning, Sister Mary directed the music and started an adult mixed choir. Practices were held in Brook Park house. The choir sang in four parts and had learned the 'Missa de Angelis', and a great number of masses sung in churches at the time, such as Farmer's, Gounod's and Hayden's. The men held a collection and bought a second-hand organ for £90. It was erected in the centre of the southern gallery of the church. Since there was no heating, an oil lamp, with water pipes attached, was placed at one side of the organ to help dry the air. One Sunday evening in 1908, the lamp burst and the organ caught fire. Fortunately, there was a parishioner praying in the church at the time and he went for help. Only the organ was destroyed. The parish priest, Canon Thomas Mangan, replaced it with a second-hand one bought for £200 from St Anne's Protestant Church in Cork. He also had electric heating installed. An electric blower was added to the organ.[37] The involvement of the sisters as directors of church music lasted until 1978. The people of Dunmanway have continued this strong tradition to the present time.

A branch of the newly founded Pioneers Total Abstinence Association was established in the convent in Dunmanway, under the direction of the Daughters of Charity, on 19 March 1906, with the registration number 18.[38] The Association operated under a tightly controlled structure emanating from a central administration based in Gardiner Street, Dublin. Each local centre was affiliated to the central council. As well as promoting total abstinence from alcohol, an important aspect of the Association was devotion to the Sacred

---

[35] PA:DC/Dunardagh/Dunmanway.
[36] P. Coste CM, *Saint Vincent de Paul: Correspondence, Conferences, Documents*, vol. 10, p. 530.
[37] PA:DC/Dunardagh/Dunmanway.
[38] Ibid.

Heart. A pioneer pin with an image of the Sacred Heart was worn as a mark of membership. The sale of the pioneer pins was administered by the Daughters of Charity, North William Street from the time of the foundation of the Association in 1898, by Fr James Cullen SJ, until 1944.[39] Three sisters were involved in the Dunmanway branch: Sister Anthony Geraghty as treasurer; Sister Gertrude Barraud as spiritual director, and Sister Gabriel Carney as one of the six members of the committee. In 1949 the branch had 1,789 members. However, in 1950 there seems to have been a disagreement about the running of the Association. The committee was disbanded by the national director of the Association, Fr O'Doherty SJ, Gardiner Street. Two of the existing members, Mary Fuller and Florence Crowley, were retained, and the convent chaplain, Fr Crowley 'was to be in charge'.[40] No explanation was given for this change. The sisters were not involved in the Pioneer Association again until they started a junior branch of the Association in the secondary school.

Indicative of the sisters' creativity in finding ways to help the people to improve their standard of living, and of more lasting influence than the blackberry and shamrock industries, was the creation of the School of Domestic Science. In 1899 the Department of Agriculture and Technical Instruction was established in Ireland, headed by Sir Horace Plunkett. He had a vision of Ireland as a place 'which would be characterised by efficient and technically proficient agriculture … a society mindful of the value of rural community.'[41] The minutes of the provincial council meeting of 19 May 1902, refer to the request by Sister O'Brien to open a technical school for girls, noting that 'permission is granted'.[42] Sisters Louise Plunkett and Vincent O'Brien of the Dunmanway community went to Belgium to study the methods of teaching Domestic Science in use in schools in Aus and Ostend.[43] On their return they started St Mary's School of Domestic Science, the first of its kind in Ireland.

Over the years the County Council gave a great many scholarships to St Mary's. The college was also sponsored by the Bishop of Ross, who saw it as a school 'for the improvement of the people'.[44] The idea of equipping people with practical skills to improve the quality of their lives is an echo of activities and recommendations of Louise de Marillac and Vincent de Paul. In 1647

---

[39] *Archives of the Total Pioneer Abstinence Association*
<http://www.ucd.ie/archives/html/collections/pioneer-association.html> accessed 20 March 2013.
[40] PA:DC/Dunardagh/Dunmanway.
[41] J. J. Kennelly, 'We Can Still Learn from Horace Plunkett', *The Irish Times* (31 March 2004), p. 18.
[42] PA:DC/Mill Hill/Dunmanway, Minutes of Council Meeting, 19 May 1902.
[43] PA:DC/Dunardagh/Dunmanway.
[44] Ibid., Newspaper cutting from *The Cork Examiner*.

Louise wrote to Sister Élisabeth Hellot in Paris asking for '100 needles, 25 or 30 thimbles, 100 little books' which she needed for teaching little girls to sew.[45] Vincent recommended that the 'children learn some trades in order to give them the means of earning their own living'.[46] Beginning with roughly thirty pupils, numbers in St Mary's increased yearly. Pupils came from Cork and Kerry, and also from Clare, Kilkenny,[47] Wexford, Waterford and Wicklow, and in pre-war days, from England and Scotland. There were summer courses to train teachers. St Mary's aimed to improve the quality of family life and the standard of living in Irish homes. Dairy farming was considered important, so the Department of Technical Instruction had a dairy built at the school. Poultry rearing was developed, and in 1927, the cows were sold and the buildings used for poultry rearing. For a while tillage ceased, but in 1943 the land was again put under tillage and cows again purchased. The Department changed the piggery into a byre with enough space for six cows, so that the students could be taught to milk. Poultry runs were also developed in a few of the fields.[48]

The Daughters of Charity had a deep appreciation of the key position and influence of the woman in the home; they were aware that if they could help girls develop good household and farm-management practice it would filter through to the whole farming community. With this in mind, students were trained in skills of butter-making, poultry-keeping, home-management, farmyard enterprises, cooking and baking, dress-making and crafts, book-keeping and typing. There was great emphasis in their training on decision making. Students were divided into groups and each student was expected to take a turn as 'housekeeper'. The housekeeper was responsible for making decisions relating to group tasks. She was also expected to keep records and give reports when the task was completed. Students therefore learned to take responsibility and to be accountable. Another area considered important was the ability of the students to express their own ideas. To this end the girls were given opportunities for debating, drama and public speaking. It was one of the aims of the college to train young women who would be able to take their place in a confident manner and make a meaningful contribution to life in rural Ireland.[49]

While it is difficult to adequately measure the contribution made by St Mary's to the life and culture of the Dunmanway area, it is clear from reports

---

[45] L. Sullivan DC, ed. and tr., *Spiritual Writings of Louise de Marillac*, p. 218.
[46] P. Coste CM, *Saint Vincent de Paul: Correspondence, Conferences, Documents*, vol. 13b, p. 75
[47] In 1907, the bishop of Ossory asked for sisters to open a college like the Dunmanway college, but the request was turned down; Minutes of Council Meeting, 26 February 1907.
[48] PA:DC/Dunardagh/Dunmanway.
[49] Interview with Sisters Vincent Hurley and Irene Sweeney, March 1985.

that the standards achieved there were of the highest order. For a hundred years the school flourished and annually around forty students were given the opportunity of this excellent course of training. At the end of each year, the students displayed their work for the families to see, and the students were also encouraged to enter their products in local competitions. Reporting on the Bandon show, the *Cork Examiner* drew particular attention to the school:

> the pupils of Dunmanway School of Home Economics [*sic*] won, in all, 1st and 2nd prize for yeast bread, 1st and 2nd prize for sponge cake, 2nd prize for handmade door mats, and 1st, 2nd and 4th prize, with championship gold medal, for churning – a record which speaks for itself where such large numbers compete at the great show.[50]

In a letter to the same paper, J. P. Rahilly extolled the merits of the Dunmanway Residential School of Domestic Science:

> I take this opportunity of publicly acknowledging the no less than wonderful achievements acquired [by my daughter] through the care, ability and kindness of the renowned teachers … and trust that other parents may be fortunate enough to come in similar touch with the Dunmanway school.[51]

Focusing on improving the quality of life in the local community was one of the chief aims of those engaged in the running of St Mary's, but this went hand in hand with forming good Christians. It was important to develop the spiritual life of the students and their understanding of their faith. For Vincent de Paul and Louise de Marillac, it was not enough to learn answers by rote. Vincent spoke to the sisters of the necessity of making sure the children had a good understanding of what they were learning: '[The Sister] shall teach catechism to her pupils, making them understand the meaning of the answers, and for this purpose she shall ask them various familiar questions in other words than those of the book.'[52] For the Daughter of Charity, telling the pupils about God was central to her ministry. Important as the verbal message was, what the sisters taught by example was more important still. A high standard was set in the Common Rules for the Daughters of Charity, Particular Rules for School Sisters: '[The Sister] will endeavour to make herself both loved and respected, so that the pupils will have in her a confidence which does not prevent respect, modesty or the silence they should observe in school.'[53] Exchanges between a teacher and pupils are deeper and more searching than

---

[50] Extract from the *Cork Examiner* handwritten in Sr Lavery's notes. PA:DC/Dunardagh/Dunmanway.

[51] Ibid.

[52] P. Coste CM, *Saint Vincent de Paul: Correspondence, Conferences, Documents*, vol. 13b, p. 180.

[53] Ibid., p. 178.

the passing on of knowledge. At the centre of the teaching/learning enterprise is the teacher, present to her pupils as a professional person and as an adult human being. As a professional teacher, she initiates things, guides and shapes the course of the discussion and leads it to a meaningful conclusion. As a mature human person, she brings to her teaching the total riches of her life: her values, her wisdom, her moral principles, her intellectual gifts, her personality and her heart. In educating the students in St Mary's, the link between learning skills and forming good Christians was always stressed.

The students' day began with mass and ended with night prayer, and throughout the day there were many things to remind them of the place of God in their lives. They were always expected to give their best for the glory of God. Special occasions in St Mary's included the May procession, the Corpus Christi procession, and the prayers around the Grotto on the feast of Our Lady of Lourdes. This latter was particularly significant for the students. Mr Mc Gann, inspector of science in the Department of Technical Instruction, donated the statues for the Grotto in gratitude for the sisters' care of his mother.[54] Each year, on the afternoon of 11 February, a number of students went to the Grotto with night lights. These would be placed in all the nooks and crannies of the area around the statues of Our Lady and St Bernadette. Just before dark, the students lit all the night lights. While not too difficult in fine weather, it was a challenge on a stormy evening in February. When it was completed the lighted Grotto could be seen for miles around the town. The people of the parish would then join the sisters and students, and the priests would lead the assembly in prayer and the singing of hymns in honour of Our Lady of Lourdes.

A great many of the students who studied in St Mary's went back to their farms with their new skills when their time of study was over. The College was noted for its ability to discern the unique gifts of students and to help them achieve their potential. J. P. Rahilly refers to the fact that 'every possible means are employed to place the pupil in the befitting groove of life'.[55] A number of students decided to dedicate their lives to God and joined the Daughters of Charity. The strong tradition of girls entering the Company goes back to the early days of the sisters in Dunmanway. The minutes of council meeting of 14 July 1889, refer to 'Miss O'Sullivan who was interviewed by Sister Visitatrice in Dunmanway with a view to entering the Community'.[56] Again on 31 October 1892, there is mention of three girls: 'Julia Hurley, Maria O'Connell, and Catherine Craven, who were postulants in Dunmanway.'[57] This tradition continued for a hundred years.

---

[54] PA:DC/Dunardagh/Dunmanway.
[55] Ibid.
[56] PA:DC/Mill Hill/Dunmanway, 14 July 1889.
[57] Ibid, 31 October 1892.

Secondary school education was the privilege of the few in Ireland in the 1920s. St Vincent's High school was discontinued when St Mary's was started in 1902, but in 1928 a Secondary Top was started in two rooms in the sisters' house.[58] In almost every decade there was a significant change in the development of this school. From its modest beginnings in 1928, it became a recognised secondary school in 1936, known as Maria Immaculata Secondary School, and was moved to a new location in a cottage on the hill beside the convent. In the 1940s the cottage was extended to provide extra accommodation for the growing numbers; in the 1950s the school began to cater for boarders; a new purpose-built school was opened in 1965; the school became co-educational in 1972; in the 1980s the secondary school and St Mary's merged. In 2002 Maria Immaculata was amalgamated with the local vocational school, Coláiste Chairbre, to form the new Maria Immaculata Community College on Bantry Road.

During all the time of its existence, great attention was paid to the quality of education provided in Maria Immaculata Secondary School. Even while it was still a very small school in the 'cottage on the hill', Maria Immaculata was known for its excellence. Writing of her experience there, a past pupil, Teresa Murray O'Donovan, boasts that 'our education at Maria Immaculata must surely rank with the best'.[59] There were only three teachers in the school in her time there: Sisters Gertrude Higgins and Magdalen O'Donnell and Miss Patricia O'Donovan who, between them, 'covered the whole secondary school curriculum … Sister Gertrude was Principal and taught all the languages: Irish, English, French and Latin, Sister Magdalen … Mathematics and Religion and Patricia O'Donovan [affectionately known as 'Miss O'] taught History and Geography.'[60] Laid on these firm foundations of excellence, the school developed through the years. One Department of Education inspector, visiting the newly equipped Woodwork and Technology Department in 1992, summed it up in the following comment: 'You have state of the art equipment and state of the art teachers.' Success was experienced right across the board: in exam results, achievements of past-pupils, games, drama, music, projects, debating, quizzes, art, enterprise, essay writing, computers, banking, technology, science, history, and all this in a great atmosphere of generosity, cooperation and fun.

The Daughters of Charity spent over a hundred years in Dunmanway. Having come there as complete strangers in 1887, they became totally inserted into the local community. Their main ministry was in education. They started

---

[58] A Secondary Top was an extension of the primary school system in areas where there was no recognised secondary school, enabling students to continue in education to Junior Certificate level within the primary school system.

[59] Maria Immaculata Secondary School Commemorative Booklet: 'A Caring Tradition', 2002, p. 7.

[60] Ibid.

St Mary's Primary School for girls and infant boys under the trusteeship of the priests of the parish. This school continues with a lay principal. Aware of the important role of women in society, the sisters brought the innovative idea of the School of Domestic Science to the town; training young women in home and farm management, they made a very significant contribution to the lives of the people of West Cork. The secondary school, Maria Immaculata, which started as a 'Secondary Top' in 1928, amalgamated with the local vocational school, Coláiste Chairbre in 2002 to form the new Maria Immaculata Community College. The Daughters of Charity were initially joint trustees of this school with the Vocational Education Committee. In 2010, the Diocese of Cork and Ross replaced the Daughters of Charity on the Board of Trustees. The Daughters of Charity withdrew from Dunmanway in 2002. Of the three sisters who closed the door of the Dunmanway convent for the last time, one went to Cork city, one to Dublin and one to Kenya.

The place once known as the 'Turret' and later as the 'convent' is all quiet and still now. In that place where the sounds of children's voices rang out for over a hundred years, where school bells told that one class had ended and another was about to begin, where the aroma of baking from the cookery kitchen made mouths water, and the scent of newly mowed grass announced the arrival of another school break, all is silence and the Turret has been restored to its original dwellers, the crows. However, the spirit that inhabited St Mary's for more than a century still lives in the people of Dunmanway and its influence goes on and on.

Chapter Eight

The Daughters of Charity of St Vincent de Paul in the Irish Workhouse System

Mary Dixon DC, Bernadette Fennessy DC, Jacinta Prunty CHF

In October 1888 the newly formed provincial council for Ireland and Britain, meeting in Mill Hill outside London, received a formal request from the elected guardians of the North Dublin Union to take charge of the workhouse infirmary. This new mission marked the first involvement of the sisters with the union workhouses and the first time they were to be employed directly by the state in Ireland. That the superiors agreed to this new project when many other demands were being made on the Company's resources was firstly because the union workhouse dealt with the poorest of the Irish poor. It was thus very much in the spirit of the Company which had long experience in the nursing of the sick poor internationally.

As a system, the union workhouses date to the Poor Law (Ireland) Act of 1838 when a version of the new English Poor Law system was introduced, amidst some opposition, to Ireland. It was intended to control the vast numbers of beggars and vagrants who thronged the streets of towns throughout Ireland and Britain, carrying (it was feared) disease as well as threatening public order. It forced Irish property owners and occupiers to pay, for the first time, through local rates, for the support of the poor. A national network of 130 unions was set up in 1838 and a workhouse was quickly erected in each to a common plan. Workhouses for the North Dublin Union, South Dublin Union and Cork Union, all opened in 1840, were designed to hold 2,000 inmates each; Limerick had a capacity of 1,600, Dunmanway and Celbridge each had a capacity of 400 (all opened 1841).[1] Relief was to be on an indoor basis only, that is, within the workhouse and furthermore was to be of such a minimal standard that it would operate as a last resort for the destitute only. A strict classification of inmates was imposed, with men separated from women and

---

[1] John O'Connor, *The Workhouses of Ireland: The Fate of Ireland's Poor* (Dublin, 1995), pp. 261–3.

children from their parents, a monotonous, demoralising regime in bleak surroundings, enclosed with a high wall and purposely designed to repel rather than attract the poor.[2] Control was in the hands of a board of guardians elected from among the more substantial ratepayers, but a rather heavy-handed centralised control was exercised by the Poor Law Commissioners, later the Local Government Board, lest any one union dare to deviate from the very mean principles upon which the system rested. By the 1880s, when the Daughters of Charity first got involved in a workhouse infirmary, the harshness and stigma of its founding philosophy was still very much in evidence though a large proportion of those reliant on the system were the sick, disabled, elderly and children for whom something more kindly – many concerned guardians and rate-paying citizens felt – could surely be offered. The sisters themselves were willing to minister in state-funded and state-regulated workhouses so that the 'real poor' might be served; they had no objection in principle to co-operating with the local authorities where the conditions of the poor might be alleviated.

North Dublin Union

From 1884 the guardians of the North Dublin Union had been in search of nuns for their workhouses, and in 1887, in response to the scathing assessment of the hospital by the Local Government Board, the guardians announced that nuns were about to take charge of it. Formal notice of the intention to appoint eight sisters of the Company of the Daughters of Charity to take charge of the workhouse was published.[3] The only concession to what was in fact a political appointment was that the Board would not require the candidates to be present for interview. The clerk of the union, Thomas B. Atkinson, informed the sisters that the advertisement for positions was by then merely a formality as 'the newspapers had already made public the intended installation of the Sisters'.[4] A nurse of the Protestant tradition was employed to care for the one hundred Protestant patients.

Following the directives of Alderman Meagher, Sister Juliette Minart, visitatrice of the Daughters of Charity, submitted the names of the eight sisters 'who were willing to undertake the charge of the sick and infirm in the Workhouse Hospital according to the terms of the advertisement'. Sister Cecilia

---

[2] Jacinta Prunty, *Dublin Slums 1800–1925: A Study in Urban Geography* (Dublin, 1999), pp. 213–7.
[3] *The Freeman's Journal*, 11 October 1888.
[4] Thomas B. Atkinson, Clerk of the North Dublin Union to the Sisters of St Vincent's, North William Street, 13 October 1888, PA:DC/Dunardagh/NDU (Provincial Archives, Daughters of Charity, Dunardagh, Dublin here abbreviated as PA:DC/Dunardagh/NDU).

Robinson was named sister servant. Her companions were sisters Galvin, Gray, Fitzpatrick, Maher, Johnson, Donnelly and Byrne.[5] It was requested that the names not be published in the newspapers and that any subsequent appointments be kept from publication.[6] Eager to see the sisters installed, Mr Atkinson called at St Vincent's North William Street a few days later expecting to find the eight sisters already there to sign their application forms. Little did he know that the sisters were 'dispersed throughout the kingdom' and had yet to be informed of their new mission. But their availability and readiness could be presumed upon; they were expected to be ready to travel, even to a foreign mission.

Dr William J. Walsh, archbishop of Dublin, was active behind the scenes. He thanked the Daughters of Charity for their 'kindness in reference to the important task we have in hand' and reiterated his confidence that the guardians 'will do everything possible to meet the views expressed by your Sisters'. His undertaking to provide £10 for each sister for travelling needs was a kindly gesture of support. Practical support came from the Sisters of Mercy in the South Dublin Union, the first nuns to serve in the workhouse system. They advised the Daughters of Charity on how to deal with the officials both before and after taking up their new duties. The Superior of the Sisters of Mercy predicted that

> it will be a most trying work especially for the first two years or so, and
> it will require Sisters with a great deal of courage, entirely devoted to
> their work and with a very kind and cordial manner with the Poor.[7]

Sister Minart and companions went to inspect the workhouse in September 1888. Accompanied by Archbishop Walsh, the principal members of the Board of Guardians, the medical staff of the Union, and the Inspector of the Local Government Board, they went through all the wards. At a later meeting a contract was agreed and the provincial council of the Daughters of Charity consented to undertake the work.[8]

The agreement reached demonstrates important aspects of the place of the Daughters of Charity in state-run institutions. Having provisionally agreed that the sisters would undertake the work, the Board of Guardians had to go through full and proper procedures. They had to be exact in maintaining the non-religious character of the state workhouse, while simultaneously allowing Roman Catholic sisters to function freely among the poor inmates, of whom

---

[5] Séance du Conseil, 17 octobre 1888. PA:DC/Mill Hill.
[6] Sr Minart to Board of Dublin Union, 20 October 1888. PA:DC/Mill Hill.
[7] Superior of the Sisters of Mercy, South Dublin Union to Superior, North Dublin Union, 1888, DC Narrative, PA:DC/Dunardagh/ NDU.
[8] PA:DC/Dunardagh/NDU.

the overwhelming majority would be of the same religious persuasion as the sisters. The guardians had to demonstrate to their superintending body, as well as to the electorate, that employing Catholic sisters was not going to make the state workhouse a Catholic institution. The positions had to be publicly advertised. The guardians had to ensure that the position of existing employees was not undermined by these new arrangements. The sisters were employed to work within the existing system, with its restrictions, regulations and budget.

On 15 December 1888, eight Daughters of Charity arrived to take up the direction of the infirmary of the workhouse in North Brunswick Street. There were 500 patients in the infirmary out of a total population 'in the house' of 2,690, with a further 690 persons on outdoor relief. However, the official date of the commencement of the Daughters of Charity work in the North Dublin Union, parish of St Paul, was 1 January 1889.[9]

Prior to the sisters' arrival at North Brunswick Street, there were frequent complaints that there were no skilled nurses or paid attendants to carry out the medical officers' orders. In the case of what were termed 'stimulants', prescribed by the medical officer for sick inmates, the cost to the North Dublin Union was much greater than that in the South Dublin Union, despite the latter having a larger number of sick. The 'great possibility' was that at least some of the supply was intercepted by the 'pauper nurses' and never reached the people for whom it was ordered. There were also 'milk frauds'.[10] It is difficult to identify any area of management that was satisfactory by the standards of the Local Government Board, or to which the sisters were accustomed to in hospitals elsewhere.

The sisters responded to the challenge. They observed the Poor Law regulations and were treated respectfully by the guardians, inspectors and other officials. The initial arrangement for £30 per annum per sister was later increased to £40 in order that the sisters might be able to pay the chaplain £60 per annum as well as providing his breakfast.[11] The priests of the Congregation of the Mission in Phibsborough were chaplains. The municipality paid for rent, rates, taxes, light and fuel, thus meeting the sisters' needs.

Medical commentators saw in the administration of workhouse hospitals 'large numbers of defects' including the neglect of the adult 'lunatic poor'.[12]

---

[9] *The Freeman's Journal*, 11 October 1888, Numbers as of 29 September 1888.

[10] *The Freeman's Journal*, 9 June 1887.

[11] Daughter of Charity Narrative, PA:DC/Dunardagh/NDU.

[12] H. Nelson Hardy, 'The medical profession, the national insurance act, and the state of poor law dispensaries in Ireland, being the first part of the Carmichael prize essay 1913' (Dublin, 1913), gives an account of the appalling practices to be found among what he calls typical workhouses, including grim, comfortless wards of undressed stone, the roofs open to the slates, patients sleeping two in a bed, no sanitary appliances so that open pails and buckets are the norm, and left un-emptied for long periods, much of the actual nursing done by pauper wards-women or inmates called 'deputies', pp. 57–63.

Many had learning needs and disabilities rather than mental illness and were housed, not cared for, in very poor conditions under the system of pauper nursing. Widely condemned, over many years, the use of 'inmate nurses' or 'deputies', paid only in extra rations and some small freedoms, was a serious obstacle to reform. Even after the arrival of the sisters to take over the running of the hospital, 'women drawn from the long-term and, by definition, destitute residents' assisted them.[13]

In 1905, the Chief Medical Officer of the North Dublin Union claimed there were 'upwards of 100' inmate nurses in the hospital wards, 'costing for food alone 3/2 d. each per week'.[14] The local government inspectors, Mr O'Connor and Dr Biggar, in their joint report for that year, pushed for the end of pauper nursing, proposing for the consideration of the Board 'the question of the training of probationary nurses in the institution and the number of nurses required in the various departments and the nursery'.[15] A probationer nurse scheme could replace the pauper nurses without burdening the ratepayers, the first, and regrettably too often the only, consideration of the guardians. Such a training scheme was proposed by Dr Powell to the Board of Guardians and to Sister Margaret O'Grady, matron. According to Dr Powell, the most important duty cast onto the guardians of the Union was 'to provide the best possible treatment, consistent with economy, for the sick poor seeking admission to your Hospitals'.[16] If they replaced inmate nurses with probationer nurses, it would, in effect, make the North Dublin Union hospital a recognised training hospital. The scheme proposed by Dr Powell envisaged the admission of thirty probationers at an entrance fee of 20 guineas each, and would entail two years of training, 'subject to superiors' in a Catholic hospital. Three visiting and two resident medical officers gave their support to this scheme. Dr Fottrell claimed that 'under a system properly organised and worked, I have no doubt much good would result. The financial part of the proposed scheme will require careful consideration.'[17] Sister O'Grady was also positive, seeing the proposed change as 'an improvement for all concerned' and encouraged by the fact that the system was in operation in the Belfast Poor Law Union and other places.[18] On 23 December 1910, the setting up of the training of probationary nurses in the institution was announced.

---

[13] Ibid.

[14] Dr Powell's proposed nursing scheme, Board Meeting, 19 October 1905, PA:DC/Dunardagh/NDU.

[15] Clerk of North Dublin Union to Sr O'Grady, 23 December1905, PA:DC/Dunardagh/NDU.

[16] Dr Powell's proposed nursing scheme, Board Meeting, 19 October 1905, PA:DC/Dunardagh/NDU.

[17] Dr W. Fottrell to Clerk of North Dublin Union, 7 November 1905 and 13 November 1905, PA:DC/Dunardagh/ NDU.

[18] Sr O'Grady to the Clerk of the North Dublin Union, 1905, PA:DC/Dunardagh/NDU.

The Easter rebellion of 1916 had its headquarters in the General Post Office in nearby O'Connell Street. The Proclamation of the Irish Republic, signed by seven of the leaders, was announced in dramatic fashion:

> Irishmen and Irish women: In the name of God and of the dead generations from which she receives her old tradition of nationhood, Ireland through us, summons her children to her flag and strikes for her freedom … We declare the right of the Irish People to the ownership of Ireland, and to the unfettered control of Irish destinies, to be sovereign and indefeasible.[19]

The one-week rebellion failed utterly as a military challenge and the leaders surrendered to prevent further bloodshed. The North Dublin Union and the work of the Daughters of Charity came unexpectedly to public notice during that time. There was a 'hidden army' of supporters, couriers, medical personnel and first-aid workers who assisted the rebels and the many hundreds of citizens caught up in the carnage. Priests and nuns gave spiritual, medical and humanitarian assistance. Brendan Mac Thormaid, author of *Deathless Glory*, recounts how James Connolly – founder of the Irish Citizen Army – before his execution, thanked Fr Aloysius, a Capuchin of Church Street (around the corner from North Brunswick Street), who was accompanying him with the last rites, saying, 'I have seen and heard of the brave conduct of priests and nuns during the week and I believe they are the best friends of the workers.'[20] Reflecting on this high praise given by Connolly to religious, Mac Thormaid gives pride of place to the Sisters of St Vincent de Paul of St John's Convent, beside the North Dublin Union:

> Evidently Commandant Daly in a dispatch to Connolly told him of the wonderful help and co-operation he had got from these dedicated nuns of the Big Bonnets at North Brunswick Street … But then those of us who know the Big Bonnets know their big-hearted dedication … In the Roll of Honour of Easter Week must go Sisters Louise, Brigid, Patrick, Monica, and Ma Soeur O'Grady.[21]

The artist Muriel Brandt has an iconic image of the same 'Big Bonnets' distributing bread to the hungry on O'Connell Street in her painting entitled *The Breadline 1916*.[22]

There is good archival evidence for the takeover of the North Dublin Union buildings by the British army on 1 September 1918.[23] A large number of

---

[19] Extract, Proclamation of the Irish Republic, 1916.
[20] Brendan M. Mac Thormaid, *Deathless Glory* (Dublin, 1966), p. 27.
[21] Ibid.
[22] M. Brandt, *The Breadline 1916*, Oil on Canvas, Crawford Art Gallery, Cork. See cover of publication.
[23] Daughter of Charity, Narrative, St John's North Brunswick Street, PA:DC/Dunardagh/NDU.

workhouses were occupied by military of opposing sides during the struggle
for independence and the ensuing civil war.[24] Whether the takeover of the
North Dublin Union buildings was as punishment for 'collusion' during Easter
Week 1916, or was simply a strategic necessity as a good vantage point with
ample space for troops, is a matter of debate. The inmates were dispersed; some
went to the South Dublin Union workhouse, others were boarded out and a
number went to families or friends. This was a time of crisis and upheaval for
the sisters. Many of those employed at the hospital were transferred and the
future for those remaining was very uncertain. The need to confirm the sisters
in the quiet possession of their convent was urged on the War Office, London,
by Fr William Byrne CM, director of the Daughters of Charity, who stressed
the 'very active part' the sisters had played in the war effort.[25] They were
involved, not only in France, but also in London, Scotland and Cork, with all
hospitals placed at the disposal of the War Office for the reception of the
wounded. After quoting instances of support from the sisters, Fr Byrne
appealed in even stronger terms:

> In view of all these facts is it too much to say that they are but
> demanding simple justice when they ask to be allowed to remain where
> they are … I make no mention of the fact that they have silently
> endured the wrenching from the work in which their heart was centred
> – that they have been deprived of their means of livelihood – their
> Convent threatened with dissolution … I can only say … on the
> strength of their services to their country's case they have a clear title to
> retain the residence they now occupy.[26]

The interest, if any, of the War Office in taking possession of the convent
quickly faded.

With the modernising of the Poor Law welfare system and the opportunity
afforded by the emptying of the workhouse, the Poor Law guardians moved
in a direction that exactly complemented the Vincentian charism of the sisters.
This was the focus on outdoor medical assistance using the dispensary structure
that had existed since 1851 and was perhaps the most positive aspect of the
Poor Law system. It was certainly the area most appreciated by the general
public, as it afforded free medical care at weekly clinics and in the houses of
the poor, including the prescribing and dispensing of drugs. For the sisters,
involvement in the outdoor medical relief of the poor of the north city would
be a remarkable, providential, recalling of the first work of the Daughters of
Charity, the visiting of the sick poor in their own homes. The guardians,

---

[24] J. O'Connor, *The Workhouses of Ireland*, p. 199.
[25] The house that the Daughters of Charity occupied in the North Dublin Union was known
as St John's.
[26] Fr William Byrne to Major Ball, 27 November 1918, PA:DC/Dunardagh /NDU.

mindful of the services these sisters had already given to the sick poor of Dublin, wanted to retain them in this new capacity. They proposed that eight sisters be retained to start the work, one sister for each dispensary district, keeping in touch with the medical officers of the districts. The guardians would provide materials for dressings and would receive written reports from the sisters. The guardians undertook to retain and maintain St John's Convent for the residence of the sisters as long as they were engaged in the work of visiting.[27] This decision was greatly welcomed, and the sisters remained in St John's for a further ten years.

Under this providential turn of events, the sisters were given 'the streets of the city' for their new apostolate of charity.[28] As the new terms of employment required, Sister O'Grady, on behalf of the visiting sisters, gave a comprehensive report to the North Dublin Union on the 24 March 1919, noting that over one thousand families had been visited since the previous November. She commented on the great poverty, suffering and wretched housing conditions they had witnessed and thanked the board members for their courtesy and assistance.[29] A formal contract was drawn up for this new work. It appointed Sister Brigid Burke as 'superintendent of the nurses in the North Dublin Urban and South City Dispensary Districts', gave her a salary of £65 per year, with apartment fuel and light. It sanctioned seven other sisters as 'assistant nurses of the same areas', each on a salary of £52 per year, with apartments, fuel and light.[30]

A few months later, Sister Brigid was assigned by the community to the North Infirmary Hospital, Cork, and submitted her resignation as superintendent of the dispensary nursing staff to the guardians. They were aghast at this sudden change and wrote to Fr Byrne expressing regret and annoyance. Declining her resignation, they demanded

> that the Superioress of the Order be informed that the Guardians wish to retain Sister Brigid's services at St John's Convent, North Brunswick Street, owing to the kindly interest she takes in the poor and for the great work she performed during the recent influenza epidemic, she being fully trained previous to her entering the Order and we consider her loss to the sick poor at the present juncture would be irreparable.[31]

---

[27] Daughter of Charity Narrative, North Dublin Union, PA:DC/Dunardagh/NDU.

[28] Company of the Daughters of Charity of St Vincent de Paul, Constitution, 12a.

[29] Report from Sr O'Grady to the Board of Guardians, 24 March 1919, PA:DC/Dunardagh/NDU.

[30] E. W. Leach, Assistant Secretary of the Local Government Board of Ireland to Secretary to Board 10 January 1920, PA:DC/Dublin/NDU.

[31] She submitted her resignation as superintendent of the dispensary nursing staff to the Chairman and Guardians of the Board on the 27 April 1920, Clerk of Union to Fr Byrne, 3 May 1920, Daughter of Charity Narrative, North Dublin Union, PA:DC/Dunardagh/NDU.

The guardians warned that the withdrawal of Sister Brigid jeopardised the position of all the sisters then employed by the Board.[32] Over the following months, letters were exchanged, including requests from three trade unions, for her return, but to no avail.[33] She was replaced as superintendent on 14 June 1920 by Sister Mullally.[34]

The Daughters of Charity spent a further nine years in this ministry. They left St John's on the 22 February 1929 after forty years of devoted service to the poorest of the poor. Shortly after their departure, newspaper reports predicted that the entire fabric of the Poor Law system, founded on the concept of indoor relief, was about to be transformed:

> Big change in Poor Law! Union may Go!
> Society of St Vincent de Paul to assist.
> Scheme that will revolutionise Dublin System.[35]

Celbridge Union Workhouse, 1892–1922

The seventh foundation of the Daughters of Charity in Ireland was established in 1892 when the sisters took responsibility for the care of the inmates of St Anne's Union Workhouse Celbridge, Co. Kildare. This workhouse was one of the first to open, following the Poor Law Act of 1838, with the first admissions on 9 June 1841. The workhouse had a capacity for 400 inmates and was one of the smallest of its kind.

The Sisters of Mercy had charge of the workhouse in Celbridge in the archdiocese of Dublin until 1892, when they were due to move to the diocese of Kildare and Leighlin. The archbishop of Dublin, Dr Walsh, was unhappy to see the Sisters of Mercy leave without being satisfactorily replaced. Since Bishop James Lynch CM and his diocese were benefiting from this transfer, Dr Walsh expected him to use his influence as a member of the Congregation of the Mission to secure the services of the Daughters of Charity. Bishop Lynch wrote to his confrère, Fr William Gavin in London on 11 February 1892 asking him to approach Sister Eugénie Marcellus, visitatrice, and 'get her to procure four sisters for the Celbridge Union, a great work of Charity'.[36] The provincial council instructed Sister Cecilia Robinson of St Vincent's, North

---

[32] Clerk of Union to Fr Byrne, 3 May 1920, Daughter of Charity Narrative, PA:DC/Dunardagh/NDU.

[33] Workers' Union (3) to Fr Byrne, 27 April 1920, PA:DC/Dunardagh/NDU.

[34] Sr Brigid Burke to Chairman and Guardians of North Dublin Union, 27 April 1920, PA:DC/Dunardagh/NDU.

[35] Newspaper cutting, 18 January 1929, 'Big Change in Poor Law', PA:DC/Dunardagh/NDU.

[36] Bishop Lynch CM to Fr William Gavin CM, 11 February 1892, PA:DC/Dunardagh/Celbridge (Provincial Archives, Daughters of Charity, Dunardagh, Dublin, here abbreviated as PA:DC/Dunardagh/Celbridge).

William Street, to visit the workhouse and submit a written report, which would be sent to the Superioress General in Paris. Sister Robinson visited Celbridge on 17 March 1892, while the Sisters of Mercy were still there. In her report she wrote that Celbridge was a healthy house and that conditions were the same as at the North Dublin Union workhouse. There were 150 inmates of whom 60 were in the hospital. Four sisters were requested, one to be matron, one as school mistress, and two others to nurse the sick. The administrators and the Board of Guardians were well disposed towards the appointment of the sisters.

Sister Robinson enclosed a letter from Fr Morrin, parish priest of Naas with her report. In it, he offered to give the Superioress General any further information she required and assured her that the Sisters of Mercy, who were transferring to Naas, had brought an 'entire reform' to the Celbridge workhouse during their years there. He also praised the Board of Guardians for their kindness and generosity and stated that it was Dr Lynch's 'most earnest wish and desire' that the sisters accept the mission. By the end of March 1892 Dr Walsh was growing impatient. He wrote to Bishop Lynch explaining that Colonel Dease, the chairman of the Board of Guardians of Celbridge

> was very anxious to know about the nuns for Celbridge. I have told him that as your lordship is charged with getting the Sisters of St Vincent for us, we may rest easy in our minds, as you will not withdraw the present Community until you have provided us with the new one.[37]

There was extensive communication between the Daughters of Charity in Dublin, London and Paris about this new mission. On receipt of the full report and recommendations, Sister Léonide Havard, the superioress general in Paris, wrote to Sister Eugénie Marcellus in Mill Hill, sanctioning the proposed arrangements for the initiation of the Daughters of Charity into Celbridge.[38] On accepting this new mission, Sister Havard remarked, 'it is right to satisfy the administration on this point as it is in the interests of our dear Masters the Poor.'[39] She then informed Bishop Lynch of the decision. Meanwhile Dr Walsh wrote to Fr Morrissey, the provincial of the Congregation of the Mission, giving his approval for the sisters' new work in Celbridge, 'the second in the Diocese since I have been placed in charge of it', and adding, 'already I am looking forward to the establishment of a third'.[40]

A memorandum in the provincial archives, Mill Hill, dated 27 May 1892, states that Colonel Dease had accepted, on behalf of the guardians, all the

---

[37] Archbishop W. Walsh to Bishop Lynch CM, 30 March 1892, PA:DC/Dunardagh/Celbridge.
[38] Sr Havard, superioress general to Sr Marcellus, 17 March 1892, PA:DC/Dunardagh/Celbridge.
[39] Ibid.
[40] Archbishop W. Walsh to Fr Morrissey CM, 18 May 1892, PA:DC/Dunardagh/Celbridge.

conditions laid down by the sisters, and had outlined their own conditions, most of which were in existence for the Sisters of Mercy. The memorandum indicated the number of inmates, the manner in which the sisters were to insert themselves in the work and how they were to behave towards the women in Celbridge:

> There are at present 134 inmates – and about 50 of them are in the Infirmary. At present there are only about 12 children. The kitchen and washhouse are worked by the women of the workhouse under the supervision of the Sisters. The Sisters have a little kitchen of their own and choose a servant from among the inmates. The Sister who is Matron is responsible for everything and will be required to have a good head, business-like habits and be very firm, as the women are sometimes very difficult to manage and may give a little trouble especially at first. The Sisters have a private Oratory with the Blessed Sacrament. Mass will be at 7.00 a.m.[41]

The sisters arrived in Celbridge in 1892. Sister Mary Nolan was appointed as sister servant and matron of the hospital, Sister Joseph Prendergast as school mistress, with sisters Vincent McKenna and Louise Madden as ward sisters.

Within six years of the sisters taking charge, they were credited by the local authorities with having wrought considerable improvements in the care of the sick. In 1898, the guardians requested two additional sisters with nursing qualifications.[42] Knowing that it was impossible to allocate any more sisters, the provincial council accepted the alternative offer that the guardians would employ and pay a qualified lay nurse with whom two sisters would work, as was done in many Catholic hospitals at the time.

World War I had a profound effect on the services of the workhouse in Celbridge. In her letters of 1915–19, Sister Mary Brady gave details of the role of the workhouse in accommodating refugees. The scarcity of provisions and the high prices made the running of the institution most difficult:

> We have a large number of Belgians at present, among them two nice old women, one is seventy years of age, the other seventy-five. They are constantly changing – they come here straight from the boat, and according as the Committee finds homes for them, they are sent away and we get a fresh lot. The constant changing makes it more difficult to manage. … Just as I was finishing this letter, forty-three more Belgians arrived, but we expect many will be going away next week.[43]

---

[41] Memo, Provincial House, Mill Hill to Celbridge, 27 May 1892, PA:DC/Dunardagh/Celbridge.

[42] Séance du Conseil, 13 juin 1898, PA:DC/Mill Hill.

[43] Sr Mary Brady to Sr Visitatrice, 17 January 1915, PA:DC/Dunardagh/ Celbridge.

The cost of all provisions, including milk, increased during the war, putting a strain on the management of the house. But despite all the hardships of the workhouse and the wartime shortages, the sisters made an effort to make Christmas 1915 special: 'Our poor people enjoyed these little feasts and tea parties, although we had not as many nice things for them as last year.'[44] The following Christmas, life was more difficult. The little extras given to the women were unavailable, as the people who used to subscribe to the Christmas festivities were 'nearly all away at the war'.[45] But even then they made the most of what was possible. The guardians had been slow to appreciate the difficulties the sisters had in making ends meet, but by January 1918, they had given 'a temporary bonus of 2 s. per week for each Sister, commencing on 1 October on account of the very high price of all kinds of provisions'.[46]

The replacement of the workhouse system became a key ambition of the Irish Free State. As a consequence, the Celbridge Workhouse was closed on 31 March 1922. The matter was recorded in the minutes of a council meeting in Mill Hill, 21 March in the briefest of terms: 'Celbridge closed by the Irish Government on 31 March 1922.'[47] There was little if any public comment outside of the immediate locality, and the sisters left quietly, moving to wherever their superiors had named as their next mission.

Abbeyleix Workhouse, 1901

Invitations to the Daughters of Charity to assume responsibility for nursing care in the workhouse hospitals of Abbeyleix, Mountmellick, Co. Laois and Rathdown, Co. Wicklow, were issued to the provincial council at Mill Hill, London, in the early summer of 1899. The provincial council decided to send the experienced Sister O'Grady of the North Dublin Union to visit Mountmellick and Rathdown and to submit a report.[48] In July 1899 a decision was made by the provincial council that the sisters would continue to staff workhouse hospitals in Ireland, contingent on the availability of daily mass.[49] The sisters were named for Rathdown, but the foundation did not go ahead because the mass arrangements were unsatisfactory and the bishop did not encourage the foundation.[50] At Abbeyleix, the local parish priest gave assurance

---

[44] Sr Mary Brady to Sr Visitatrice, 14 January 1916, PA:DC/Dunardagh/Celbridge.

[45] Sr Mary Brady to Sr Visitatrice, January 1918, PA:DC/Dunardagh/Celbridge.

[46] Ibid.

[47] Séance du Conseil, 21 mars 1922, PA:DC/Mill Hill.

[48] Séance du Conseil, 15 juin 1899, PA:DC/Mill Hill.

[49] Ibid., 3 juillet 1899, PA :DC/Mill Hill.

[50] *Mais toujours avec la condition que les sœurs n'iront pas à cet Hôpital si elles ne peuvent pas être assurées d'avoir la Messe tous les jours.* Séance du Conseil, 25 juin 1899, 10, 17, 31 juillet 1899, PA:DC/Mill Hill.

that mass would be celebrated in the workhouse four times during the week, all year round, and on the other days mass would be available in the nearby church at times that would allow the sisters to discharge their hospital duties.[51]

The response to the requests for sisters for Abbeyleix and Mountmellick was quickly cleared with the Bishop of Kildare and Leighlin.[52] Contracts were drawn up for both houses, the near-identical conditions a reflection of the uniformity of the Poor Law system, which left very little room for local difference.[53] The guardians at Abbeyleix were assured that, in so far as possible, one sister would have a nursing certificate and the other three would have a minimum of one year's hospital experience.[54] Over the summer of 1901, the final arrangements were put in place: the salary would be £50 per annum for the sister with nursing qualifications and £30 each for the others.[55] Sister Murphy of the North Dublin Union was named sister servant and with her companions, sisters Gordon, Buckley and Rennie arrived in Abbeyleix on 7 September 1901.[56]

The hospital was still in a very primitive state. Like other union workhouses in Ireland, there had been few improvements in the previous sixty years. The 1902 report of Dr Joseph Smyth, medical inspector for the Local Government Board of the Abbeyleix hospital, pointed out areas needing improvement: 'The maternity ward had only one bed with a straw tick, which should be burned;' in the infirmary only twelve of the beds had wire fittings, the other forty just straw ticks; the 'pipes were out of order'; there was overcrowding in the nursery and in the wards; there was no proper lock-up for poisonous or important medicines; 'Higginson's syringes should be suspended at full stretch with the nozzles downwards.'[57] Dr Smyth's report was presented by the Local Government Board to the guardians requesting that these matters be given their careful attention. Acknowledging the improvements already made by the Daughters of Charity, the report added:

> It is only fair to state that the Infirmary has been but a short time under the care of the Sisters of Charity, and that already they have accomplished great improvements which are very much appreciated.[58]

[51] Séance du Conseil, 3 juillet 1899, 10 juillet 1899, PA:DC/Mill Hill.

[52] Ibid., 17 juillet 1899, PA:DC/Mill Hill.

[53] Ibid., 10 juillet 1899, 31 juillet 1899, PA:DC/Mill Hill.

[54] Ibid., 26 novembre 1899, PA:DC/Mill Hill.

[55] Ibid., 30 juin 1901, PA:DC/Mill Hill.

[56] Ibid., juillet 1899–juillet 1901, PA:DC/Mill Hill.

[57] Report of Dr Joseph Smyth presented by H. W. Swaine (Secretary) Local Government Board, Dublin, to the Abbeyleix Union, 15 July 1902, PA:DC/Dunardagh/Abbeyleix.

[58] Report by Dr J. Smyth, presented by H. M. Swaine (Secretary) Local Government Board, Dublin to the Abbeyleix Union, 15 July 1902, PA:DC/Dunardagh/Abbeyleix.

The Daughters of Charity with their charism of 'serving Christ in the poor' with compassion and love needed a great spirit of faith in their new environment. Dr Smyth advised close personal supervision of the wards. He insisted that the sisters make the patients' beds themselves, which he said was among

> the most important duties of hospital nursing … Only in this way can they counteract the tendency of patients to make the bed a place of concealment for things that are objectionable, such as dirty clothes, bottles, soap, bread, tobacco pipes, matches, dirty rags, and all sorts of rubbish.[59]

Within the first three months of the sisters' arrival in Abbeyleix, the guardians decided that in order to reduce the running costs of the workhouse the number of sisters could be reduced by one. Sister Rennie was withdrawn and sent to Lanark, Scotland. The guardians later requested a sister to be matron of the hospital. Sister Catherine Harrington was proposed, but before her appointment was finalised, they had changed their minds and named a lay person.

In 1903 the Vice-Regal Commission on Poor Law Reform was set up. All workhouses then in operation were inspected and 743 witnesses interviewed. Its first and unequivocal recommendation was that the workhouse system should be abolished. It stated that the poverty of Ireland could not be dealt with adequately by the poor relief law, but rather by the development of the country's resources. It recommended that the various classes of inmates in the workhouses be segregated into separate institutions, and that the infirm or aged be transferred to county institutions, to which it gave the name 'County alms-houses'. After the Easter Week rising of 1916, the movement for self-government grew and with it the desire to dismantle the workhouse system. The first programme of Dáil Éireann[60] made this a key policy objective:

> The Irish Republic fully realises the necessity of abolishing the present odious, degrading and foreign poor law system, substituting therefore a sympathetic native scheme for the care of the nation's aged and infirm, who shall no longer be regarded as a burden but rather entitled to the nation's gratitude and consideration. Likewise it shall be the duty of the Republic to take measures that will safeguard the health of the people and ensure the physical as well as the moral well-being of the nation.[61]

---

[59] Report by Dr Joseph Smyth presented by H. M. Swaine, Local Government Board to Board of Guardians, Abbeyleix Union, 11 July 1902, PA:DC/Dunardagh/Abbeyleix.
[60] Dáil Eireann: lower house of Parliament in the Irish Free State (1919–49) and Republic of Ireland (1949–present time).
[61] Quoted in O'Connor, *The Workhouses of Ireland*, pp. 197–8.

During the War of Independence and the ensuing civil war, military forces often occupied the workhouses, as already noted in respect of the sisters' work in the North Dublin Union. Some workhouses were burnt down, others deteriorated, thirty-three became county homes, thirty-two were converted to district hospitals or fever hospitals, nine to county hospitals, and most of the others were closed.[62] Abbeyleix workhouse became a hospital, first known as St Vincent's County Hospital and later as The District Hospital, Abbeyleix.

The Laois County Board of Health had replaced the various boards of guardians in the county, with much wider powers and working under immense pressure from the electorate who were expecting real, tangible improvements. In 1924, they required that nurses be properly trained. This entailed that candidates on the nursing staff in Abbeyleix must have resided for not less than two years in a general clinic or hospital recognised by the minister, 'and after examination must have obtained from such Hospital a Certificate of Proficiency in Nursing'.[63] There was also a decision in 1934 to replace the old hospital with a new building.

The first five months of 1934 were times of extreme tension for the Daughters of Charity in Abbeyleix, arising from: plans for the building of a new district hospital; the demolition of the old workhouse building, including the convent; a financial crisis regarding hospital funds and labour protests by the unemployed in the town. While the demolition of the centre block of the old hospital was underway, the patients and staff needed to be accommodated elsewhere.[64] The acting secretary of the Laois County Board of Health, Mr O'Gorman, outlined the arrangements agreed with the Minister that the nursing sisters were to be accommodated in the new part of the rear block, the ordinary medical and surgical cases to remain in this block and maternity cases to be provided for suitably in the same block.[65]

Two rooms were to be allotted to the sisters in the rear of the building with the patients. There were disagreements between the committee members, labour unions, architect and secretary. The accommodation offered was turned down as 'totally unsuitable ... even as a temporary measure'.[66] However, this was only one of the problems in Abbeyleix.

There was serious unemployment in the 1930s, and a lot of unrest caused by delays in the building of the hospital which would have provided local

---

[62] J. O'Connor, *The Workhouses of Ireland*, p. 199.

[63] Secretary, Local Appointments Commission St Stephen's Green, Dublin to Sr Superior, Abbeyleix, 16 December 1927, PA:DC/Dunardagh/Abbeyleix.

[64] Secretary, Laoighis County Board of Health and Public Assistance to (Sister) Matron, District Hospital, Abbeyleix, 19 February 1934, PA:DC/Dunardagh/Abbeyleix.

[65] Ibid.

[66] Sr Anne Thomson Visitatrice to the Acting Secretary District Hospital, Abbeyleix, 1 March 1934, PA:DC/Dunardagh/Abbeyleix.

employment. The contract price for the hospital was £32,000 and a large proportion of that would have gone on wages in Abbeyleix and environs. Both the Abbeyleix branch of the Irish Labour Party and the Fianna Fáil cumann demanded a speedy resolution to these problems.[67] On 20 March 1934, about seventy unemployed men marched through the main street of Abbeyleix and up to the district hospital, carrying a banner with the inscription 'Abbeyleix unemployed demand work or home assistance'.[68] The sisters, still in the confines of the hospital, felt at risk and the sister servant, Sister Vincent Coveney, wrote to the visitatrice, Sister Anne Thomson, 'we have the Police guarding us night and day here and all doors are bolted tightly.'[69] The people did not intend any harm to come to the sisters. A union representative claimed, 'The Workers of Abbeyleix did not in any way want to interfere with the Nuns, and whenever they looked for protection, they always got it from the Workers.'[70]

Another problem related to hospital funds. The sister responsible for the accounts appears to have lacked judgement in not requiring receipts. £1,000 was unaccounted for and the cash books were mislaid. There was a public investigation into the finances of the hospital in 1934 and this was a serious blow to the sisters' reputation.

A decision was made in May 1934 to withdraw the sisters from Abbeyleix. Although the problem concerning accommodation was the main reason for the withdrawal of the sisters, the labour unrest and the financial embarrassment combined to precipitate their departure on 25 May 1934. Sister Thomson wrote to Bishop Cullen of Kildare and Leighlin regarding the withdrawal of the sisters from Abbeyleix Hospital:

> It is with regret that I have to inform your Lordship that on account of impossible conditions brought about by the Committee we are obliged to withdraw our Sisters from Abbeyleix, at least until the new building is ready and suitable accommodation can be given them. It is really a sorrow for us to leave those poor people in the County Home, and we feel convinced that your Lordship will realize we should not have taken such a step without absolute necessity. May 25th is the date fixed for the withdrawal of the Sisters.[71]

---

[67] Fianna Fáil was one of the major political parties in Ireland. A cumann: a local branch of the party.
[68] Newspaper Account (untitled), 20 March 1934, PA:DC/Dunardagh/Abbeyleix.
[69] Letter from Sr Coveney to Sr Anne Thomson, 22 March 1934, PA:DC/Dunardagh/Abbeyleix.
[70] Newspaper Account (untitled), 20 March 1934, PA:DC/Dunardagh/Abbeyleix.
[71] Sr Anne Thomson to Bishop Cullen of Kildare and Leighlin, 23 May 1934, PA:DC/Dunardagh/ Abbeyleix.

St Vincent de Paul, 1581–1660   St Louise de Marillac, 1591–1660

Crest and Motto of the Daughters of Charity

Sœur de S.ᵗ Vincent de Paul
missionnaire de charité.

Sœur de S.ᵗ Vincent de Paul
cuisinière des pauvres.

Sœur de S.ᵗ Vincent de Paul
pharmacienne des pauvres.

Early representations of the Daughters of Charity

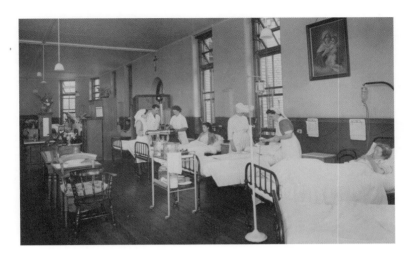

Female Ward, North Infirmary, Cork, 1947

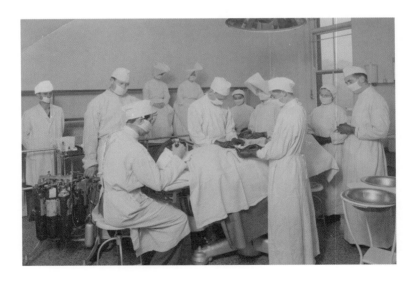

Operating Theatre, 1947–48,
North Infirmary

Sr Marie Mc Kenna, Tutor, 1962

The Breadline 1916
The Daughters of Charity of St Vincent de Paul
dispensing bread in 1916

St Vincent's, Fair Street,
Drogheda, Louth

St Vincent's, North William
Street, Dublin

St Vincent's Hospital,
Fairview, Dublin

North Infirmary Hospital, Cork, 1914

St Vincent's, Abbeyleix, Louth

St Vincent's,
Mountmellick,
Laois

St Anne's, Celbridge, Kildare

St Mary's,
Dunmanway, Cork

St Vincent's,
Clonard Gardens,
Belfast

Our Lady's Home,
Henrietta Street,
Dublin

St John's,
North Dublin Union, Dublin

St Vincent's, Cabra, Dublin

On hearing that the sisters were leaving there was strong local reaction. Requests for them to remain appeared in the local newspapers. A resolution was adopted by 'a large and representative public meeting' held in the town on Friday 4 May 1934:

> It is not our wish that you vacate the Convent, and the duties by which you have so faithfully devoted your lives to the service of God and the afflicted. We have experienced your extreme kindness and advice on several occasions when through illness or accident, like the Good Ministering Angels of Mercy, your careful and attentive hands were ever ready to soothe the sick and wounded ... We have long spoken of you as our Sisters of Charity; in fact the works have become household words, and will we hope be the words of future generations ... We request you, through your Superiors to remain in our service in your Hospital Convent.[72]

The sisters in nearby Mountmellick were lobbied, in the hope that representations from there might carry weight with the provincial leadership. The acting secretary asked Sister Brendan Malone, matron of Mountmellick if she could prevail on her superiors to retain the sisters in Abbeyleix as 'there are sure to be considerable changes in the Management of the Board's affairs within a very short time'.[73]

From May until September 1934, there were repeated pleas to Sister Thomson and to Fr John O'Connell, to allow the return of the sisters to Abbeyleix. *The Kilkenny People*, in an article headed 'Calamity that nuns left', quoted Mr Bartley, the new commissioner for administering the Laois Board of Health:

> It was a grave error on the part of my predecessors that they did not make an effort to keep them here ... I think it would be a wonderful thing for the sick poor who are sometimes forgotten by their own friends to have a nun by the bedside when they are dying to say the prayers for the dying.[74]

None of the pleas were answered. Thus, the Abbeyleix chapter for the Daughters of Charity was finally closed.

---

[72] Letter from a large representative public meeting to Matron and Daughters of Charity, 4 May 1934, PA:DC/Dunardagh/Abbeyleix.
[73] M. O'Gorman (Acting Secretary) to Sr Mary Brendan Malone, County Home, Mountmellick, 18 May 1934, PA:DC/Dunardagh/Abbeyleix.
[74] The Kilkenny People, 30 June 1934, PA:DC/Dunardagh/Abbeyleix.

Mountmellick Workhouse, 1902

The workhouse in Mountmellick Co. Laois, was built 1842–44, on a six-acre site half a mile to the south of the town. It was designed by George Wilkinson, the Poor Law Commissioners' architect, on the austere style of other workhouses. Declared fit for the reception of paupers on 31 August 1844, it received its first admissions on 3 January 1845.[75] The building had accommodation for 800 residents. During and after the great famine, 1845–47, many of the destitute were housed there. From 1895 to 1900 it had also served as a prison. There is a reference to this in notes in the archives of the Daughters of Charity:

> When the sisters came many of the rooms still had barred windows. There was also a gallows which for some reason or other had never been removed. On a level with it was the loft door out of which the condemned man left the 'condemned cell' to meet his God within the next few minutes, stared at by the crowd gathered in the courtyard below to watch the scene. How many men thus met their fate is known to God alone.[76]

It was in the late 1890s that the guardians of the Union decided to engage nuns to run the workhouse hospital. On 6 June 1899, Fr David Doyle, parish priest of Mountmellick, wrote on their behalf to Sister Eugénie Marcellus requesting sisters for the hospital:

> I shall take it as a great favour if you kindly let me know as soon as possible if your esteemed Community could undertake to supply the sisters that may be necessary … I think at least three sisters would be required.[77]

Sister Marcellus visited Mountmellick to explore the situation and was interested in the project. It is clear from the correspondence between her and Fr Doyle that an essential condition was the availability of daily mass for the sisters. She was satisfied by the assurance given her by Fr Doyle that

> the Sisters who come will not be deprived of the spiritual advantages of attending daily mass … celebrated each morning at 7.30 a.m. in the parish church, about five minutes' walk away … and if the morning is wet they could have the hospital horse and trap.[78]

---

[75] J. O'Connor, *The Workhouses of Ireland*, p. 262.
[76] Daughters of Charity, Narrative, PA:DC/Dunardagh/Mountmellick (Provincial Archives, Daughters of Charity, Dunardagh, Dublin, Mountmellick, here abbreviated as PA:DC/Dunardagh/Mountmellick).
[77] Fr Doyle to Sr Marcellus, 6 June 1899, PA:DC/Dunardagh/Mountmellick.
[78] Ibid.

Even though the guardians had invited the sisters to take over the workhouse hospital and the Daughters of Charity had accepted the invitation, it was still necessary to advertise the positions in the local papers. On 20 February 1902, an advertisement for 'a matron at a salary of £40 per year, one trained nurse for the Infirmary at £40 yearly, and two Assistant Nurses at £30 yearly' appeared in the *Leinster Leader* and the *Leinster Express*.[79] On 10 March, the clerk of the Union, Richard Goodbody, wrote to Sister Marcellus to inform her that 'four Sisters of Charity had been elected to fill the advertised positions in the Workhouse'.[80]

Preparations for the accommodation of the sisters in the workhouse building were completed, and on 10 October 1902, four Daughters of Charity arrived in Mountmellick: Sister Patricia O'Mahoney, as matron and sister servant, accompanied by sisters Mullally, Klanser and Forge. The sisters were happy with the accommodation provided for them and particularly with 'the little Oratory where the Blessed Sacrament was reserved'.[81] It became possible for them to have daily mass in the workhouse chapel.

When the sisters arrived in Mountmellick, there were over three hundred and fifty inmates in the workhouse, of which sixty were in the hospital. These were mainly the elderly, but there were also people with physical and intellectual disabilities and single mothers and their children. The sisters 'were untiring in their devotion to the poor, working long hours under primitive conditions to bring relief and consolation to the sick and suffering'.[82] They worked to improve the standards of care and compassion, and while they did their best to improve conditions, it must be remembered that they were working within the Poor Law regulations and within very tight budgets. As well as tending to the physical and social needs of the people, they also took great care of their spiritual needs.

Though engaged initially to take charge of the workhouse hospital, the sisters took on other duties as time went on. On 14 October 1911, a sister was appointed by the guardians to take charge of the fever hospital; on 10 December 1919, a sister was appointed to care for 'imbecile epileptics' and another to care for the old men.[83] The workhouse in Mountmellick became the County Home under the jurisdiction of the Local Government Board of Queen's County. When Sister Brendan Malone was matron, the entire administration of the County Home was handed over to her.[84] As had happened in the other

---

[79] *The Leinster Leader* and *The Leinster Express*, 20 February 1902.
[80] R. Goodbody to Sr Marcellus, 10 March 1902, PA:DC/Dunardagh/Mountmellick.
[81] Daughter of Charity, Narrative, PA:DC/Dunardagh/Mountmellick.
[82] Ibid.
[83] Ibid.
[84] Ibid.

workhouses, the sisters gave dedicated service to the poor people of Mountmellick. In July 1966, it was the first of the County Homes to become an up-to-date geriatric hospital. Parts of the old buildings were reconstructed, others adapted and all decorated and made bright and comfortable for the old people. The high walls surrounding the building were demolished and the whole appearance of the home improved.[85] At the official opening of the refurbished buildings, Bishop Patrick Lennon asked for God's continued blessing 'not on the stones and mortar but on the patients, staff, sisters, nurses and on all who have devoted their lives to the service of the sick, the elderly, the lonely and all those in need'.[86] The hospital was officially opened by Sean Flanagan, minister for health. The Daughters of Charity continued to care for the elderly there until 1987.

Conclusion

The employment of the Daughters of Charity of St Vincent de Paul in the Irish workhouse system from 1888 to 1934 is a complicated story as so many different places were involved, with their own boards of guardians, local priorities and local politics, and over a period when the Poor Law system itself was reconstituted. The Daughters of Charity were by no means the only nuns employed in workhouse hospitals from the later nineteenth century onwards; the work of the Mercy Sisters and the Sisters of St John of God must also be noted. Though the Poor Law Commissioners were at first reluctant to have nuns – any nuns – in charge of workhouse hospitals, fearing that their non-religious character might be diminished, in the unions where the Daughters of Charity were employed they managed to win both official and public approval over time, and for very good reasons.

While the Poor Law was a recognition, however begrudging, of state responsibility for those who could not maintain themselves by their own unaided efforts, the Daughters of Charity demonstrated that state care could be done not only with economy, efficiency and transparency, but also with great compassion and respect for the person. Always careful to agree contracts, the sisters were able to work within the restrictions of this system, slowly making improvements, and raising the standard of nursing, nurse training, and hospital care more generally. Beginning in North Brunswick Street, the Daughters of Charity served in six of the country's workhouses but many other requests (directed to Mill Hill) had to be turned down. The sisters' contribution to the development of the dispensary system in the North Dublin area was

---

[85] Daughters of Charity, Narrative, PA:DC/Dunardagh/Mountmellick.
[86] Report of the sisters in Mountmellick, 1981, PA:DC/Dunardagh/Mountmellick.

also significant. Their flexibility and mobility were great assets in these enterprises. Working in state-run institutions but with strong, integrated community structures, they were enabled to move from a place when their services were no longer required and go to where there was greater need. That they managed to work with the different authorities at national, diocesan and local level, in a time of political conflict is a remarkable testimony to their personal resilience and willingness to endure much for the sake of their real masters, the poor. Their contribution has always been appreciated, as is evident from the many testimonials presented when the community was withdrawn from a particular hospital and the sisters missioned to somewhere else.

Chapter Nine

St Vincent's, Cabra, Dublin:
Opening the Door to Education for Children
with Special Needs

Claire Sweeney DC

Go to serve [these little ones] with charity, gentleness, and affection.[1]

The Special Olympics 2003 was a most memorable event for Ireland. The players in the Olympics, all people with special needs, touched hearts in an extraordinary way. They helped people experience what being truly human means in a society that has become very materialistic. Society's perception of people with special needs, evidenced during those special days in 2003, bears little resemblance to society's perception of them at the beginning of the twentieth century. The pioneering work of the Daughters of Charity in the field of children with intellectual disabilities made a major contribution to this change in perception.

'Opening the door to education for children with special needs' was chosen as the subtitle for this chapter specifically to underline the fact that it deals only with the educational aspect of the services of the Daughters of Charity to persons with intellectual disabilities. The service began at the end of the nineteenth century and now serves up to 1,500 people with special needs. Characterised by respect and love, the services focus on enabling the individual to develop to full potential. The educational development dealt with in this chapter is just one aspect of the total picture.

The Cabra Auxiliary
Ireland in the second half of the nineteenth century conjures up a picture of hunger, poverty and displacement in the minds of most people. The country

---

[1] P. Coste CM, *Saint Vincent de Paul: Correspondence, Conferences, Documents*, vol. 9 ed. and tr. Marie Poole DC (New York: New City Press), p. 106.

had suffered a severe famine, with its consequent disease, death and emigration. The workhouse system had been set up as one of the measures to deal with the problems created by the famine.[2] Despite the fact that there was considerable provision of Catholic orphanages run by religious organisations from the 1850s, and despite the introduction of industrial schools from 1868, there were still large numbers of children attached to the workhouse in the second half of the nineteenth century. The problem of providing schooling for these children was compounded by the fact that the workhouse system did not allow the children to be educated at the local national schools. It was part of the workhouse policy to segregate the children so as to make them more conscious of their pauper status. At the same time there was growing awareness that the workhouse environment was not suitable for the moral development of children, and so a decision was made to build schools on separate locations, but within the workhouse system.

The North Dublin Union built a school in Cabra in 1884 for the children of the North Dublin Union, located at North Brunswick Street. It became known as the Cabra Auxiliary. It was built in the austere style of the workhouse, and situated on twenty acres of land near the Phoenix Park. It had been intended as an agricultural school 'primarily for boys who had parents in the workhouse'.[3] However both boys and girls were brought there from the North Dublin Union. A number of teachers and pauper assistants were transferred with the children, and six Dominican nuns from a convent nearby were engaged to teach the girls.

In 1892, the Dominican nuns decided to withdraw their services from the Cabra Auxiliary in order to devote their time to providing services for deaf children. The Daughters of Charity, who were serving in the North Dublin Union, were invited by the Board of Governors to replace them. When the chairman of the Union heard that the Daughters of Charity had agreed to replace the Dominican nuns, he asked them to take over the entire running of the Cabra Auxiliary. Sister Catherine O'Grady, sister servant of the North Dublin Union community, a key figure in the negotiations between North Dublin Union authorities and the Daughters of Charity in London, wrote to Sister Éugenie Marcellus, visitatrice, 'Some of the Guardians have called in private to ask me to write to you … [They] want everyone to know that the Sisters are to be the heads of the institution, acting of course, under the Guardians.'[4] Archbishop William J. Walsh, who had been involved in the

---

[2] See Chapter Eight, 'The Daughters of Charity of St Vincent de Paul in the Irish Workhouse System'.

[3] Report of the Reformatories and Industrial Schools Commissioners, 1884.

[4] Sr O'Grady to Sr Marcellus, 18 August 1892, PA:DC/Dunardagh/Cabra (Provincial Archives, Daughters of Charity, Dunardagh, Blackrock, Dublin, here abbreviated as PA:DC/Dunardagh/Cabra).

coming of the Daughters of Charity to North Brunswick Street in 1888, was also putting pressure on them to take over the running of the Cabra Auxiliary. Sister Marcellus wrote to him on 22 August 1892, pointing out that the Daughters of Charity did not have enough sisters at that time to take over the whole establishment as the guardians wished, but would be willing to replace the six Dominican Sisters. There was a possibility that 'in a few months' time they 'should probably see [their] way to complying with the further requirements of the Guardians'.[5]

Another issue for the sisters was the care of teenage boys. Sister O'Grady wrote to Sister Marcellus, 'The Guardians also wish that the Sisters should of course undertake the charge of the boys and be their responsible people for the Institution.'[6] Taking charge of the boys as well as the girls would require more staff, but a bigger problem lay in the fact that the provincial council was wary of agreeing to undertake the care of teenage boys in industrial schools and other residential settings, as seen in the numerous requests, and almost as many refusals, between 1885 and 1925.[7]

Following on the above correspondence, Fr William Gavin CM, Director of the Daughters of Charity, went to Dublin for a meeting with the guardians of the Union. Sister O'Grady reported to Sister Marcellus on this meeting saying that 'Fr Gavin was very impressed by the determination [of the guardians] to secure the services of the Sisters' and saw no reason why the Sisters should not take over 'the whole thing'.[8] She believed that the work would be very suitable for them, 'It is a grand work, nothing but the real poor.'[9] Here, as in other places, the sisters were endeavouring to be true to the dictum of Louise de Marillac in 1660: 'Oh what a happiness it would be, provided God were in no way offended, if the Company had only to serve the totally destitute.'[10] It is clear from Sister O'Grady's letter that the guardians wanted to appoint the Daughters of Charity to run the Cabra Auxiliary and were doing all they could to get the agreement of the Local Government Board to appoint the number of sisters required, and to set up proper financial arrangements for them.[11] There were two difficulties with this: as shown above, the Daughters of Charity did not have enough sisters to send and the Local Government Board was reluctant to agree to the appointment of 'nuns' to run the institution because of the religious tensions existing at the time.

---

[5] Sr Marcellus to Dr Walsh, 22 August 1892, PA:DC/Dunardagh/Cabra.
[6] Sr O Grady to Sr Marcellus, 18 August 1892, PA:DC/Dunardagh/Cabra.
[7] Minutes of Council Meetings, PA:DC/Mill Hill.
[8] Sr O'Grady to Sr Marcellus, 18 August 1892, PA:DC/Dunardagh/Cabra.
[9] Ibid.
[10] L. Sullivan DC, *Sister Rosalie Rendu: A Daughter of Charity on Fire with Love for the Poor* (Chicago, 2006), p. 833.
[11] Sr O'Grady to Sr Marcellus, 18 August 1892, PA:/DC/Dunardagh/Cabra.

The second half of the nineteenth century was a time of much proselytising, and this gave rise to a great deal of mistrust between Catholics and Protestants in many areas. The fact that archbishops Paul Cullen and William J. Walsh had on previous occasions advised the sisters not to accept government grants, lest they be compromised in religious matters, is indicative of Catholic mistrust, while the satirical pamphlet *The Pope is in the Poorhouse*, distributed in Dublin, shows Protestant mistrust of Catholic activity.[12] Because of these religious tensions, the Local Government Board had reservations about giving a religious order complete authority in a publicly financed Poor Law institution.

In the end, agreement was reached and six Daughters of Charity were sent to take over the entire running of the Cabra Auxiliary in September 1892. They were sisters Margaret Galvin, as matron, Mary Flanagan, Mary Hook, Margaret Lane, Margaret McKenna and Mary O'Sullivan.

Some of the residents were children whose parents were in the workhouse in North Brunswick Street; others were vagrants. Some had physical and/or intellectual disabilities. The sisters applied themselves to the work with the devotion that is characteristic of their Company.

Although it had been agreed to take on boys as well as girls, the initial arrangement was for six sisters only, who, having been unanimously elected by the Board of the North Dublin Union on 22 September 1892, would take 'charge of the several departments of the Children's Home of Cabra Auxiliary Workhouse'. Sister O'Grady warned the Visitatrice to ask the North Dublin Union for sufficient personnel to run the school, 'They say that if you don't ask for them in the beginning, they will not give them after but with difficulty.'[13] In 1893, four more sisters were appointed: sisters Prendergast, Haggerty, Cutler and Sullivan. Returns for 1910 show that there were 400 children in Cabra, many of them sick children, and the entire staff – teaching, caring, cooking, and maintenance – consisted of only fifteen sisters, one male teacher, a Protestant teacher, a few assistants, and a man to keep guard at night.

The influence of the sisters in the running of the Auxiliary was curtailed by workhouse regulations. Although the 1895 Local Government report states that 'the schools are very efficiently run by the Sisters of Charity of St Vincent de Paul who have entire charge of the food, clothing, discipline as well as instruction', it was the workhouse authorities who decided the daily routines.[14] The sisters had to follow the dietary arrangements determined by the guardians, whose decisions were closely monitored by the Local Government

---

[12] J. Robins, *From Rejection to Integration: A Centenary of Service of Daughters of Charity to Persons with a Mental Handicap* (Dublin, 1992), p. 1.
[13] Sr O'Grady to Sr Marcellus, 18 August 1892, PA:DC/Dunardagh/Cabra.
[14] Local Government Report 1895, PA:DC/Dunardagh/Cabra.

Board. The clothes of rough wool worn by the children and made in the workhouse had a uniform style with the telltale stamp of the North Dublin Union, as another way of reminding the children that they were paupers. A strict routine was followed: breakfast was at 6.00 a.m. followed by an hour's religious instruction and lessons; practical training at 2.00 p.m.; supper at 5.30 p.m. followed by more lessons, with a short time left for recreation before bed at 7.00 p.m. in winter, and 8.00 p.m. in summer. An interesting part of the routine was the daily walk of the children in the Phoenix Park. The purpose of these walks was to let the public see 'how clean and neat in appearance and how orderly in behaviour' the children were.[15] It was considered important to make a good impression on the general public as the children would be looking for employment later on.

The guardians maintained strict supervision of the institution through regular visits and through the weekly report which was required from the matron. There were also frequent examinations by the inspectors of schools on behalf of the Commissioners of National Education. A report in January 1893, a few months after the sisters had taken over, goes as follows, 'General proficiency fairly good and the copybooks are kept free from blots. The children were poorly prepared in grammar. Answering in geography was but middling.[16] The report of the 12 January 1894 commends the sisters for

> the improvement in the appearance and demeanour of the children since the school was placed in their charge … The tone of the school is bright, and in addition to the ordinary course, instruction is successfully given in kindergarten with musical drill … A very manifest improvement has been effected in reading … general proficiency is very good.[17]

The report of 1895 also commended the school: 'reading good, writing careful, spelling fair.'

Reports of inspectors of the Local Government Board in the 1890s were also very favourable. It is clear that the sisters introduced higher standards of cleanliness, and the cared-for appearance and good health of the children was a matter of comment in the reports of the inspectors. Although the Board had been reluctant to sanction the appointment of the Daughters of Charity to run the Auxiliary, it was quick to acknowledge the improvements that had taken place even within one year. It is worth noting, however, that they gave the credit to the guardians rather than to the sisters:

> There is a marked improvement in the Cabra Auxiliary. The children look better and healthier … The whole institution has evidently

---

[15] *The Freeman's Journal*, 3 April 1895.
[16] Report of the Local Government Board of Inspectors, PA:DC/Dunardagh/Cabra.
[17] Ibid.

benefited considerably by the increased attention given to it by the guardians, who now visit it regularly.[18]

Since the Cabra Auxiliary was situated on twenty acres of land, the boys in residence had opportunities to learn the skills of farming. This was useful, as they could be employed as farm labourers later. It appears there were no other forms of training for the boys at that time. However, in 1910, tailoring and boot-making were transferred from the main workhouse to the Cabra Auxiliary and this provided a good opportunity for training.[19] Training opportunities suitable for the girls was an easier matter, as they involved areas in which the sisters were proficient, including sewing and knitting, laundry, arts and crafts, general housekeeping and poultry.

There were a number of sick children in the Cabra Auxiliary from the beginning, although in the early years most of the sick children were kept in the parent house at North Brunswick Street. In 1907, a special committee was set up to look into overcrowding in the workhouse hospital. The committee suggested 'that accommodation be provided at the Cabra Auxiliary for twenty of the grown sick children in the workhouse'.[20] The sisters agreed to take these children but this did not solve the problem at the workhouse. The minutes of the meeting of the guardians, 25 January 1910, indicate that there were still 140 children at North Dublin Union and 95 of them were sick. Of these '21 were classed as insane epileptics and 4 as lunatics'.[21] In 1911 all these children were transferred to Cabra. When the North and South Dublin Unions amalgamated in 1918, the children from the South Dublin Union Auxiliary, Pelletstown, Dublin, were also transferred to Cabra.[22] Requests were made to the commissioners of the newly created Dublin Union in 1924, 'to provide special accommodation for the handicapped children who were then residing in asylums and workhouses'.[23] This led to a further increase in the numbers in the Cabra Auxiliary.

St Vincent's

When the Free State government set about reorganising the Poor Law system in 1925, one of the first things it did was to abolish the workhouse as an institution. An order was issued to the sister servant, Sister Teresa McKenna at

---

[18] Report of the Local Government Board of Inspectors, PA:DC/Dunardagh/Cabra.

[19] North Dublin Union, Copy of Committee Proceedings, 1911 (Dublin), p. 22.

[20] Report of the Special Commission of the Board of Guardians (Dublin, 1907), p. 2.

[21] North Dublin Union, Copy of Committee Proceedings, 1910, p. 15.

[22] J. Robins, *From rejection to integration: a centenary of service of Daughters of Charity to persons with a mental handicap*, p. 32.

[23] National Archives, Department of Health file, National Archives of Ireland, A131/147, p. 57.

the Cabra Auxiliary on 28 November 1925, informing her of the termination of employment of the fifteen sisters, the chaplain and the seven lay people.[24] The children were to be boarded out. This could not be achieved in full due to the numbers of children with disabilities. In January 1926 'the normal children were withdrawn for boarding out, but a few physically and mentally defectives were left under the care of the sisters'.[25]

It appears that the termination of employment was never put into effect. When the Cabra Auxiliary, as a Poor Law institution, came to an end, negotiations between the Daughters of Charity and the Irish government about providing accommodation for children with intellectual disabilities began. The first move was made by Archbishop Edward Byrne of Dublin who was concerned that Catholic children were being cared for by the Protestant Stewart's Hospital. He asked the Daughters of Charity in Cabra Auxiliary to care exclusively for children with intellectual disabilities. At the same time the Irish government began its negotiations with the sisters. Father John O'Connell, director of the Daughters of Charity, led the negotiations on behalf of the sisters. In response to a letter from Dr O'Dwyer, Commissioner, requesting that the sisters lease the Cabra Auxiliary for the purposes of starting a home 'for mentally defective children and imbeciles',[26] Fr O'Connell wrote, 'We shall be glad to take on the new work of caring for the mentally deficient children in Cabra.'[27]

When the need for a Poor Law school ceased, the sisters made the necessary changes and turned what was a school for 'workhouse children' into a special care centre for children with intellectual disabilities, and they called it St Vincent's. They agreed to take 'all mentally deficient children or imbecile children who shall be sent to them by the commissioners'.[28] As St Vincent's was the only Catholic home for children with intellectual disabilities in Ireland at the time, children from workhouses all over the country were transferred there. By the end of 1926, there were 118 children with intellectual disabilities in St Vincent's, 73 girls and 45 boys.[29] Approximately 80 per cent of them were supported by health boards, the rest were private cases. Those referred by health boards were paid for at county level. The sum agreed between the commissioners and the Daughters of Charity was '12/6 d. per week per head'.[30]

---

24 Condon, Clerk of the Union to Sr Teresa McKenna, 28 November 1925, PA:DC/Dunardagh/Cabra.
25 Returns from St Vincent's, 1926, PA:DC/Dunardagh/Cabra.
26 O'Dwyer to Daughters of Charity, 18 August 1925, PA:DC/Dunardagh/Cabra.
27 O'Connell to O'Dwyer, 25 August 1925, PA:DC/Dunardagh/Cabra.
28 Copy of Agreement, 22 May 1930, between Commissioners of the Dublin Union and the Daughters of Charity, PA:DC/Dunardagh/Cabra.
29 North Dublin Union, copy of Committee Proceedings (Dublin, 1927) p. 90.
30 O'Connell to Dwyer, 25 August 1925, PA:DC/Dunardagh/Cabra.

When the Cabra Auxiliary ceased to be a Poor Law school in 1925 and became St Vincent's Centre for the care of children with intellectual disabilities, it lost its recognition as a school. However, having been a school, it maintained an orientation towards education. Some of the sisters who had been teachers in the Poor Law school stayed on to care for the children with intellectual disabilities. The fifth annual report of the Department of Local Government, reporting on St Vincent's, stressed that it was not merely a custodial centre 'but in a real sense a school, a place where instruction suitable to the capacity of the child is imparted, and occupation and recreation organised to help in its training and education'.[31] However, the Department of Education was unwilling to recognise it as a school. Dissatisfied with this, the sisters decided to use pressure to achieve school status. In a letter to the sister servant, Sister Brady, Fr John O'Connell says that the sisters should impress upon the Department that they 'propose to provide, as far as possible, suitable trades – boot-making, tailoring, gardening for the boys; for the girls – basket-making – the sisters will know – but that this will take capital expenditure.'[32] Much of the emphasis on training is a carry-over from the days of the Poor Law school. The trades of boot-making and tailoring continued to be taught because the equipment was still there; and since the children had to be dressed, it was all the better if clothes and shoes could be made on the premises.

St Vincent's was recognised as a school by the Northern Ireland Department of Education in 1940, but not by the Department of Education in Dublin. Sister Louise Burke became principal in 1944. She made a very determined effort to fit the school into the structures of the national school system in the hope of making it more acceptable to the Department of Education in Dublin. Trained teachers were appointed to the staff, and boys and girls were integrated in classes. In 1946 a formal application for recognition was made by the sisters to the Department of Education, asking for a pupil–teacher ratio of 20:1. In 1947, recognition was granted, but the special consideration for a 20:1 pupil–teacher ratio was rejected. It was to be on the same basis as that pertaining in the mainstream national school system. According to this, the numbers on roll in St Vincent's only warranted four teachers, but the sisters had nine teachers employed there. The nine teachers were retained, and the community of the Daughters of Charity paid the salaries of five of them from their own funds. This was a very heavy financial burden on St Vincent's but it would have been too difficult for the teachers, both physically and emotionally, to have taken any more than twenty of these children in a class. Having smaller

---

[31] Fifth Annual Report of the Department of Health and Local Government (Dublin, 1930), p. 94.
[32] O'Connell to Sr Brady, 1930, PA:DC/Dunardagh/Cabra.

classes made it possible to develop a curriculum that was suited to the needs of the children.[33]

Curriculum development

The fact that the Daughters of Charity in Ireland and Great Britain formed one province at the time and that there was frequent exchange of sisters throughout the province, greatly influenced the development of services for people with intellectual disabilities in Ireland. In 1924, the Daughters of Charity had opened a centre for children with intellectual disabilities in Rosewell, Scotland. Some sisters from Rosewell came to work in St Vincent's. As services for people with intellectual disabilities were developing well in Scotland, the sisters who came brought new ideas. Moreover, sisters from Ireland were sent to do courses in England and Scotland.

Sister Louise Burke, first principal of St Vincent's, and Sister Gertrude O'Callaghan, who succeeded her, had both studied in Great Britain – Sister Louise at Jordan Hill Training College, Glasgow, and Sister Gertrude at Queen Anne Street, London. These two sisters had considerable input into the type of curriculum that developed at St Vincent's and later in other similar schools run by the Daughters of Charity. The curriculum that was developed in St Vincent's, though influenced by what was happening in Great Britain, was distinct from it, concentrating on the needs of the particular group of children in St Vincent's. The Scottish system tended to have an academic bias, since the schools for children with intellectual disabilities were run in close conjunction with the mainstream primary schools. The English system had less emphasis on the academic, though language skills were considered very important. In the English system, training in crafts and manual skills was emphasised and project work was seen as an effective means of getting the children involved in their own learning.

In constructing the curriculum in St Vincent's, a selection was made of the best elements of the two systems, and these were adapted to what was suitable for the Irish setting. Religion, language, nature study and storytelling became core subjects; crafts were central to the curriculum and included rug-making, knitting, embroidery, flower-arranging, weaving and stool-making. Great attention was given to physical development and motor coordination, with particular emphasis on eurhythmics and various forms of dance. In the evenings and at weekends the girls helped with household activities, while the boys helped on the farm. All spent some of their leisure time continuing the crafts begun in the classroom. St Vincent's also had its choir and percussion

---

[33] Interview with Sr Louise Burke DC, St Teresa's, Blackrock, 15 April 1985.

band. Specialist teachers were employed for music and physical education, and paid for from the private funds of the Daughters of Charity. St Vincent's became famous for its annual concerts, to which members of the departments of Health and Education were regularly invited. On such occasions, St Vincent's produced a fine display of craft too.[34]

St Michael's, Glenmaroon, expanding the service

Overcrowding became a serious problem in St Vincent's in the late 1940s. Despite the fact that the St John of God Brothers had opened a home for boys with intellectual disabilities in Stillorgan, Co. Dublin in 1930, and that the Daughters of Charity had opened a home for women with intellectual disabilities in Clonsilla, Co. Dublin in 1944, there were still over 500 residents in St Vincent's. It became impossible for St Vincent's to accept all the applications received. When the sisters decided not to take any more boys, the commissioners complained that they were breaking the terms of the 1930 agreement which obliged them 'to take all mentally handicapped children referred to them by the Commissioners'.[35] Fr Joseph Sheedy, Director, in turn pointed out that the commission had already broken the agreement by failing to remove boys from St Vincent's 'when they reached 16 years of age'.[36]

The overcrowding in Cabra was eased somewhat in 1950 when the Department of Health offered the sisters the house of Sir Ernest Guinness at Glenmaroon, Co. Dublin, on condition that they open a home to care for 200 children with intellectual disabilities. The sisters accepted this offer. By degrees the girls, who had mild intellectual disabilities were transferred from Cabra to the house at Glenmaroon, which became known as Holy Angels. In 1956, a special purpose-built school, St Michael's, was opened there with an enrolment of 175 pupils.

The sisters and staff in St Michael's were visionary in curriculum development. Since this school was not obliged to follow a set programme laid down by the Department of Education, it became possible to develop a curriculum suitable to the needs of the students. It concentrated on simulating life situations in the classroom and on giving the pupils social competencies. There was an awareness that pupils would be embarrassed in later life if they were unable to read simple instructions or make necessary calculations in the working or social areas of life. Basic skills were taught through life-simulated situations. This helped to overcome some of the pupil resistance to learning.

---

[34] Interview with Sr Louise Burke DC, St Teresa's, Blackrock, 15 April 1985.
[35] Mrs McKean to Fr Sheedy, 29 January 1947, PA:DC/Dunardagh/Cabra.
[36] Fr Sheedy to Mrs McKean, 31 January 1947, PA:DC/Dunardagh/Cabra.

The curriculum was broad and was kept concrete and experiential, and project work was widely used. There was also great emphasis on dance, music, choral speaking, swimming and art. The pupils of St Michael's were able to take their place in open competition in these areas and achieved a great deal of success. This helped in building self-confidence and fostered the growth of other personal qualities, such as concentration, interest, observation, and persistence. Games, music, dance and crafts provided valuable opportunities for fun and enjoyment and for social training.

Because it was a residential school, the pupils in St Michael's had further opportunity in the evenings of being involved in practical activities. Each unit had its own kitchenette and the children helped in the preparation and serving of meals. Pupils were encouraged to make their own beds and be responsible for their personal belongings. This training was important in preparing the girls for the world of work, not only in developing skills, but also in the cultivation of good habits and a right attitude to work. In their final years in St Michael's there was strong emphasis on pre-vocational training. Pupils were given simulated and real opportunities for interviews and were taken on visits to different work places. They were also given simulated practical experience in handling unemployment, insurance, trade union membership, personal budgeting and banking.

The authorities and staff in St Michael's were very aware of the need to work in conjunction with parents. It was important for teachers to be aware of the parents' expectations and to help them to understand the problems the child with intellectual disabilities is likely to face, so that they were realistic in their ambitions. The fact that the school population came from all over the country made liaising with parents difficult, and often involved a lot of travelling. However, the collaboration between parents and teachers became established practice within the Daughters of Charity services for people with intellectual disabilities. This has been one of their great strengths and has made developments within the service in general possible.[37]

Education for children with moderate intellectual disabilities
The opening of St Michael's as a school for children with mild intellectual disabilities, 1955, meant that St Vincent's lost its status as a school, as it was again caring for people with moderate and severe intellectual disabilities, and at that time the Department of Education did not consider it a duty to provide education for these children. The Daughters of Charity entered into negotiations with the Department of Education to have school status restored.

---

[37] Interview with Sr Gertrude O'Callaghan DC, St Michael's, Glenmaroon, 23 April 1985.

In June 1962, a letter from Seán Ó Conchobhair, Secretary of the Department of Education, to Sister Rosalie Hurl, sister servant of St Vincent's, expressed regret that the Department could not 'recognise as national schools, institutes whose purpose is to provide training facilities for children who are for the most part in the moderately subnormal category'.[38] Around the same time Dr Patrick Hillery, minister for education, made the same point, but qualified the Department's position by saying that it was waiting on the findings of the Commission on Mental Handicap. This attitude of the Minister and his department is hard to understand in view of the fact that eight years earlier an expert committee of the World Health Organisation had stated:

> Unless a child is so severely abnormal as to be completely incapable, his education should be the responsibility of the public education authority, even though the child is in fact in a hospital or medical institution.[39]

For whatever reason, the Department of Education did not wait for the report of the Commission on Intellectual Disabilities before making its decision regarding St Vincent's. This report was not published until 1965, but in July 1963 the Department announced its intention to recognise St Vincent's as a school for children with moderate intellectual disabilities.[40]

Commission on Mental Handicap 1965
The report of the commission on Mental Handicap, 1965, emphasised the need for special educational facilities for children with intellectual disabilities.[41] It acknowledged that it was difficult for these children to develop mentally or socially in the mainstream classroom. It made the point that because of difficulty in concept formation, and because of limited vocabulary, defective speech, weak memory and lack of concentration, it was virtually impossible for them to make progress in ordinary conditions. It pointed out that this inability to develop led to frustration and unacceptable behaviour patterns. It claimed that even at play the child with intellectual disabilities was disadvantaged because of slowness in understanding and poor motor coordination and that failure to learn and to win acceptance in the school community could destroy self-confidence and lead to aggression or withdrawal.

The report contended that it was considered possible, through special education programmes, to help the pupil with intellectual disabilities to achieve security and happiness in life. In order to do this, the programmes would have

---

[38] Seán Ó Conchubhair to Sr Rosalie Hurl, 30 June 1962, PA:DC/Dunardagh/Cabra.
[39] WHO, Technical Report Series, no. 75, *The Mentally Subnormal Child* (Geneva, 1954), p. 21.
[40] Department of Education to Sr Rosalie Hurl, 24 July 1963, PA:DC/Dunardagh/Cabra.
[41] Commission of Enquiry on Mental Handicap, Report (Dublin, 1965).

to be directed towards personal development in the widest sense, and avoid
the exclusive pursuit of narrow educational or vocational objectives. The
fundamental objectives of such a programme would include: (1) The systematic
development of behaviour patterns which are socially acceptable during and
after school life; (2) Training in sensory perception and discrimination; (3)
Physical development including muscular coordination; (4) Language
development and speech training.[42] Most of the ideas put forward in this report
had already been incorporated into the curriculum developed in St Michael's
and St Vincent's.

There were two other developments in the Daughters of Charity education
services for people with intellectual disabilities in the 1950s. In 1951,
Woodstown House, Lisnagry, Co. Limerick was purchased by the Daughters
of Charity and opened as a home for girls with intellectual disabilities. This
centre developed as a service for people with severe and moderate intellectual
disabilities and was recognised as a school in 1964. In 1959, another school
for children with mild intellectual disabilities was opened in St Teresa's,
Blackrock, Co. Dublin. It was to be both residential and day, and it developed
along the lines of St Michael's, Glenmaroon. These schools played an important part in the development of special education in Ireland.

A training course for teachers of children with intellectual disabilities [43]
Although some of the sisters involved in special education in Ireland went to
do courses in England and Scotland, it was not possible to send every teacher.
The sisters who had been most involved in developing the schools for children
with special needs were, therefore, very conscious of the need for special
training facilities for teachers of children with intellectual disabilities in Ireland.
The Department of Education officers were also aware that teachers dealing
with children with intellectual disabilities were finding regular teacher training
inadequate.

In the late 1950s, an t-Uasal Tomás Ó Cuilleanáin, inspector of special
schools, approached Sister Gertrude O'Callaghan, principal of St Michael's,
Glenmaroon, with the request that a teacher from a school in Blanchardstown,
Co. Dublin, be allowed to sit in on some classes in St Michael's. This request
was granted. Subsequent to this, a week's course was held in St Michael's for
teachers of children with intellectual disabilities. It was a combined effort
between St Michael's and St Augustine's, Stillorgan, the school run by the St
John of God Brothers.

---

[42] Commission of Enquiry on Mental Handicap, Report (Dublin, 1965), p. 86.
[43] Interviews with Sr Gertrude O'Callaghan, Sr Louise Burke, and Dr Donal Cregan CM,
January–April, 1985.

Negotiations had already begun between Sister Louise Burke and Tomás Ó Cuilleanáin on the feasibility of setting up a special course for teachers of children with intellectual disabilities. In February 1960, Tomás Ó Cuilleanáin wrote a report for the Department of Education, outlining the need for such specialist training in Ireland. Around the same time, Sister Louise Burke approached Dr Donal Cregan CM, president of St Patrick's Training College, Drumcondra, to discuss the possibility of setting up this new course under the auspices of the college. She then approached an t-Uasal Seán Ó Conchubhair, secretary of the Department of Education, to gain the Department's approval. This was granted and the course started in 1961 in rooms belonging to the Dominican Order, in Little Denmark Street, Dublin. Sister Louise Burke became the first director of the course.

To be eligible to do this course, one had to be a fully recognised teacher with some experience in teaching children with intellectual disabilities. There were fifteen on the first course. Starting as a one-year course in Little Denmark Street, it later moved to premises within St Patrick's Training College and developed into a two-year programme. The special training given to teachers on this course was to have a major impact on the quality of education offered in special schools in the decades which followed. The Daughters of Charity were major contributors, especially in the early years. Sister Louise Burke and Sister Gertrude O'Callaghan lectured to the students, visited the schools involved, assessed and evaluated the teaching, and made their own schools available as models for developing schools.

Conclusion

The developments in education for persons with special needs discussed in this chapter had taken place by the 1960s. Not only did the sisters have a vision of what was needed, but they also had the courage to negotiate with the relevant personnel in the Department of Education and in St Patrick's Training College in order to translate their vision into action. The sound judgement of the sisters has been confirmed by Department of Education legislation in recent times. Referring specifically to students with special needs, the White Paper on Education *Charting our Education Future* (1995) stated: 'All students, regardless of their personal circumstances, have a right of access to and participation in the education system, according to their potential and ability.'[44] The Education for Persons with Disabilities Bill (2002) recommended the provision for further education 'to assist people with disabilities to leave school with the skills necessary to participate in society ... and to live independent and full lives ...

---

[44] An Roinn Oideachais, *Charting our Education Future* (Dublin, 1995), p. 24.

in consultation with the parents'.[45] With regard to teacher training, *Charting our Education Future* notes among the principal needs of teachers, the skill 'to develop to their fullest potential those students with special needs'.[46] The role of parents and the community in general in the education of children is also highlighted:

> A central feature of the reform of the education system is the em-powerment of boards of management and parents to take greater responsibility for the quality of educational provision in the school and for the promotion of closer co-operation between the school and the wider community.[47]

This current legislation is stipulating the approach the Daughters of Charity were taking in education as far back as the 1960s, showing how progressive they were fifty years ago in their approach to education for persons with special needs. They envisioned a better quality of life for the people in their care, and with the help of the children's parents and friends, they and their colleagues worked unceasingly to open the door to education for children with intellectual disabilities.

---

[45] Education for Persons with Disabilities Bill, 2002, as Passed by Seanad Éireann <http://www.oireachtas.ie/viewdoc.asp?fn=/documents/bills28/bills/2002/1702/b17b02s.pdf> accessed 7 January 2013.
[46] *Charting our Education Future*, p. 127.
[47] Ibid., p. 140.

Chapter Ten

Our Lady's, Henrietta Street, Dublin:
Accommodation for Discharged Female Prisoners

Bríd O'Neill DC, Eileen Devlin DC, Jacinta Prunty CHF

Work with prisoners was among the earliest of the charitable ministries undertaken by the Daughters of Charity. Vincent de Paul, co-founder of the Company with Louise de Marillac, was involved first-hand in work with prisoners, held in the foulest of conditions in Paris and Marseilles. Vincent's care for the galley slaves was recognised in his appointment in 1619 as chaplain general of the galleys.[1] The Daughters of Charity began to work with these men in the prisons and on the ships in 1640.[2]

It was for the care of female prisoners discharged from Mountjoy Prison that the Daughters of Charity were brought to 10 Henrietta Street in 1899. While the role of prisoners' aid societies to reduce reoffending was long recognised, Ireland lagged well behind Britain in this work. Under the General Prisons (Ireland) Act 1877, the chief secretary of Ireland had the power to certify prisoners' aid societies. A sum not exceeding £2 per prisoner could be paid to such societies by the governor of the prison. The society undertook to apply the sum for the benefit of the discharged prisoner. Alternatively, this modest grant could be paid directly to the prisoner on their discharge.[3] Irish charities were slow to benefit from the funding available under this Act, as noted in the report of the General Prisons Board for 1879–80. Only the Belfast Prison Gate Mission had been certified by then, despite the high level of recommitments to Irish prisons.[4] It was in response to public calls for the

---

[1] P. Coste CM, *Saint Vincent de Paul: Correspondence, Conferences, Documents,* vol. 1, ed. and tr. Marie Poole DC (New York: New City Press), p. 118.

[2] P. Coste CM, *Life and Labours of St Vincent de Paul* (New York: New City Press, 1987), pp. 319–24.

[3] Prisons Act (Ireland), United Kingdom Acts of Parliament of 1877, 40 & 41 Vic., c. 49, sec. 44.

[4] The Harcourt Road asylum, founded 1821 by two Protestant ladies, members of the Society of Friends, and by Dr Orpen, accommodated four or five female Protestant ex-prisoners by 1880 and did not apply for certification. The Prison Gate Mission was not eligible for certification as it 'is not confined in its constitution or objects to Protestants'. James G. Alcorn, 'Discharged Prisoners' Aid Societies', *Irish Quarterly Review* (December 1881), vol. 8, pp. 217–23. By certifying societies on a strictly sectarian basis, the legislators aimed to limit the practice of prozelytism among charities.

establishment of prisoners' aid societies that the Dublin Discharged Female Roman Catholic Prisoners' Aid Society was founded in April 1881 by a lay committee.

In the promotion of aid societies for discharged women prisoners, the 'moral and personal influence' of committee members and managers was emphasised. In the 'great scheme' of reforming women prisoners, it was necessary to import 'the most zealous and active in the cause and these we will find to be persons in religious communities, or animated by strong religious feelings'.[5] While the earliest reports of the Discharged Female Roman Catholic Prisoners' Aid Society have not survived, it can be deduced from correspondence with the superiors of the Daughters of Charity that the Society had every intention, from the outset, of working in partnership with a religious community. By 1895, the Society had its own fine premises, at 10 Henrietta Street which it titled 'Our Lady's Home'.[6] At the Society's earnest request, Sister Felicité Hurley and two companions arrived on 6 April 1899 to take charge of the day-to-day management of this institution 'and to carry on the work of the Discharged Female Roman Catholic Prisoners Aid Society'.[7]

The geographical location of 10 Henrietta Street – close to but not on the doorstep of Mountjoy Prison – made it an ideal location for 'rescue and reform' work. Mountjoy Prison was opened on 27 March 1850, for male prisoners; in September 1858 a female prison distinct and separate in its management from the male prison was added to the Mountjoy complex. The first women prisoners were transferred from Cork on 20 September 1858; the women from Grangegorman and Newgate in Dublin soon followed.[8] By the 1880s most female prisoners from all over Ireland were confined in Mountjoy.[9]

In the 1730s, 10 Henrietta Street was built as the family home of the Gardiners. Henrietta Street, one of the earliest and most ambitious development projects of the Georgian period, was itself the creation of Luke Gardiner. The span of the street's social history is fascinating. Designed and developed as a prime aristocratic area, adjacent to the central north side axis

---

[5] J. G. Alcorn, 'Discharged Prisoners' Aid Societies', p. 220.

[6] Contracts of sale relating to 10 Henrietta Street are dated 4 May 1895 and 17 June 1895; a conveyance dated 2 August 1895 transfers ownership to Eliza Browne, Baroness O'Hagan, and the Hon. Francis O'Hagan. The premises consisted of 10 Henrietta Street and the plot of ground at the rear fronting on Dominick Street. A further conveyance is dated 22 April 1898, where the property is in the names of Eliza Browne, the Rt Honourable Gasten, Thomas William Monsell Baron Emly, John Mulhall and Valentine Grace. The premises no. 10 never actually belonged to the Prisoners' Aid Society. Provincial Archives, Daughters of Charity, Dunardagh (here abbreviated as PA:DC/Dunardagh/Henrietta Street).

[7] PA:DC/Dunardagh/Henrietta Street.

[8] T. Carey, *Mountjoy: The Story of a Prison* (Cork, 2000), pp. 80–5.

[9] Ibid.

of Capel Street, Henrietta Street was an enclave of the oldest and grandest houses in the city. The street was host to many famous figures of wealth, privilege and power, including bishops and leading politicians and was one of the most exclusive and sought-after residential addresses in the city.

However, its period of pre-eminence and grandeur was to be relatively short lived. The street's decline commenced with the Act of Union in 1801 and some of its illustrious residents moved to other prestigious areas of the city, including Merrion Square. By the 1850s a slow but inexorable decline had set in; the conversion of palatial houses to offices was quickly overtaken by the spread of tenements, marked by a concentration of acute poverty and social margin-alisation. It was the declining social status of the street that allowed such a fine property to be purchased by the trustees of a lay charity and that later enabled adjoining properties to be bought.

Prisoners' Aid Societies, under the General Prisons (Ireland) Act 1877, were formed 'for the purpose of finding employment for discharged prisoners, and enabling them, by loans and grants of money, to live by honest labour'. In practice, each society was to aid prisoners after their discharge by providing suitable lodgings, furnishing temporary maintenance and subsequently exercising a 'friendly supervision' over them, or as one promoter summarised it, 'getting them swallowed up in the tide of life'.[10] It was expected that the small gratuities per person from the General Prison Board would be supplemented by charitable subscriptions and bequests. The local authorities (the municipal corporations and grand juries) could also contribute a sum per person from local taxation (the rates), as they did already to support children in reformatories and industrial schools.

The contract drawn up between the committee of the Discharged Female Roman Catholic Prisoners' Aid Society (a certified society under the 1877 Act), and the Superioress General of the Daughters of Charity of St Vincent de Paul in Paris, dated 15 March 1899, reflects the statutory constraints under which this Dublin charity operated as well as the standard conditions the sisters attached to any new undertaking. The sisters were also subject to the Society's own founding rules (reprinted as a preamble to each annual report), which allowed it to appoint 'a matron and other officers and agents to act under their direction, in administering the aid and exercising the supervision contemplated by the Society' (rule v). In addition, the sisters could be withdrawn from Henrietta Street 'at any time or for any reason' by request of the archbishop of Dublin, William Walsh, or of their own superioress general, each party giving the other at least three months' notice.[11] In agreeing to be bound so closely to

---

[10] P. G. Alcorn, 'Discharged Prisoners' Aid Societies', p. 222.

[11] Original agreement between Committee of Our Lady's Home and Superioress General of the Daughters of Charity relating to conditions in which the sisters take care of Our Lady's Home, Paris, 15 March 1899, PA:DC/Dunardagh/Henrietta Street.

the work of this Prisoners' Aid Society, which was itself closely tied to the Catholic archdiocese of Dublin (with the archbishop named as one of its trustees), the Daughters of Charity appointed to Henrietta Street were constrained in what they could initiate and had to justify what might be viewed as the slightest deviation from the written regulations, or from what the archbishop of Dublin might approve. However, the work was incontrovertibly one very close to the founding spirit of the community and one for which the sisters were, as it was to prove, eminently well equipped.

In carrying out the core object of the Society, 'to aid Roman Catholic prisoners after their discharge from prison, and to enable them by employment, grants and loans, to live by honest labour' (rule ii) certain women committee members, individually approved as visitors by the prison authorities, first made contact with the female prisoners before their discharge, and were 'thus able to prevent their drifting away, and returning to former associates and surroundings'.[12] The contract under which the Daughters of Charity took charge of 10 Henrietta Street specified that the ladies of the committee visited the prison three times weekly and at their weekly meetings decided on the girls whom they considered suitable for admission to the home. The sisters also visited the prison each Wednesday.[13] On the day of their discharge each prisoner was met by a representative of the home and offered help, beginning with breakfast. 'Those who desire to be employed are given daily work. Any who desire to enter penitentiaries are secured admission, and those anxious to become dealers are given the necessary goods.'[14] Changes at short notice to the schedule of court appearances or the internal bureaucracy of the prison system could result in fruitless visits and endless waiting by the prison visitor. The prison authorities, on the whole, cooperated with the Society, as indeed they were obliged to under statute.[15] Particular care was extended to discharged prisoners on their way to the country who, though provided by the prison board with their railway tickets, were 'in danger of being led astray by evil companions or designing persons between their discharge and the departure of trains.' The hospitality of 10 Henrietta Street was extended to such women until they were accompanied to the train and seen off safely.[16]

The work of this Prisoners' Aid Society was financed from the small gratuities allowed on a prisoner's discharge, the subscriptions of members of

---

[12] Annual report of the Dublin Catholic Discharged Female Prisoners' Aid Society (henceforward DCDFPAS), 26th report of 10 Henrietta Street and 2nd report of 7 Synnott Place, 1 May 1906 to 1 May 1907 (Dublin, 1907), pp. 7–8.

[13] PA:DC/Dunardagh/Henrietta Street.

[14] Annual report of the Dublin Roman Catholic Discharged Female Prisoners' Aid Society (henceforward DRCDFPAS), 31st report (Dublin, 1912), p. 7.

[15] Sr Felicité to Miss Rafferty, 14 January 1914, PA:DC/Dunardagh/Henrietta Street.

[16] DRCDFPAS, 28th report for 1918 (Dublin, 1919), p. 6.

the Society ('[The Society] shall consist of all annual subscribers of five shillings and upwards,' rule i), other donations and bequests actively solicited by the members of the Society, small-scale fundraising events such as bridge tournaments and raffles, and whatever small sums towards their support might be raised from the work of the women assisted by the Society, both residents and externs. Under rule v, the committee was empowered to pay 'such salaries as they may think proper' to a 'matron, officers and agents' to pay rent for 'any house or premises hired for the use of said Society' and to pay for 'the necessary repairs and furniture for same and other incidental expenses'. Under this rule and out of a very modest, uncertain income flow, the Society contracted itself in 1895 to provide the Daughters of Charity with suitable accommodation, furniture and household linen. They were to have a private oratory in the house and were also able to attend the Dominican church in nearby Dominick Street. The running expenses of the home, as well as light and fuel, were paid by the committee along with £30 a year for each sister.[17] Public thanks were extended to the sisters at every annual general meeting, 'as they manage to combine the greatest amount of comfort for the inmates with the minimum of expense'.[18]

The rules of the Society made clear that direction or control of all aspects of the work ultimately rested with the committee even when (after 1899) the Society entrusted the day-to-day management of its home to a religious community. While after 1899 the matron was allowed to admit applicants pending the committee's decision, and discharge inmates 'for reasons she may consider sufficient', she was directly responsible to the committee for seeing that its rules and regulations were 'strictly carried out' (regulation 3). Financial accounts and the names of all admitted and discharged were regularly submitted to committee meetings; in her journal, the matron would also bring to the committee, 'a statement of any matter she may consider material in connection with the working of the Institution' (regulation 3). Committee members were entitled to visit the home at any time and to enter into a book kept for that purpose, any observations they wished to make; they could bring this to the next committee meeting (regulation 2). There was, therefore, a very open and effective relationship between the lay society, the Daughters of Charity and the circle of benefactors and supporters, all working towards the same end: 'the work of rescue and reformation' of women who had spent time in prison, giving them the chance 'of regaining their self-respect and becoming useful members of society'.[19] In short, 10 Henrietta Street held out the hope for a fresh start in life.

---

[17] Original agreement, 15 March 1899, PA:DC/Dunardagh/Henrietta Street.
[18] DCDFPAS, 26th report (Henrietta St), 2nd report (Synnott Place) for 1906/07 (Dublin, 1907), p. 5.
[19] Ibid.

The 'ongoing friendly supervision' of discharged prisoners that was expected of prisoners' aid societies under the 1877 Act was undertaken with particular care by the Daughters of Charity as they grappled with the perennial problem of finding gainful employment and safe accommodation for them. Our Lady's Home could be a temporary stop over only, assisting in the transition back to the 'real' world. For the first years of the charity, the girls were placed on probation in the house by the prison authorities for eighteen months, after which some at least emigrated (26th report, p. 5). On the advent of the sisters in 1899, the Society rejoiced that emigration was no longer necessary; but rather the girls were 'placed in situations both in Ireland and England, and remained in touch and under the influence of the Home' (26th report p. 5). Occasionally these situations were further afield, as reports from France and Cape Town, South Africa testify.[20] Small numbers had a welcoming family to receive them. A few, usually older women, chose to enter the 'old-established refuges' or Magdalen asylums, but most entered the workforce, or at least tried to earn their own living in an over-supplied labour market.[21] While keeping 'in sympathetic touch' with all the girls sent to 'situations', the sisters repeatedly provided short-stay accommodation for former residents temporarily unemployed.[22] Selections from the many letters received from former inmates demonstrating their 'kindly and grateful feelings' were appended each year to the published reports.[23] One small indication of positive experiences may be gleaned from a reference to the fact that former inmates who obtained situations 'generally come to the Home to have their aprons and print dresses made, and give many orders for such work'.[24]

From its foundation, the Society had to balance its primary obligation to discharged prisoners with the great need to assist young women 'in imminent peril of being led into crime, but who have not actually become criminals'.[25] While saving girls from the ignominy of prison was undoubtedly a charitable work that the members of this society were ideally placed to advance, it had to be presented as an adjunct to the core work 'which in no way, pecuniary or otherwise, interferes with the proper care and attention which the Committee gives to discharged prisoners, or the proper application of the funds of the Society'.[26] The care of young women 'exposed to danger' was recognised as an area of urgent need by the Daughters of Charity on taking over the

---

[20] DRCDFPAS, 33rd report for 1913 (Dublin, 1914), pp. 9–10.
[21] DCDFPAS, 26th report (Henrietta Street), 2nd report (Synnott Place), 1906/07 (Dublin, 1907), p. 7.
[22] DCDFPAS, 29th report for 1909 (Dublin, 1910), p. 7.
[23] DCDFPAS, 26th report (Henrietta St), 2nd report (Synnott Place) for 1906/07 (Dublin, 1907), pp. 8–9.
[24] DRCDFPAS, 33rd report for 1913 (Dublin, 1914), p. 8.
[25] DCDFPAS, 29th report for 1909 (Dublin, 1910), p. 7.
[26] Ibid.

management of Henrietta Street, but one where they needed to tread carefully. An application by Sister Felicité to Archbishop William Walsh to open a night school in the basement of 10 Henrietta Street was refused in January 1904.[27] Permission for 'a class' was grudgingly allowed a few weeks later 'pending the procurement of more suitable place, apart from the inmates of the Home'.[28] A night school for factory girls was soon underway; within a year the average nightly attendance was one hundred.[29] Alongside religious instruction the girls were taught laundry work, cooking, sewing, 'and all housewifery, which helps to their future comfort and well-being'.[30] Subsequent reports make brief, generalised reference to the provision of 'useful employment and training' at Henrietta Street to large numbers of young women.[31] By 1910 this 'second task, the provision of employment for women and girls who are exposed to temptation and in sore need of food, clothing and protection' was advertised in a more public way.[32] However, its nature as 'a separate work which the Committee undertook voluntarily in addition to their already serious responsibilities' was always spelled out.[33]

The unwillingness of the Archbishop to permit the expansion of the sisters' sphere of operations was, in part at least, tied to his anxiety to ensure that priority was given to female prisoners. Most former prisoners were reluctant to submit 'to what they regard as the rigid discipline of a convent' thus every effort had to be made to protect the essentially lay character of the home.[34] A request to extend the number of sisters from three to four in May 1907 was sanctioned 'only on the distinct understanding that the number of sisters is not to be further increased' lest it dissuade the very girls 'for whose special benefit the Home was established' and for whom, in advance of the sisters' arrival, it had been 'so long and so successfully worked'. While recognising that the general efficiency of the home under the stewardship of the sisters had been 'admirably maintained', his observation that several recent admissions had been outside that class of women 'for which it was primarily intended, and from which it takes its name' further underscored his anxiety that the sisters concentrate their attentions on the discharged prisoners.[35]

---

[27] Denis Pettit, Archbishop's House, to Sr Felicité, 22 January 1904, PA:DC/Dunardagh/Henrietta Street.

[28] Denis Pettit, Archbishop's House, to Miss Matthews, 20 February 1904, PA:DC/Dunardagh/Henrietta Street.

[29] DCDFPAS, 26th report (Henrietta Street), 2nd report (Synnott Place), 1906/07 (Dublin, 1907), p. 6.

[30] Ibid.

[31] DCDFPAS, 29th report for 1909 (Dublin, 1910), p. 7.

[32] DCDFPAS, 33rd report for 1913, p. 6.

[33] DCDFPAS, 39th report for 1919, p. 4.

[34] William Walsh to Mrs Browne, 31 May 1907, PA:DC/Dunardagh/Henrietta Street.

[35] Ibid.

Though never limited to that group, the focus of Our Lady's Home, as established by the Prisoners' Aid Society, was to be 'discharged first-committal prisoners', for whom the best hopes could reasonably be entertained. The statistics demonstrate that these were indeed the most amenable to 'rescue and reform'; of the twenty-four 'first offenders' in 10 Henrietta Street placed in situations between May 1906 and 1907, twenty-two have 'done well', demonstrating what can be done with first offenders, and 'most gratifying to those who have worked amongst them'.[36] The constraints which this policy imposed on the Society and on the sisters, who were required to carry out its wishes, is exemplified in the crisis surrounding the extension of responsibility to another discharged prisoners' home and the resulting divisions in the committee.

Several of the ladies on the managing committee of the home at 10 Henrietta Street also served in a similar capacity to the Holy Family Home, which undertook the same work of rescue and assisting Discharged Prisoners, but deals with other than First Offenders. It was founded by Miss R. ffrench, a prison visitor and committee member of Our Lady's Home and also 'resident member of the committee' to the Holy Family Home. This institution was located at 7 Synnott Place in the same part of the city. A resolution was passed at the annual meeting in May 1906 to extend the responsibility of the Prisoners' Aid Society to this smaller home, and half of all subscriptions, donations and the prison grant (amounting to £120 2 s. 3 d.) was handed over to this second home.[37]

Comparisons drawn between the two operations served only to highlight the gulf between them: from May 1906 to May 1907, Our Lady's Home received thirty-eight girls, placed out twenty-four who had completed their probation and accommodated fifty at the end of the year. Holy Family Home received fifty-six women over the same period, five completed their probation and were placed out and given outfits, thirty-three stayed such a short time that they were neither placed out nor given outfits and eighteen were still resident in the home. The verdict was that this was 'a much more difficult and a much more disappointing work'.[38] In their dealings with repeat offenders supporters were reminded of the gospel injunction 'to forgive even up to seventy times seven' and to console themselves with the knowledge that, at the very least, 'even in the short periods that some of them remain, we keep them free from sinning and of causing other people to sin also'.[39]

---

[36] DCDFPAS, 26th report (Henrietta Street), 2nd report (Synnott Place), 1906/07 (Dublin, 1907), p. 6.
[37] Ibid., p. 7.
[38] Ibid.
[39] Ibid.

The strain of running two committees, with several members common to both, under the umbrella of the Dublin Catholic Discharged Female Prisoners' Aid Society, appears to have precipitated multiple crises internally, exposing deep divisions between the founding members or 'old guard' and newcomers. At a meeting held sometime between May and October 1907, a resolution was passed to remove Mrs Emily Clarke, honorary treasurer for twenty-seven years; this 'regrettable proposal' resulted in 'a counter-proposition to remove from the Committee the members who were mainly responsible for it'.[40] This in effect removed all the old committee members and replaced them with an entirely new group. The conciliatory efforts of Mr Ignatius Rice (a law agent), who proposed several members of the old committee to serve on the new, came to nothing as the old members were so incensed they refused to cooperate in any capacity. The majority of members in attendance at the meeting, although sympathetic to the work of the Synnott Place Home with 'the older class of Discharged Offenders', considered that it could not be legally taken over as it had its own independent committee, which was not answerable to the Society despite being largely funded by it. Members who were 'actively identified with the policy which the meeting had decided to alter, namely, the taking over of the Synnott Place Home and Committee as then constituted' could hardly be elected onto the new committee. The new committee 'far from being anxious to depose any of the active members of the old committee, or put any indignity upon them' did everything possible to win their support, including offering to co-opt them onto the committee and seeking mediation through the Archbishop's house, but to no avail.[41]

In October 1907, the archbishop of Dublin, William J. Walsh, formally withdrew approval of the 'Henrietta Street Institution' 'with which [he had] found it impossible to continue to cooperate in any way'.[42] In a severely worded letter to the Provincial Superior of the Daughters of Charity, he ordered that his name be removed 'from the list of persons willing to receive subscriptions', on the basis that he did not recognise the new committee and refused to listen to explanations or petitions of any sort.[43] But the Archbishop's disapproval notwithstanding, the new committee had been validly elected according to the rules of the Society and the members were entitled to take charge. Sister Felicité Hurley was in an invidious position as she could not take sides. The stalemate continued to March 1908 when, to spare the deposed members of the

---

[40] Undated, unsigned letter to Archbishop William Walsh. From content end of March 1908, correspondent, probably Ellen Carew Rafferty, writes as instructed by the committee of the DRCDFPAS, PA:DC/Dunardagh/Henrietta Street.

[41] Ibid.

[42] William J. Walsh to Sister Provincial, 12 October (no year), PA:DC/Dunardagh/Henrietta Street.

[43] Ibid.

committee from the 'painful ordeal' of meeting with their successors, the books and papers of the Society

> were brought to His Grace by one of the ladies and they were sent by him last Friday to the sister superior at the Henrietta Street home, with a letter explaining the circumstances and asking her to have the papers handed over at the first opportunity to whoever may be the proper person to receive them.[44] The role of go-between was hardly a pleasant one, but at least the proper administration of the charity could be resumed. Dr Walsh, 'unable to recognise even the existence of this [new] Committee', remained steadfast in his resolve to have nothing to do with Henrietta Street, 'neither directly nor indirectly', despite entreaties from within and without the Society over the following months and years.[45]

That the Society weathered the 'succession crisis' of 1907–8 was due largely to the good sense and outstanding administrative capacities of Miss Carew Rafferty, the daughter of a generous benefactor, William A. Rafferty of Kilternan, Co. Dublin, and a committee member in her own right prior to her election as honorary secretary. She continued as secretary until 1923 and was instrumental in the transfer of the Society's work into the hands of the sisters. She later entered the Daughters of Charity and worked in England. She was subsequently appointed the English language secretary in the motherhouse in Paris.[46]

Miss Rafferty had enjoyed a professional partnership and close friendship with Sister Felicité Hurley, from the arrival of the sisters in 1895. Sister Felicité was an exceptionally capable woman, whose capacity for business and sound judgement, administrative skills and 'unflagging efforts' on behalf of the Society were fuelled 'by an ardent desire to help every erring girl, and to do it quickly'. This was referred to in the report of the Society following her death in 1918.[47] The good relations that existed between Miss Rafferty and Sister Felicité are evident from the easy tone of their correspondence and the frank disclosure of day-to-day difficulties; together they kept the institution afloat through tumultuous years.[48]

---

[44] Michael J. Curran, secretary (to Archbishop Walsh) to Miss Rafferty, 23 March 1908 (signed 27/8/08 also), letter damaged by fire, PA:DC/Dunardagh/Henrietta Street.

[45] Michael J. Curran, secretary (to Archbishop Walsh) to Miss Rafferty, 1 April 1908; see also, same to same, 10 April 1908 (signed 14/4/08 also); both letters damaged by fire, PA:DC/Dunardagh/Henrietta Street.

[46] Manuscript history Dunardagh, PA:DC/Dunardagh/Henrietta Street.

[47] *DCDFPAS*, 38th report for 1918, p. 4.

[48] For example, see Sr Felicité to Miss Rafferty, 14 January 1914, PA:DC/Dunardagh/Henrietta Street.

The possibility of extending the range and quality of the services that could be offered in Henrietta Street and the numbers that could be served, presented itself in concrete form in September 1908, a landmark in the history of Henrietta Street. Mrs Emily Clarke, took pleasure in announcing the purchase of 9 Henrietta Street, adding, 'and that I intend presenting it to your community as a gift from me.' The only proviso attaching to the gift was that the house should be used 'for the extension of the work of the "Prisoners Aid Society" as long as the Society requires it'.[49] In November 1908, a deed of gift was drawn up by Mr Brady, solicitor, on behalf of Mrs Emily Mary Clarke, Frankfort, Blackrock, Co. Dublin, in respect of the Daughters of Charity. It was stipulated that the Prisoners' Aid Society would have the use of 9 Henrietta Street for the extension and carrying out of its work, paying rent, taxes and keeping the premises in repair, but if and when the Society discontinued with the services of the sisters, they (the sisters) should have the premises for their own purposes.[50] Repairs were quickly put in place in 9 Henrietta Street, 'doors of communication' were opened between houses 9 and 10, enabling an increase in the dormitory accommodation and the provision of 'a large recreation hall for the girls, who heretofore have had no large room for the purpose'.[51] Plans were afoot by March 1910 to devote part of the new house to workrooms, 'where daily employment will be given to prisoners who are unable, from various causes, to enter the Home'.[52] Unskilled, discharged women prisoners found it practically impossible to enter the labour market in a city with little factory employment; yet extern employment was crucial to the aims of the Society; 'the recall to better ways of those who have made themselves amenable to the law.'[53]

The saga of the 'hand laundry' opened February 1911 in the basement of 9 Henrietta Street, replaced two years later by the 'new laundry' or 'electric laundry' to the rear of the premises, reveals the many obstacles in the way of providing extern employment for poor and vulnerable women and girls on a profitable basis. There was already a laundry in house 10, which by the end of 1907 was supplied with gas to heat the irons and electric light.[54] It was used firstly as a laundry of what was a large household (about fifty residents and three sisters in December 1907). Laundry work was one of the subjects taught to the factory girls in the basement night-school established in house 10 in

---

[49] E. M. Clarke to Sr Felicité, 30 September 1908, PA:DC/Dunardagh/Henrietta Street.

[50] Letter from Mrs Clarke to Mr Brady, member of committee, 19 November 1908, PA:DC/Dunardagh/Henrietta Street.

[51] DCDFPAS, 29th report for 1909 (Dublin, 1910), p. 8.

[52] Ibid.

[53] DCDFPAS, 38th report for 1918, p. 4.

[54] DCDFPAS, 26th report (Henrietta Street), 2nd report (Synnott Place), 1906/07 (Dublin, 1907), p. 5.

1904; presumably the evening students were taught these skills in the same room used by the resident girls by day.[55] Laundry from charitable individuals was also gratefully received in house 10, and made up by far the greatest portion of the house's income: from 1 March–31 December 1909, laundry receipts came to £1,613 or about 80% of total income. To set this in context, the prisons' board annual grant came to £50 and the rest of the income was derived from subscriptions, donations, bequests and interest on investments. Up to 1914, annual income slightly exceeded expenditure, but without the excess of laundry receipts over laundry expenses, the home could not have continued. The laundry in house 10 continued to operate alongside the experiments opened in the basement and rear of house 9; it was a public laundry registered under the Factory Act and open to inspection.[56]

One of the first projects in 9 Henrietta Street was the equipping of a 'hand laundry' in the basement, for the employment of 'discharged prisoners who are unable to enter a Home'; it was in use from February 1911.[57] The women received breakfast, dinner, tea and 'a small monetary remuneration per day'; the average number regularly employed in its first year was seven.[58] But there were problems with the project from the outset. The committee had to admit, with regret, that 'discharged prisoners of this class rarely continue in regular employment though every effort is made to induce them to do so'.[59] Sewing as an alternative to laundry work was always available to those who preferred (and the items made were sold on the premises) but the attractions were not sufficient to draw the very persons it was designed to assist.[60] There was also some concern with the 'bad use' to which the women sometimes put their earnings, but this was beyond the scope of the Society to regulate.[61]

The basement situation of the hand laundry quickly proved to be most unhealthy for both workers and sisters and the committee was forced to replace it. The architect submitted plans in July 1912 for a laundry and stables to the rear of house 8, incorporating a two-bedroom house over two floors.[62] The laundry itself was to include reception and delivery areas, wash house, large ironing room and heating chamber. Reservations about the very large sum of money to be spent on what was still merely a hand laundry were expressed by

---

[55] DCDFPAS, 26th report (Henrietta Street), 2nd report (Synnott Place), 1906/07 (Dublin, 1907), p. 6.

[56] Manuscript history undated, PA:DC/Dunardagh/Henrietta Street.

[57] *DCDFPAS*, 31st report for 1911, p. 7.

[58] Ibid.

[59] Ibid.

[60] Ibid.

[61] Ibid., p. 8.

[62] MS plans of Laundry & C. for the CFDPA Society, Henrietta Street, Dublin by J. Geoghegan, MHIAI, 37 St Stephen's Green, 8 feet to an inch. Also plan dated 18 July 1912 (colour), 44 feet to an inch, PA:DC/Dunardagh, Henrietta Street.

the Provincial of the Daughters of Charity in August 1912 with the gentle note saying, 'I presume all details have been carefully considered and that the plan is suited to the requirements of the work.'[63] However, when the building contract was signed 11 October 1912,[64] the final cost was £1,362.[65] Funded mostly from legacies and from the current account, this new laundry was opened on 1 March 1913. It boasted electric power and light, which were described as 'more economical, cleaner and easier to work than steam or gas'.[66] But the scale of operations, despite its expensive construction and fittings, continued to be very modest; the average number of regular workers employed during its first year was six and it contributed only a fraction (around 14 per cent) to the total laundry receipts.[67] The numbers fluctuated; fourteen discharged prisoners worked there in 1919, six in 1923 and the numbers of extern workers never reached the figures that would justify the huge outlay on construction and fitting-out.[68]

While the new laundry was under construction to the rear of house 9 and under the direction of the Society, 8 Henrietta Street was purchased outright by the Daughters of Charity, for use as a night refuge for poor women. The signatories were Revd W. Byrne CM, Sister Josephine O'Driscoll, a representative of the provincial council and Sr Felicité Hurley and Sister Josephine Corcoran of Henrietta Street. The sisters received possession of the house on 11 January 1913. The cost of the new house, £300, was met by a donation of £200 from a Mr M. Lawlor, 6 Upper Prince Edward's Terrace, Blackrock, and a donation of £100 from Mrs Clarke, who had already generously purchased 9 Henrietta Street. 'Good Mrs Clarke', as she was referred to by Sister Felicité, also furnished 8 Henrietta Street, providing beds and bedding, tables and chairs. The night refuge was opened on 1 July 1913 and continued until 1961. It provided residential accommodation for twelve ladies. Among those who were first to take advantage of the night refuge were homeless prisoners; in 1923 twelve prisoners availed of the facility, while the total number of women provided with supper, bed and breakfast was 6,934.[69]

---

[63] Sr Marcellus, provincial, St Vincent's Mill Hill, to Dear Madam, 31 Aug. 1912, PA:DC/Dunardagh/Henrietta Street.

[64] Articles of Agreement between Catholic Female Discharged Prisoners' Aid Society and Christopher J. Dowdall, 30 Synge Street, contractor, 6 September 1912; Agreement between Messrs Francis Carr and Company, 27 North Frederick Street, and the RC Female Discharged Prisoners' Aid Society of 9 Henrietta Street Dublin, the architect Mr Joseph A. Geoghegan, 37 St Stephen's Green Dublin, 11 October 1912, PA:DC/Dunardagh/Henrietta Street.

[65] DCDFPAS, 32nd report for 1912, p. 7.

[66] DCDFPAS, 33rd report for 1913, p. 7.

[67] Refers to the receipts from the 'electric laundry' in no. 9, of which £198 out of £1370, DCDFPAS, 33rd for 1913, p. 7.

[68] DCDFPAS, 39th report for 1919 (Dublin, 1920), p. 5; DCDFPAS 42nd report for 1923, p. 5.

[69] DCDFPAS, 33rd report for 1913, p. 10; DRCDFPAS, 42nd report for 1913 (Dublin, 1924), p. 6.

The year in which both the night refuge and the new laundry were opened, 1913, turned out to be a year of 'exceptional trial for the poor' as labour unrest reached crisis point in the Dublin Strike and Lockout. The Prisoners' Aid Society and the sisters combined to extend services 'to a body of poor women who through feebleness and otherwise are disqualified to compete with the ordinary worker'.[70] It was the outbreak of war in 1914, which resulted in rampant inflation especially in fuel and food prices that exposed the precarious state of the funding upon which the Society's work was based. The Easter Rebellion of 1916 and the political and military upheavals that ensued until the end of the civil war in 1923 were also factors that led to the decision to restructure the Henrietta Street institution.

From 1909, when 9 Henrietta Street was acquired, there was significant expansion in the works and expenses of the Society. By the provision of food and clothing to prisoners on their release, opening workrooms and a laundry for the employment of those who could not enter Our Lady's Home, the Society had indeed helped many 'to regain their self-respect and to withstand temptation'.[71] But few of those assisted by the Society were able to contribute towards their own support, at least in the short term. Our Lady's Home was always intended to be a place of transition, one of the chief aims of the Society being 'to restart the girls as soon as possible in the world as respectable, self-supporting members of society'.[72] Just as they were acquiring the skills and experience that might make them useful employees, they were moved on. The constant turnover of girls 'prevents any of the inmates being considered economic workers' and made comparison with commercial undertakings most unfair.[73] From 1914 onwards, the institution was plunged into debt.[74] By the end of 1918 the Society was almost £900 in debt, due largely to matters outside the control of the committee, namely the rise in the costs of fuel and light from £555 in 1917 to £1,304 in 1918.[75] 'With a settling of prices after the war, and a recasting of prices based on the new order of things' the committee looked forward to a time when the home would once more be self-supporting.[76] In the meantime the level of debt continued to climb. By the end of 1919 the Society was in debt to the extent of £1,245.[77] This had not gone unnoticed by the Provincial Superior at Mill Hill and Sister Josephine Bacon, the sister servant, had to explain matters. Committee members valiantly organised

---

[70] DCDFPAS, 33nd report for 1913, p. 6.
[71] DCDFPAS, 38th report for 1918, p. 4.
[72] Ibid.
[73] Ibid.
[74] DCDFPAS, 39th report for 1919, p. 5.
[75] DCDFPAS, 38th report for 1918, p. 4–6.
[76] DCDFPAS, 38th report for 1918, p. 6.
[77] DCDFPAS, 40th report for 1920, p. 3.

numerous fundraisers but the proceeds were used to meet urgent current needs rather than clearing the debt.[78] The replacement of the motor van in 1919, without which the laundry could not operate at all, cost nearly £500 and was met by the proceeds of a flag day.[79] Guinness shares were sold in 1920, as an emergency measure. While they realised £1,042 the committee was then at the loss of the dividends, which were an important part of its annual income.[80]

The shifts in political power on the national stage and the crisis engendered by the 1916 Easter rebellion was played out at committee level in the Prisoners' Aid Society, with the forced deposition of its nationalist president, Count George Noble Plunkett and vice president, Countess Josephine Mary Plunkett by a unionist committee member, J. C. Gaisford St Lawrence of Howth Castle. After lengthy and sensitive negotiations throughout 1915, Gaisford St Lawrence had been persuaded to lend his illustrious name to the Society as a trustee.[81] At the first committee meeting to be held after the rebellion, on 17 May 1916, he went to great efforts to ensure 'the position of our President and Vice President as arising out of the recent rebellion' were considered. Gaisford St Lawrence informed Miss Rafferty that 'as an officer in His Majesty's service, and also as a loyal subject' whether or not he continued as trustee and committee member 'must depend on what decision is arrived at by the Committee'.[82] While the committee tried not to become entangled in political questions – its membership, though all Roman Catholic, represented a wide span of sympathies – Gaisford St Lawrence persisted in seeking the expulsion of the Plunketts. Countess Plunkett offered her resignation but it was first rejected by the committee; Gaisford St Lawrence insisted he would continue as a member only on condition that Countess Plunkett's resignation was accepted without comment and that Count Plunkett was asked to send in his resignation.[83] Finally forced to withdraw, Josephine M. Plunkett paid a warm tribute to 'the kindly feelings of my co-workers when we did what we could in common for the good of the Society' and the 'loyal and sympathetic way' in which the members met any suggestion she offered.[84] She concluded her letter with a cryptic reference to the political dramas then unfolding which would eclipse the likes of Gaisford St Lawrence of Howth: 'The temporary power

---

[78] DCDFPAS, 39th report for 1919, p. 3; flag day DCDFPAS, 42nd report for 1923, p. 6.
[79] Ibid., p. 3.
[80] DRCDFPAS, 40th report for 1920 (Dublin, 1921), p. 3.
[81] See series of letters requesting Mr Gaisford St Lawrence of Howth Castle to take on the trusteeship, along with Father Walshe, provincial of the Vincentians, following on the deaths of Mrs Clarke and Mrs Wilfred Fitzgerald. Lawrence, Howth to Miss Rafferty, 18 March 1915; Laurence, Howth to Miss Rafferty, 29 March, 1915, PA:DC/Dunardagh/Henrietta Street.
[82] Lawrence, Howth Castle to Miss Rafferty, 17 May 1916.
[83] Lawrence, Howth Castle to Miss Rafferty, 27 June 1916.
[84] Josephine M. Plunkett to Miss Rafferty, 29 July 1916.

that now controls our lives – and deaths – have seen fit to select me for distinction. To the will of the Higher Power I bow and say "Thy Will be done".'[85]

The role of honorary secretary was a difficult one for Miss Carew Rafferty during this crisis, as family connections certainly placed her on the side of the 1916 rebels. The solicitor Michael Cartan O'Meara, who served as trustee to the Prisoners' Aid Society up to 1915, shared the task of sorting out the 'hopelessly insolvent' estate of the executed rebel leader, P. H. Pearse with Miss Rafferty's father, William Arthur Rafferty of Springfield, Kilternan, Co. Dublin.[86] A serious blow to the Society and to Miss Rafferty personally was the death of Sister Felicité Hurley in 1918, after twenty years as superioress of Our Lady's Home. In the report for the following year, condolences were extended to the family of the late Mr Rafferty, 'a very kind benefactor of the society' who had a lifetime interest in the work of the home, at the time of his death, his older daughter was serving as honorary secretary and his younger daughter as honorary treasurer.[87]

The economic climate at the close of World War I did not allow the Society to return to solvency and there were countless other charities competing for funds. During 1920 the 'disorganised state' of the country prevented members of the Society from coming in touch with many girls to whom they could have rendered assistance, most especially 'country cases'.[88] The long-established practice of meeting women each morning on their discharge from Mountjoy Prison had to be discontinued, 'until Dublin becomes more normal again'.[89] The ranks of loyal members and benefactors were thinned a little due to the deaths of Emily Clarke, Sister Felicité, William Rafferty, Fr Grimley (parish priest and trustee) and others. The possibility of ever again operating debt-free seemed remote. A fire in the laundry in August 1921 was another setback. Pressures were mounting internally to entrust the work of the Dublin Discharged Female Roman Catholic Prisoners' Aid Society, in its entirety, to the Daughters of Charity of St Vincent de Paul.

There was, however, one important area in which positive progress could be recorded, namely, in relations with the Archdiocese of Dublin. The Society had been fortunate in securing the services of Lord Chief Justice Molony as president, and those of his wife, Mrs T. Molony, as a committee member, following on the forced resignation of Count Plunkett in 1916. On the succession of Dr Edward Joseph Byrne to the Archdiocese of Dublin, the Lord

---

[85] Ibid.
[86] See Articles of Agreement between P. H. Pearse and the Intermediate Board of Education, 20 Feb. 1911; Michael Cartan O'Meara to W. A. Rafferty Esq., Springfield, Kilternan, 20 October1916, PA:DC/Dunardagh/Henrietta Street.
[87] RCDFPAS, 39th report for 1919, pp. 3–4.
[88] RCDFPAS, 40th report for 1919, p. 4.
[89] Ibid.

Chief Justice was among the first, in November 1921, to congratulate him formally, on behalf of the committee of the Catholic Discharged Female Prisoners' Aid Society, and to draw his attention to its 'most excellent work' over many years. While mentioning the 'little difficulty' the Society had with his predecessor, he was nevertheless sure that Dr Walsh had always recognised that the Daughters of Charity of St Vincent de Paul, who managed the institution 'were doing a great service to some of the poorest of the poor and the most wretched of the wretched'.[90] The carefully-crafted letter met with a generous response, a note requesting him to convey to the members of the Society 'that their work has my cordial appreciation, and will receive all due encouragement', enclosing £50 as a subscription towards the working expenses of the charity.[91]

The question of disbanding the committee and giving the sisters full control and responsibility for the work was addressed by Fr John O'Connell CM in 1923. The provincial of the Vincentian Fathers, Fr Joseph Walsh, who was one of the trustees from 1912, also appears to have been strongly in favour of the change, which was presented in the context of 'increasing the usefulness of the Charity and reorganising some of its spheres of activity' rather than as a takeover.[92] Negotiations were entered into with the Archbishop and with Lord Chief Justice Molony in his role as president of the Prisoners' Aid Society. In November 1923, Miss Rafferty, honorary secretary, reported: 'The Committee think that the time has come when the sisters should be more intimately associated with the management and control of the institution, and intend at the annual meeting [in May 1924] to submit proposals with that object in view.'[93] The Archbishop was also fully in favour. In March 1924, Fr O'Connell reported to the Lord Chief Justice: 'Nothing could be more encouraging for the community than the commendatory terms in which His Grace gives his sanction to their taking over Our Lady's Home and nothing could be more pleasing to them than his beautiful well-deserved tribute to the splendid work of the Committee during these past years and his hope that its members would not cease to give their assistance in the new conditions.'[94] The likely transfer was made public at the annual meeting of 5 May 1924 in 10 Henrietta Street, when the committee announced its opinion that 'the time has come when the sisters should be more intimately associated with the management and control

---

[90] Lord Chief Justice (stamped notepaper, unsigned) to Dr Byrne, 7 November 1921.
[91] Edward Byrne to 'My dear Lord Chief Justice', 4 May 1922.
[92] DCDFPAS, 42nd report for 1923, p. 4.
[93] Original letter from Miss Carew Rafferty to Fr O'Connell CM, 9 November 1923, PA/DC/Dunardagh/Henrietta Street.
[94] Fr O'Connell CM to Lord Chief Justice, 31 March 1924; see also letter from E.J. Byrne, archbishop of Dublin to Lord Chief Justice, 19 March 1924, PA/DC/Dunardagh/Henrietta Street.

of the institution' and furthermore, that proposals to this effect would be submitted at the 1925 annual meeting. Lord Chief Justice Molony had already provided the best possible public endorsement of the transfer in a speech to the Statistical and Social Inquiry Society of Ireland earlier in 1924 and quoted by the Prisoners' Aid Society in its own report. From his own 'intimate acquaintance' with the Society he claimed:

> I know of no other higher form of Christian Charity than is exemplified in the lives of the Sisters who manage that institution, and who are happily, and to their minds amply rewarded, by the remembrance of the many discharged prisoners whom they have restored to the paths of virtue and given the means of honest employment.[95]

The committee handled the transfer well by giving ample notice in public and by ensuring that all members, not just the committee, had a voice in the decision. Endorsements by such high-ranking figures as the Lord Chief Justice, the Archbishop of Dublin and the Provincial of the Vincentians were also useful. A new committee was subsequently formed composed for the most part of Vincentian priests and Daughters of Charity, but a small group of lay people continued to act as trustees and the work retained the name of the Prisoners' Aid Society.

The new management arrangements made extensions and changes to the work simpler, but the core business of 8–10 Henrietta Street continued as before. In 1924, at the request of Archbishop Edward Joseph Byrne, the sisters opened St Brigid's Hostel at 9 Henrietta Street for nuns, business girls and students. As well as meeting a need for respectable, city-centre accommodation, the hostel was a source of income for the intern works. In 1929, the sisters were asked to provide Penny Dinners for the poor and needy of the area and a hall was constructed at the end of the garden opening on to Henrietta Lane where they were served daily.[96] In 1925, part of 8 Henrietta Street (the premises first used as a night refuge for poor women) was set up as a day nursery and became one of the longest-running nurseries in the city. To complement the services of the nursery, a club for mothers was established. The nursery was later renovated and modernised to a high standard, catering for thirty-four pre-school children.

---

[95] DRCDFPAS, 42nd report for 1923 (Dublin, 1924), p. 5.
[96] Manuscript history, PA:DC/Dunardagh/Henrietta Street.

The story of the involvement of the Daughters of Charity in Henrietta Street with the Prisoners' Aid Society from 1899 to 1925, as told in this chapter, points to many of the characteristics of the approach of the Company in their service of people in need. It demonstrates that the Daughters of Charity endeavour to remain faithful to their founding principles of seeking out the most vulnerable in society; furthermore it shows their willingness to work in whatever roles are required of them in a project, in this case moving from being in charge of the day-to-day running of the institution (1899) to overall responsibility of the project (1925) when the Prisoners' Aid Society was no longer financially viable. During the history of the project their collaboration and adaptability, in the interests of development and expansion of the work, demonstrated an attitude that was characteristic of the tradition of the Company from the beginning. The fact that the dominant people of the Prisoners' Aid Society were influential in the Dublin of their time mirrors their founder's genius in engaging the rich on behalf of the poor.

Being always open to the needs of the poor, they facilitated the development of the services: accommodation and rehabilitation of women prisoners (1899); night school for factory workers (1904); night refuge for the poor (1913); hostel for nuns, business girls and students (1924); day nursery (1925) and 'penny dinners' (1929). All these innovations reflected the pressing needs of the time and point to the creative and organisational ability and energy of the sisters in charge. All that took place in the evolution of the work is a reflection of the passion of the Daughters of Charity for the service of the poor as expressed in their motto: 'The charity of Christ crucified urges us.'

Chapter Eleven

Invitation to the Daughters of Charity to Belfast, 1895–1900

Anna Byrne DC

> You will easy know a doffer'
> When she comes into town,
> With her long yellow hair,
> And her ringlets hangin' down,
> And her rubber tied before her,
> And her picker in her hand,
> You will easy know a doffer,
> For she'll always get her man.[1]

This popular West Belfast linen factory ditty of the late nineteenth century depicts a light heartedness among the mill workers. A former mill worker reflected: 'I couldn't get the pickers and things on me quick enough … You were so proud … You thought it was great comin' out after work with them shakin' in front of you … like a horse and his bells were comin'.'[2] An observer considered, 'They must be quare and happy in the mill, because the mill girls are always smilin'.'[3]

Cheerful accounts from workers and their contemporaries testify to the resilience and camaraderie among female employees. However, this could deflect attention from the harsher aspects of daily life, as working conditions in the West Belfast linen mills, the particular focus of this chapter, were anything but wholesome. It was because of the abject poverty associated with

---

[1] 'The Doffer's Song'. A doffer was a girl who took off (doffed) the full bobbins of spun yarn and replaced them with empty bobbins in the spinning rooms. Eilis Brennan, Evelyn Cardwell, Carmel Gallagher, Bill Crawford, Deirdre Brown and Andrew Anderson, *Linen: Continuity and Change: The Story of the Irish Linen Industry* (Ulster Folk and Transport Museum: Belfast, 1988), p. 39.

[2] Ibid., p. 38. Pickers were tools for dealing with thread which had wound itself around the rollers when breaks had occurred.

[3] Ibid.

this industry, in which very many Catholics toiled, that the Daughters of Charity of St Vincent de Paul were invited to Belfast in 1895, and to the west of the city in particular.

In 1852 there were twenty-eight linen mills in Belfast, eight of which were located on the Falls Road. This district was to witness intensive and rapid development over the nineteenth century as long-established cotton mills were converted to the more profitable wet-flax spinning process. Dozens of new mills were opened and intervening parcels of land were hastily built upon to provide the burgeoning workforce with housing of a minimum standard. The census of 1901 revealed that only 39 per cent of the population was born in the city; many of the newcomers were Roman Catholic and from the lowest strata of the rural poor. By 1901 the Falls-Smithfield area held the largest concentration of Catholics in the city, with 40 per cent of the total Catholic population. The vast bulk of all manual workers, 74 per cent, lived in districts strictly segregated on the basis of Protestant or Catholic religious affiliation. In addition to spatial segregation, Catholics were constrained from entering business or the professions by the lack of educational opportunity, and many obstacles placed in their path by the social and economic elites. Census returns between 1861 and 1911 indicates a higher illiteracy rate among Catholics than among Protestants; this is easily identified in the business and the professional fields, see Figure 11:1.

Of the fifty-five linen mills and factories in the city in 1857 only three were owned by Catholics.[4] This disparity was mirrored in the professions. The

Figure 11:1 Education and Religion, Belfast 1861–1911

Year	% Roman Catholic in total population	% Roman Catholic in school population	% Illiterate Roman Catholic	% Illiterate Protestant
1861	34	28	30	11
1871	32	28	28	10
1881	29	27	21	8
1891	26	25	14	7
1901	24	23	12	6
1911	23	22	7	2

Note: Illiteracy was measured for the population aged five years and over, except in 1911 when the age taken was nine years and over.[5]

---

[4] A. C. Hepburn, 'The Catholic Community of Belfast, 1850–1940' in Max Engman, ed., et al., *Ethnic Identity in Urban Europe* (New York, 1992), p. 47.
[5] Ibid.

percentage of Catholic lawyers and doctors increased from 10 per cent to 12 per cent between 1857 and 1911 despite the substantial increase in the Catholic population.[6] The income differential between the sectors was considerable. Hepburn in his calculation of a mean valuation of economically active male households in 1901 concludes that Catholic professional and business classes had a mean figure of £15.28 while the corresponding figure for semi- and un-skilled workers was £4.82. Wages for manual workers in all sections of industry were low. Among the linen workers of West Belfast, where women made up the highest proportion of all employees, wages were still lower. The concept of equal pay for equal work was unthinkable at the time. Women mill workers were locked into a cycle of subsistence wages and poverty; support and access to education were required in order to break out of the poverty trap. Bishop Henry Henry, Roman Catholic bishop of the diocese of Down and Connor (1895–1905), was acutely conscious of the scale of the problem in what he referred to as 'the Catholic end of the city' where there were 'over 20,000 Catholics, mostly working people'. In his search for a 'zealous community of nuns' to whom he might entrust his plans for the educational, pastoral and moral care of the child factory workers or 'half-timers' and their families, he applied in the first instance to the provincial of the Daughters of Charity of St Vincent de Paul in Mill Hill, London.[7]

The initiative to invite the Daughters of Charity was taken by a friend of the Bishop, Mr Edward Mac Creanor, who knew the community in Drogheda (founded in 1855). This Catholic gentleman was among the first members of the Society of St Vincent de Paul in Belfast and a leading businessman in the city who had his home in Omeath, Co. Louth.[8] With extensive first-hand knowledge of living conditions throughout the city, he was an articulate advocate on behalf of the poorest Catholics, associating the intended new foundation with the Vincentian spirit of the good work already undertaken locally. He declared:

> In all Ireland there is no better or more deserving field for the good and dear family [*sic*] of the great St Vincent de Paul to secure a grand harvest for God's glory, the salvation of souls, and the reduction of heresy and schism.[9]

The expected cooperation between the lay Vincentian workers and the religious sisters is spelled out more clearly in the information provided by

---

[6] Ibid.
[7] Letter of 17 September 1896, PA:DC/Dunardagh/Belfast (Provincial Archive, Daughters of Charity, Dunardagh, Dublin, here abbreviated as PA:DC/Dunardagh/Belfast).
[8] See postscript, Edward Mac Creanor to Sr Provincial, 11 October 1895, PA:DC/Dunardagh/Belfast.
[9] Edward Mac Creanor to Sr Provincial, 11 October 1895, PA:DC/Dunardagh/Belfast.

Bishop Henry Henry on the system of home visitation that was already in place. Bishop Henry said, 'We have in the city about 200 girls who are affiliated to the Mother House of St Vincent de Paul, who do much in that line;' that is, visiting the poor, the sick and the dying in their own homes and giving them whatever spiritual and temporal aid was in their power.[10] This was the work of the Ladies of Charity.

In his repeated entreaties to the superiors of the Daughters of Charity for a Belfast foundation, Mr Mac Creanor laid heavy emphasis on the financial and political pressures under which the 'poor, hard-struggling Catholics' of the city operated. Admitting that he had pressed the case on the basis of outdated information ('gleaned about twenty five years ago respecting the establishment of a House of your Order'), nevertheless he felt a special case could be made for Belfast, and for supporting a newly appointed bishop:

> As his Lordship has been so recently consecrated, as his See is one of the largest, and certainly the most difficult in Ireland, owing to the numerous and powerful combinations for crushing and thwarting Catholic progress, as pointed out in my letter of the 11th of Oct., I have only to beg of you to keep Belfast favourably in memory, with the view of founding a house of your good dear sisters there, and on the easiest terms at the commencement.[11]

The smallness of the Catholic middle class, relative to the large mass of poor Catholics in need of assistance, placed Belfast in a category of its own, at least according to the promoters of the new foundation:

> It is all uphill work for the Catholics of Belfast, as immense numbers of poor are to be taught and cared for, and comparatively few are possessed of means to pay for this work. The calls on these persons for the promotion of religious undertakings are heavy and increasing.[12]

The discrimination which Catholics suffered was emphasised, as were the pressures on Catholics to neglect or abandon the practice of their faith, with Belfast depicted as 'the centre of the most determined Calvinism, Protestantism, Orangeism, Freemasonry and anti-Catholic Exclusiveness'.[13]

His Vincentian credentials, previous contacts with the Daughters of Charity, and readiness to contribute financially towards the costs of the new foundation, made Mr Mac Creanor the ideal lobbyist for the Belfast house of charity. It was on the appointment of his close friend, Henry Henry as bishop on 20 August 1895, that he acquired a suitable plot of ground for the proposed

[10] H. Henry to Sr Provincial, 17 September 1896, PA:DC/Dunardagh/Belfast.
[11] Edward Mac Creanor to Sr Austin, 21 September 1895, PA:DC/Dunardagh/Belfast.
[12] Edward Mac Creanor to Sr Provincial, 11 October, 1895, PA:DC/Dunardagh/Belfast.
[13] Ibid.

new school and associated convent and began a process to 'select a community at once to take charge of this plot and look after the buildings'.[14]

There had been a marked reluctance on the part of consecutive bishops of Down and Connor to allow religious congregations into the diocese. In the case of Belfast at least, this was partly due to the difficulties of getting title to land, as evidenced in the correspondence from the 1850s onwards.[15] However, on 6 January 1854 the Sisters of Mercy arrived on the invitation of Bishop Cornelius Denvir. They were the first sisters in the diocese since the reign of Queen Mary. Their sphere of influence was mainly in the north of the city with their principal foundation, St Paul's Convent, on the Crumlin Road. The Dominican Sisters were invited in 1870 to provide for the education of middle-class girls on the Falls Road. St Dominic's was established as a fee-paying second-level school for both day girls and boarders. St Catherine's Primary School was opened in 1870. It catered for girls until they were fourteen years of age and was organised in line with Cabra's commitment to a 'poor school'. This meant that a night school was conducted for the benefit of young women who worked in the local mills, the curriculum comprised of literacy lessons and instruction in Christian doctrine.[16] The Bon Secour Sisters were invited to Belfast in 1872 by Bishop Dorrian (1865–85), who purchased Clonard Lodge on the Falls Road to accommodate them. This house was formerly owned by William Ross of Ross's Mill. While the main apostolate of the sisters was giving medical assistance in the homes of those who could pay, they also ran a small hospital.

On his appointment, Bishop Henry invited three religious congregations from continental Europe to the city, a bold attempt to provide for the spiritual and educational needs of (in particular) the deprived western sector where the numbers of Catholics continued to soar. The Redemptorists, an international missionary order founded in Naples in 1732 by Alphonsus Maria de Liguori (1696–1787), were invited in 1896 to serve the spiritual needs of the migrant workers in the linen mills to the west of the city, beyond the parish of St Mary's (see Map 11:1). Bishop Henry felt the diocesan clergy could not meet the pastoral needs of their congregation as they were without sufficient church accommodation or priests enough to hear their confessions. Clonard Monastery was developed as their headquarters.[17]

The De La Salle Brothers, a French congregation renowned for their educational work, were invited to provide primary education to the young factory boys or 'half-timers'. They opened St Gall's school in Waterville Street in 1900

---

[14] H. Henry to Sr Provincial, 17 September, 1896, PA:DC/Dunardagh/Belfast.
[15] Dr Cullen 1854, Dublin Diocesan Archives.
[16] M. Duggan OP, *In Search of Truth: Journeys of Nineteenth Century Irish Dominican Women* (Dublin, 2010), p. 141.
[17] J. Grant, *One Hundred Years with the Clonard Redemptorist* (Dublin, 2003), p. 35.

followed in 1901 by another primary school, St Finnian's, in response to the huge pressure on accommodation. The Daughters of Charity in their turn were asked to establish a girl's school for 'half-timers'. Both were hastened, no doubt, by the state's efforts to extend education to all children under the Education Act of 1870, though school attendance was not compulsory in Ireland until the 1890s. Belfast provided ample scope for religious congregations from France or elsewhere whose special concern was the education of poor children, once the contentious issue of accommodation could be solved.

In the invitation extended to the Daughters of Charity to come to Belfast the unique character of the city was emphasised again and again. Unlike Dublin or Cork with monastic origins, Belfast was planned by landlords in the early seventeenth century and quickly became the most heavily industrialised centre on the island. Belfast was the main production centre for the linen industry which was concentrated in Ulster; in fact it accounted for 80 per cent of linen spinning capacity in Ireland in the 1890s. Alongside textiles came ship building, while engineering serviced the mills and the shipyards as well as being a major sector in its own right. The sectarian divisions in the city were longstanding and were reflected at every level of production and in every sector. Far from easing with expanding opportunities for merchants and factory owners, they sharpened in the later nineteenth century, making the city renowned internationally, at least in Catholic circles, for its bigotry. There was also the gender balance, or imbalance, with the ratio of women to men mill workers approximately 3:1, and many households, especially in the poorest areas, headed by women. The Daughters of Charity, therefore, were invited to live among and minister to the mill workers in a ruthlessly expanding industrial city, which was also avowedly sectarian.

The position of the children who worked in the factories and mills of west Belfast as 'half-timers' was the most urgent concern, according to both Mr Mac Creanor and Bishop Henry. In the negotiations of 1895 'a convent national school for girls working as half-timers in Mills, with as much other supervision of these girls as possible is the first work aimed at by the Bishop for the sisters'.[18] The same point is repeated a month later lest there be any misunderstanding: 'the work of schools – Day and Evening for poor children, the majority of whom would be workers in mills' was the principal work for which the Bishop sought sisters.[19] At least 275 of these child workers, who attended school on alternate days, were on the rolls of Catholic schools in the Falls district in 1896; the Bishop was anxious 'to gather all these children into one school under a community of nuns who would look after them carefully not only when in school, but at their homes'. Through the 'half-timers' pupils in the school the

---

[18] Edward Mac Creanor to Sr Austin, 21 September, 1895, PA:DC/Dunardagh/Belfast.
[19] Edward Mac Creanor to Sr Provincial, 11 October 1895, PA:DC/Dunardagh/Belfast.

sisters would come into contact with their parents and older siblings, 'and exercise a civilizing religious influence over them'. What was proposed was in effect a home-school liaison scheme, where the sisters would carefully watch over their charges as they grew into adulthood, support the parents in their rightful tasks, and through their pastoral care and the advantages of education try to counteract the bad influences to which the children were too often subjected, particularly the evil of drunkenness.[20]

Home visitation was also specifically mentioned by Bishop Henry in his letter of invitation; visiting the poor in their homes, and care of the sick poor especially of the dying was an integral part of their charism that would surely find scope among the burgeoning Falls Road population.[21] The Daughters of Charity were not curtailed by 'enclosure' as nuns were, so they could visit the people in their homes. The ministry to the mill workers extended to the possibility of providing accommodation for newly arrived migrants. Mr Mac Creanor held out the hope that as soon as possible after their arrival and the successful establishment of the school for 'half-timers' the sisters would open 'a house of residence for these girls, to take them out of lodging houses which are far from satisfactory retreats in many cases'.[22] The sisters were also invited to work with the many single girls employed in 'the different works' in the city who had no option but to go to 'lodgings that are often unsafe for them, and become ruined before they know their danger'.[23] Although all observers would indeed agree that 'a Boarding House for such people would be a great boon', establishing the school and associated home visitation would have to take priority.[24]

The mission of the Daughters of Charity was unique among religious in Belfast. It had a family focus, but with a specific interest in the development of women and was spatially limited to the Lower Falls area. The sisters were to: provide an education for the young girls who worked as 'half-timers'; offer support for female mill workers; accommodate vulnerable 'working girls'; and finally visit families in need in their homes in the locality.

From invitation to arrival

There is evidence that a certain Canon Rooney had written to the Superioress General of the Daughters of Charity in Paris, as early as 1883, and asked the superiors to send some sisters to care for orphans. In his letter he referred to Belfast as the 'centre of Protestantism in Ireland' feeling no doubt that this

---

[20] Bishop Henry to Sr Provincial, 17 September 1896, PA:DC/Dunardagh/Belfast.
[21] Ibid.
[22] Edward Mac Creanor to Sr Austin, 21 September 1895, PA:DC/Dunardagh/Belfast.
[23] Bishop Henry to Sr Provincial, 17 September 1896, PA:DC/Dunardagh/Belfast.
[24] Ibid.

would be a good enough ploy to have his request granted. While it was refused, it seems that it was just not opportune at the time as the response is hopeful, *pour le moment c'est impossible.*[25] Despite being turned down, Canon Rooney's request undoubtedly brought the cause of Belfast to prominence in Paris and prepared the ground for a more favourable response at a later date.

The Society of St Vincent de Paul was introduced to Belfast in 1850 with the opening of St Mary's conference in Chapel Lane. It is likely that Canon Rooney heard of the sisters through this society. Although the lay organisation founded by Frédéric Ozanam (1813–1853) had spiritual rather than structural links with the Congregation of the Mission and the Daughters of Charity, as children of a common father – St Vincent de Paul – they could be expected to be working towards the same ends, in fruitful partnership. Mr Mac Creanor, as an active member of the Society, certainly saw his petition to Paris for a foundation of the Daughters of Charity in this spirit of mutual collaboration. This possibility is also noted in Bishop Henry's letter of 17 September 1896.[26]

On his appointment to the bishopric of Down and Connor, Bishop Henry took up the negotiations anew, urging that the sisters might arrive in Belfast for Easter of 1896. Mr Mac Creanor, acting in unison with his bishop, also petitioned for a speedy decision, writing frequently, and leaving a city address whenever business held him in Belfast – 'The Union Hotel, 5 Donegal Square, W. Belfast' lest there be any delay in receiving letters.[27] Despite the energy and expectation of the Belfast parties, there was a further delay of over four years, largely due to the insistence by Paris on adhering to their standard contract, referred to by Mr Mac Creanor as 'the conditions on which you usually accept foundations'. He had to admit that neither he, nor his bishop, were aware 'of the extent of the difficulties involved in the undertaking', that is, that the superiors of the Daughters of Charity in Paris, relying on the information forwarded from Mill Hill, required that both parties to a new foundation sign a contract which detailed the financial and other bases upon which the house would be run.[28] Such negotiations and decisions took time, so that it was simply impossible to 'furnish a foundation sooner than at about a year from the time of application'.[29] Assurances that 'the income derived from the schools would produce much of the means of support from the outset' needed to be spelled out in hard currency, while the high costs of purchasing the site, and erecting the convent and school buildings, made it clear that local donations would be fully subsumed into establishing the project.[30]

---

[25] Minutes of the provincial council meetings, 1883, PA:DC/Mill Hill/Belfast (Provincial Archives, Daughters of Charity, Mill Hill, London, here abbreviated as PA:DC/Mill Hill).
[26] Letter to Sr Provincial 17 September 1896, PA:DC/Dunardagh/Belfast.
[27] Edward Mac Creanor to Sr Austin, 21 September 1895, PA:DC/Dunardagh/Belfast.
[28] Ibid.
[29] Edward Mac Creanor to Sr Provincial, 26 November 1895, PA:DC/Dunardagh/Belfast.
[30] Edward Mac Creanor to Sr Provincial, 11 October, 1895, PA:DC/Dunardagh/Belfast.

Precise detail was needed in Paris regarding the accommodation for the sisters; Bishop Henry was not able to furnish this, as the convent was not yet built, nor in fact was the site even purchased at the time of application. A lack of understanding in Paris of the difficulty Catholics had in acquiring property in Belfast probably contributed to the hold up. Property in the town was controlled by one landlord family, the Chichesters (Earls of Donegall) and from 1647, later marquises controlled the town exclusively.[31] In late-nineteenth-century Belfast a prospective leaseholder had to provide a letter of reference from a clergyman in order to proceed with the purchase of property in the city. This of course identified clearly to which religious tradition the prospective tenant belonged. There was much unease and suspicion among the Protestant majority around the possibility of Catholics acquiring property.[32] Catholic institutions were particularly opposed, as highly visible testimonies to the increasing numbers of 'Romanists' in the city.

Ongoing negotiations with the Daughters of Charity were handled largely by Mr Mac Creanor on behalf of Bishop Henry. Writing to the provincial headquarters at Mill Hill outside London in October 1895, he asks that they might forward to him a copy of the 'conditions on which you usually accept foundations'.[33] In the planning of any new foundation, the sisters dealt directly with the local bishop as early as possible in the negotiations, a practice that was to prove again and again essential to their long-term success, despite the delays that were incurred in the initial stages. Edward Mac Creanor had to justify his role as go-between by explaining that the newly appointed bishop had a massive backlog of work, 'as his see is one of the largest and certainly the most difficult in Ireland, owing to the numerous and powerful combinations for crushing and thwarting Catholic progress'.[34] In this same letter he appeals to the superiors to make the founding of the house on the 'easiest terms at the commencement'.

A plan to build a house for the sisters with a small garden beside the school in Dunlewy Street fell through as it would be too expensive and would take too long to build.[35] Mr Mac Creanor continued to be actively involved until the sisters arrived. It was he who negotiated that Clonard House would be the first home of the sisters when the Redemptorist community moved to their new monastery. Victor and James Kennedy owned Conway Mill and lived in Clonard House. They sold it to the estate agents, Robert John and Thomas

[31] R. Gillespie and Stephen A. Royle, *Irish Historic Towns Atlas, No. 12, Belfast, Part I, to 1840* (Royal Irish Academy in Association with Belfast City Council, 2003), p. 2.

[32] A. C. Hepburn, 'The Catholic Community of Belfast, 1850–1940', p. 45.

[33] Mr Mac Creanor to Sr Provincial, 21 September 1895, PA:DC/Dunardagh/Belfast.

[34] Edward Mac Creanor to Sr Provincial, 26 November 1895, PA:DC/Dunardagh/Belfast.

[35] PA:DC/Dunardagh/Belfast.

Edward McConnell who wanted to develop the area. Their intention had been to extend the street network and improve access to the area.

A solicitor called Henry Maguire acquired the property for the Bishop. The original site comprising some 14 acres was divided and the house and a strip of land around it (3 acres, 2 roods, and 20 perches) was sold to the Bishop for £2,360 plus a head rent to Mr Kennedy of £100 per annum. This head rent was purchased from the trustees of the Kennedy estate in June 1917 at eighteen years purchase, total cost being £1,816 16 s. 4 d. The diocese met the overall expenses and the house was given to the sisters rent-free. They were, however, to meet the cost of minor repairs. Fr Joseph Walsh a priest of the Congregation of the Mission helped with the negotiations in regard to the property. A detailed agreement was drawn up and eventually signed by Bishop Henry and Sister Marie Kieffer, superioress general on 31 May 1900.[36] The cost of refurbishment of the house was met by Mr Mac Creanor through a donation of £500, a considerable sum at the time. The agreement drawn up by Bishop Henry and Sister Kieffer included a sum of £30 a year to be given by the bishop for the maintenance of each sister, this money was paid quarterly and in advance.

The acquisition of premises, though fraught with difficulties, was not the only reason behind the delay. It was realised, well into the negotiations, that as the sisters were to teach in the school they were to be paid by the government;[37] they would, therefore, need to hold teaching qualifications recognised by the state. The dearth of suitable sisters exacerbated the delay; three of the first group of five named for Belfast in January 1900 never arrived. They were deemed to have inadequate qualifications to be assistant teachers in the new St Vincent's school.[38] In April 1900, sisters Frances Hickey and Alice O'Sullivan were named as replacements and were joined by Sister Elizabeth Whitehill from Dunmanway in July 1900. The selection of qualified personnel was crucial because the school for the 'half-timers' was the lynchpin on which the whole venture depended. Mr Mac Creanor spelled out with admirable clarity, 'A convent national school for girls working as half-timers in mills with as much other supervision of these girls as is possible is the first work aimed at by the bishop for the sisters.'[39]

On 1 May 1900, four sisters arrived in Belfast. Sister Josephine Graham was to be the sister servant while also working as the support person for the women in the mills and visitor to their homes. Sister Frances O'Donnell was appointed as the first principal of the school. The sisters took over the newly

[36] PA:DC/Dunardagh/Belfast.

[37] Bishop Henry to Sr Provincial, 17 September 1896, PA:DC/Dunardagh/Belfast.

[38] Ibid.

[39] Edward Mac Creanor to Sr Provincial, 26 November 1895, PA:DC/Dunardagh/Belfast.

completed St Vincent's School on their arrival. While Clonard House was being refurbished the sisters lived in temporary accommodation in the Dominican Convent on the Falls Road. Unlike the arrival of the sisters in Drogheda in 1855, which was marked with a spectacular civic and ecclesiastical welcome, the opening of a new foundation of Daughters of Charity in Belfast was without fanfare or public acclaim. No record has been found in the local press marking the occasion. A quiet, unobtrusive start was well advised, as antagonism in the city towards Catholics was too easily roused. It is possible that a lesson was learned from the experience of the founding of the Dominican Convent on the Falls Road some twenty years previously. At that stage it became clear that a 'Papist' monastery was certainly not welcomed in Belfast. On arrival in 1870 the Dominican Sisters had to engage, with the help of a local business man and friend, Mr Sheils, a group of young men who slept in the grounds of the convent and were to be 'ready to "beat off" the Orange men with sticks and clubs'.[40]

St Vincent's School

Over five hundred child factory workers or 'half-timers' enrolled in St Vincent's School (see Map 11:1) on its opening day, 1 May 1900, along with 380 'full-timers' or regular school children. The presence of so many wage-earning girls witnesses to the importance of child labour to the Belfast mills, and to the Falls Road and Shankill families of West Belfast for whom every few pence counted in the weekly struggle to 'get by'. It is also a testimony to the slow pace at which the regulation of child labour advanced in the United Kingdom: in 1833, the working hours of factory children aged 8 to 13 were limited to nine hours per day; by 1847 the nine-hour day was to include three hours of schooling, between 6.00 a.m. and 3.00 p.m. The age at which children could work was slowly raised: from ten years in 1875, to 11 years in 1891 and to 12 years in 1901.[41] The school-leaving age too, was discretionary for the most part and was dependent on the passing of what was known as Standard IV; some achieved this at 11 years of age or even earlier. Arguments in favour of retaining girls in school were gaining ground, despite the protests of industrialists and those most wedded to the political philosophy of laissez-faire. The issue of early school leaving was raised in public debates and conferences: the fact that 'an immense proportion' of children ended their education 'just as they were growing really capable of profiting by it'. It was felt that girls in particular were

---

[40] M. Duggan OP, *In Search of Truth: Journeys of Nineteenth Century Irish Dominican Women*, p. 141.
[41] Ulster Folk and Transport Museum, Education Services, *Linen: Continuity and Change: The Story of the Irish Linen Industry*.

abandoned at a critical juncture, 'just as the time approaches when they will be surrounded with moral dangers'.[42] While child protection (from overwork) and investment in education were being debated in Westminster and elsewhere, St Vincent's through its two shifts, morning and afternoon, provided girl factory workers aged 11 and upwards, with what for some was their first experience of a 'proper' school.

In the request to the Daughters of Charity, Bishop Henry envisaged a school that would serve educational, spiritual and material needs, in the spirit of their patron, St Vincent de Paul. He was particularly vexed by what he saw as the widespread lack of parenting skills, 'A large number of their fathers and mothers indulge in drink and neglect them in their young days.'[43] While it is impossible to judge the degree to which the school answered these needs, an inspector's report of 27 May 1903 assessed the progress of the pupils as 'excellent' a noteworthy plaudit after only three years' operation, and considering that many were malnourished or otherwise unable to give their full energies to lessons.[44] All pupils, whether half-timers or full-timers, followed the same curriculum to a greater or lesser extent, consisting of English, arithmetic, geography, handiwork and music. The high demand for places was sustained by the continuing population increases in the Falls Road and Shankill districts. By 1923, when the Londonderry Education Act was passed which forbade the 'half-time' system, St Vincent's had to be extended to include more classrooms for infant classes.

Support for female migrant workers

In his letter of request to the superiors of the Daughters of Charity, Bishop Henry identified two other areas of need in which the sisters living in the locality could be involved. The first one involved home visitation 'assisting in relieving the poor and assisting the dying' and the other one, not realised until 1917, was to provide accommodation for the many girls working in the city and living in 'lodgings that are unsafe to them'. While acknowledging the support given by the Society of St Vincent de Paul he continues to say that 'a boarding house for such people would be a great boon'.[45] This second strand of the remit, to provide support for the female mill workers, was carried

---

[42] E. M. Field, 'The Care of Girls Leaving Elementary Schools' in *Women Workers: papers read at a conference convened by the Bristol and Clifton Ladies' Association for the care of girls, in November 1892* (London, 1893), p. 200.

[43] Bishop Henry to Sr Provincial 17 September, 1886, PA:DC/Dunardagh/Belfast.

[44] District Inspectors' observation book; inspection carried out by Mr C. Bartley, PA:DC/Dunardagh/Belfast.

[45] Bishop Henry to Sr Superior, 17 September 1896, PA:DC/Dunardagh/Belfast.

through specifically by Sister Josephine Graham, who was assigned to visit the women in their homes or lodgings and to give encouragement and whatever material aid she could furnish. Her visiting district was in the parish of Shankill at the heart of the linen-making industry. This parish was part of the parish of Belfast, which later was divided into the parishes of St Peter and St Paul.[46] St Peter's Church, now the Roman Catholic cathedral, was opened in 1866, and St Paul's in 1887; however, St Paul's only became a separate parish in 1905.

The other key industries for which Belfast was renowned – shipbuilding, engineering, rope and tobacco manufacture – had a predominantly male workforce, skilled and better paid. The linen industry of West Belfast contrasted with this. Its location was determined by the local geography: the mills were sited along the same side of the Falls Road to take best advantage of the many rivers flowing down from Divis Mountain. The working environment in the mills and social conditions in the densely packed surrounding area made West Belfast one of the most deprived areas in any British Isles city of the time; the *Irish News* of 24 October 1896 reported that 'Belfast had an average death rate, in the previous 20 years nearly 20 per cent higher than that of the 23 largest English towns'.[47] Mill work was difficult and injurious to health – a change from former times when the linen was processed mainly out of doors as a cottage industry in the rural areas. Despite improved mechanisation and the new large-scale manufacturing processes of the city mills, the making of linen continued to be labour-intensive, back-breaking and dangerous work. It required large numbers of dexterous, painstaking and biddable workers, willing to endure very long hours for minimal pay; the steady throng of uneducated women migrating to Belfast provided the necessary labour force. These were the women Sister Josephine was to befriend and assist.

Some insights into the realities of life as a mill worker can be gained by examining the stages of the linen-making process.[48] Each step in the manufacturing process had its own specialist building, sometimes referred to as a 'room'. (Map 11:1 shows the spatial distribution of the production of linen in West Belfast.) In the machine and preparing 'rooms' the air was laden with flax dust called pouce. The spinners and weavers had to bear constant moist conditions and heat, ideal for the spread of disease. 'Mill girls worked long hours, for mostly uncaring employers, in dark, fetid rooms, often up to their ankles in water.'[49] A respiratory condition called phthisis, a form of tuberculosis, was widespread; it was long accepted among medical officers that it resulted from the conditions endured by the workers. A study in the 1870s,

---

[46] A. Macaulay, *Down and Connor: A Short History* (Du Signe, 2000).
[47] Ulster Folk Museum, *Linen: Continuity and Change*.
[48] 'The Linen Trade' <http://www.thebanfordhaungtons.co.uk>
[49] P. Collins, *The Irish News, Centenary Edition*, 2000, p. 36.

undertaken by Dr C. D. Purdon, the leading certifying surgeon in the Belfast Factory District, pointed out that the death rate in the 'preparing' rooms was the worst with a figure of thirty-one per thousand.[50] These workers were mainly women, and if employed constantly in this dusty environment, rarely lived beyond 30 years of age.[51] Death from phthisis, like other forms of tuberculosis, was slow and tortuous, and invariably hit young adults in what should have been their most active years of work and child-rearing.

Moreover, care for women who were pregnant did not fall within the remit of the mill owners. Maternity leave was unheard of and, due to financial pressures, women had to return to the workplace as soon as possible after giving birth.

> Again and again medical officers deplored the return of mothers to work only a few days after giving birth: such women suffered 'prolapse of the womb, uterine displacements, chronic leucorrhoea, and ulceration.' Babies and small children were 'minded' by old women or older children. Dr Purdon found workers 'leaving the care of their offspring to the "Baby Farmer," who feeds them on improper diet – tea and whiskey – and in order to keep them quiet, different preparations of opium'. The sale of laudanum and opium, more cheaply bought than whiskey, he discovered was 'enormous and increasing'. 30.1% of the factory class died under the age two-and-a-half years.[52]

Mrs Elizabeth Mc Cann (nee Laverty 1882–1950) migrated from Ballymoney and worked in the Blackstaff weaving and spinning mill situated in 77 Springfield Road. She gave birth to Joseph Collin, her sixteenth child, on the evening of 15 January 1926 having worked in the mill that morning and returned to work the following day.[53] Elizabeth's oldest daughter Mary joined her in the mill until its closure when she was forced to migrate to the United States in search of employment. It was into this discouraging situation that the Daughters of Charity had been invited thirty years previously to attend to the social and pastoral needs of the mill workers in their homes.

The division of work in the mills of West Belfast was on the basis of religious affiliation. Protestant women, especially Presbyterians, were given preferential treatment; they held the more prestigious jobs, which of course gained a higher, albeit small, wage. The more attractive jobs of the time included milliners, dressmakers, seamstresses and machine workers, all at the cleaner end of the linen-making process. Higher remuneration was not the

---

[50] Ulster Folk Museum, *Linen: Continuity and Change.*
[51] Ibid.
[52] J. Bardon, *Belfast: An Illustrated History* (Belfast, 1982), p. 126.
[53] Interview with Joseph Collin McCann, 14 December 2006.

only benefit of these posts. Most importantly, they did not have the health risks associated with jobs of a lower status. Some Catholic women managed to get jobs as spinners, but most were confined to the preparing rooms, with their attendant health hazards.[54] The rest of the economically active female population had to make do with menial work as washerwomen, factory labourers, street traders and servants, which allowed them barely enough to eke out a meagre existence.

While it is obvious that prospects for the newly arrived migrant to Belfast were modest enough, industrial employment was still preferred by many rural girls, holding out the possibility of independence and marriage and stimulated chain migration to the city. The rate of urbanisation in Belfast, illustrated in Figure 11:2, far outstripped any other city or town in Ireland.

Figure 11:2 Rate of urbanisation in Belfast

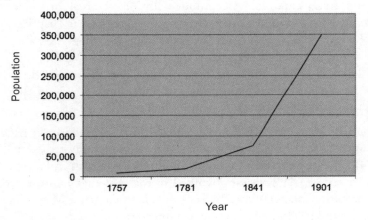

Inter-regional migrants came mainly from the surrounding counties of Antrim, Down, Armagh and Tyrone, making Belfast's population almost entirely Ulster in origin. Figures for 1759 estimate the Roman Catholic percentage at 6.6 per cent; by 1861 the Catholic percentage reached a peak of 34.1 per cent. By 1901, the Catholic percentage had fallen to 24.3 per cent, but that was within a greatly enlarged administrated area. The 1901 census reveals how spatially concentrated the Catholic population was, with 40 per cent to be found in the Falls-Smithfield ward of West Belfast, leading to serious overcrowding and tensions at the interface with similarly poor and densely packed industrial–residential areas dominated by Protestant workers.

---

[54] J. Grant, *One Hundred Years with the Clonard Redemptorists* (Dublin, 2003), p. 29.

The amelioration of the worst aspects of factory employment was a slow, tortuous process. Industrialists as a group lobbied strenuously against state regulation of the hours and conditions of labour. They were supported in their opposition by well-meaning sympathisers who feared any limitation on the hours women might work would throw them out of employment.[55] It was only through a succession of factory acts, where each clause was hotly contested, that limits were placed on the hours a woman or child might work, minimum sanitary provisions were specified, basic health and safety regulations imposed, rules laid down for the regulation of unhealthy trades and processes, and the responsibility of the employer for the condition of the workplace spelt out. The Factory and Workshop Bill of 1895 was stripped of several clauses, including those restricting the overtime worked by women in the 'sweated trades' before it became law in Ireland and Britain.[56]

The restriction of the 'legal working day' for textile factories employing women and children to twelve hours was a single achievement, while by the end of the decade there was a grudging acceptance that the protection of workers did not in fact undermine the economic viability of the industries thus regulated.[57] But even where the minimal provisions of the factory acts were met, the improvements in the position of the employees were modest. Trade unionism was still underdeveloped among the largely female mill workers of Belfast. In other sectors trade unionism was well established; unions of Belfast metal workers dated from 1826, when the Iron Moulders Union was formed, and other unions representing the interests of heavy trades quickly followed.[58] Possibly because there were few male employees among the great mass of low-paid workers, the linen industry failed to unionise. Religious divisions also served to overshadow grievances common to Protestant and Catholic mill workers and to dissuade workers from confronting a largely Protestant management.[59]

The women mill workers were provocatively, but not inaccurately, described as 'linen slaves' by the socialist and trade unionist James Connolly on a visit to Belfast in 1913. The historian J. C. Beckett argues that unionised groups did in fact contribute to the divisions in the city, stating that 'unionised groups formed Belfast's artisan and largely Protestant working class elite'.[60] It is difficult to discuss the involvement of the sisters when they first arrived as it was new territory for them. It is likely that Sister Josephine made tentative steps in her

---

[55] S. Webb, 'Women and the Factory Acts', *Fabian Tract*, 67 (London, 1896), pp. 3–4, 9.

[56] Ibid., p. 9.

[57] Ibid., p. 10.

[58] P. Bew, 'Politics and the Rise of the Skilled Working Man' in J. C. Beckett et al., *Belfast: The Making of the City* (Belfast, 2006), p. 143.

[59] M. Green, *Mill to Millennium* (Belfast, 1996), p. 20.

[60] Ibid.

involvement in the mill workers' lives by getting to know them in their homes when called to assist an ill or dying person. Direct involvement in the mills was unlikely until the sisters had established themselves and they did so through the 'half-timers' from St Vincent's school. Integration into an established system and community takes time.

Accommodation for migrant workers

Charged with home visitation, the Daughters of Charity were very quickly face-to-face with the harsh realities of domestic life in West Belfast. The background statistics reveal some of the peculiarities inherent in the housing situation. The Royal Commission on Housing in Ireland in 1885 identified that Belfast had some of the best houses in the United Kingdom; in fact the housing stock quadrupled between 1870 and 1900, and most of these were for rent. However, in 1900 at least ten thousand of the houses lay vacant as those in need of housing could not afford the rent and the available houses were for the most part located too far from the mills in the west of the city.[61] Subletting and overcrowding were widespread in West Belfast in the 1890s, while ownership of the housing stock was concentrated in the hands of mill owners, who gave little thought to their tenants' welfare. Inspectors' reports testify to appalling conditions:

> 1800 houses … in stinking unpaved courts … so that it would seem to be an understood law of nature that the indigent do not actually require as much fresh air as the wealthy … The great majority of the poorer class of houses … consist of four rooms … each of seven to ten feet square … in two storeys [and] we have known … so many as eighteen or even twenty persons sleeping within them.[62]

The overcrowding problem was exacerbated by the fact that much of the finishing process on fine linen articles was done in the homes. These workers were known locally as 'spriggers' and often consisted of mothers and daughters working together. They were at the bottom of the pay scale and their working conditions were deplorable. 'They worked long hours in ill-lit homes for a few pence an hour. This was known as 'sweated' labour, and the labour movement fought long and hard to eradicate the practice.[63]

Young migrant workers sought the cheapest possible accommodation in the shadow of the mills. Poor families, though already overcrowded, were quick to take in paying lodgers to supplement their modest incomes, while some

---

[61] J. Bardon, *Belfast: An Illustrated History* (Belfast, 1982).
[62] Ulster Folk Museum, *Linen: Continuity and Change.*
[63] P. Collins, *The Irish News*, p. 36.

premises were devoted entirely to this class of resident, who would endure minimal standards for the few short hours they would not be at work. In his initial invitation to the Daughters of Charity, Bishop Henry wanted the sisters to provide supervised accommodation for girls who were forced to seek lodging in these homes. He hoped that the sisters might take the young women 'out of the lodging houses which are far from satisfactory retreats in many cases'.[64] Although the contract of 31 May 1900 stipulated the provision of hostel-type accommodation it did not to materialise until 1917 when the sisters themselves with some local people organised a sale of work and a bazaar. The modest proceeds of this venture with other donations were used to build a hostel on the junction of Clonard Street and Dunmore Street. Although not used as a residential building since 1958 the derelict building is still referred to with affection by the older local people as 'the Home'.

Conclusion

Belfast in the late 1800s was a unique city on the island of Ireland with a developing industrial economy. Urbanisation had made an indelible mark on the lower course of the River Lagan. Rural to urban migration was the main process that fuelled the exponential growth of the city which was segregated on sociocultural grounds. Intra-regional migrants came primarily to work in the manufacturing industry which characterised contemporary Belfast as the main industrial core of the island. The geography of opportunity determined the location of particular industries in the city. The stretch of land to the west, with many streams from Divis Mountain, favoured the siting of linen mills in the Smithfield ward. Moreover the population structure, particularly in West Belfast, was skewed in favour of females in the working and hence child-bearing cohorts. It was to the densely populated lower Falls-Smithfield area of the city that the Daughters of Charity were invited with a specific mandate to minister to women.

The invitation extended to the Daughters was precise. The dearth of provision for the education of girls referred to as the 'half-timers' was recognised by Bishop Henry. The De la Salle Brothers had started St Gall's school for boys who worked in the mills, the Daughters of Charity were then charged with staffing St Vincent's as a sister school for girls. This was to be the focus of work and the means of financial support for the four specially selected sisters who arrived, without fanfare, on 1 May 1900. In due course, other sisters came to join the local community in Clonard House – or 'the Convent' as it was referred to – and began home visitation. The third request of Bishop Henry, that of providing suitable accommodation for Catholic female

---

[64] Bishop Henry to Sr Provincial, 17 September 1896, PA:DC/Dunardagh/Belfast.

migrants, seeking employment particularly in the mills, took longer to fulfil. The hostel or 'the Home' as it was affectionately known was not available for occupation until 1917, nine years after the death of Bishop Henry. In conclusion, a significant point to note is that at the time of writing the work for which the Daughters of Charity were invited by Bishop Henry into the Diocese of Down and Connor in the latter part of the nineteenth century, is still the main work of the sisters in Belfast – education, home visitation, and hostel work.

Map 11:1 West Belfast linen production in the early 1900s

Areas of linen production

1. Clonard House
2. Site for 'Home' built 1917
3. St Vincent's School for half-timers,
   Dunlewey Street

Chapter Twelve

Irish Daughters of Charity on International Mission Service

Louise O'Connell DC

This is how you should act if you are to be good Daughters of Charity, going wherever God may wish to send you; to Africa, into Africa, to the army, to the Indies, to whichever places ask for you; it does not matter; you are Daughters of Charity and so you must go.[1]

The Company of the Daughters of Charity has been missionary from its foundation days in 1633 in Paris. The founders, Vincent de Paul and Louise de Marillac, were always ready to respond to requests for new missions in France, but 'in the beginning the field of action for the Daughters of Charity was limited to Paris'.[2] In 1638, the works began to expand beyond the capital with the foundation of a mission in St-Germain-en-Laye. After that, new foundations were springing up across France. They numbered fifty by 1648. In 1652 a group of sisters went to Warsaw in Poland. Aware that there might be difficulties when the second group of three sisters joined the first group in Poland, Louise de Marillac wrote on 19 August 1655:

I beg you to open wide this heart to allow our three Sisters to enter into this cordial union so that the last three arrivals will be indistinguishable from those who arrived first ... never speak Polish among yourselves without letting our Sisters know what you are saying. This will help them to learn the language more quickly.[3]

The great missionary expansion of the Daughters of Charity came in the nineteenth century; this was due to internal and external circumstances. The social and political turmoil of the French Revolution scattered many religious communities to find refuge in other areas within France or in adjoining countries. The Daughters of Charity were dispersed in many directions, some

---

[1] P. Coste CM, *Saint Vincent de Paul: Correspondence, Conferences, Documents*, vol. 1, ed. and tr. Marie Poole DC (New York: New City Press), p. 105.
[2] J. M., Román, *St Vincent de Paul: A Biography*, tr. Joyce Howard DC (London, 1999), p. 471.
[3] L. Sullivan DC, ed. and tr., *Spiritual Writings of Louise de Marillac: Correspondence and Thoughts* (Brooklyn: New City Press, 1991), p. 478.

returned home, others formed groups in areas far from Paris, others suffered persecution, imprisonment and some were martyred. Those sisters who were martyred at Arras and Angers, have been beatified; the Sisters of Arras in 1920,[4] the Sisters of Angers by Pope John Paul II on 19 February 1984 together with ninety-seven other martyrs.

In the early 1800s the community of the Daughters of Charity was reassembled under Sister Antoinette Deleau and began to recover from the devastation of the Revolution. On 25 March 1813, Napoleon 'ordered the City to purchase and hand over to the Sisters of Charity their present motherhouse at rue du Bac'. In the 1830s the motherhouse on the rue du Bac in Paris became the focus of attention due to the apparition of Our Lady to a young seminary sister, Sister Catherine Labouré. The story of the apparitions and the many graces and conversions attributed to the Miraculous Medal brought worldwide attention to the chapel in rue du Bac and to the Daughters of Charity. Many young women flocked to the motherhouse in Paris.[5] When Sister Marie Azais was directress of formation (1846–8) there were 500 seminary sisters in the motherhouse.[6]

Leadership in the Congregation of the Mission helped in the revitalisation of the primitive spirit of the founders; Fr Jean-Baptiste Etienne was superior general from 1843–74 and Fr Antoine Fiat from 1878–1914. During their time in office the Daughters of Charity took root in North and South America, in Asia, the Middle East, in Africa and in several countries in Europe.[7]

Because of religious persecution in Ireland, many young men from Ireland discovered their missionary vocation in France. There were up to fifteen Irishmen in the Congregation of the Mission in the time of Vincent de Paul.[8] In 1647, during the Cromwellian persecution, a group of six of these Irish Vincentians, four priests and two clerical students, arrived in Ireland to give missions. One of them, Thaddeus Lee, not yet ordained, was martyred in the presence of his mother.

With the gradual lifting of the Penal Laws, especially after Catholic Emancipation in 1829, there was a growing awareness of possibilities to participate in the Catholic International Missionary Service. The young indigenous congregations in Ireland were aware of the charitable activities of the French Daughters of Charity through Church leaders of the time. Mary Aikenhead, foundress of the Irish Sisters of Charity, showed awareness of the

---

[4] J. P. Sheedy CM, *A Short History of the Sisters of Charity of St Vincent de Paul* (London, 1951).
[5] Ibid., pp. 34–7.
[6] Notes on lives of deceased sisters, PA:DC/Taiwan (Provincial Archives, Daughters of Charity, Taiwan here abbreviated as PA:DC/Taiwan).
[7] P. Renaudin, *The Sisters of Charity* (Paris, 1930).
[8] J. M., Román, *St Vincent de Paul: A Biography*, pp. 394–5.

work of the Daughters of Charity: 'Once more she [Mary Aikenhead] discussed with Anna Maria and Dr Murray the possibilities of a new religious order that would visit the poor in their homes, something on the lines of the French Daughters of Charity.'[9] Miss Margaret Aylward's 'first structured work among the poor of what soon became her adopted city was through the Ladies' Association of Charity of St Vincent de Paul for the Spiritual and Temporal Relief of the Sick Poor'.[10] They were very active in the poverty-stricken areas of the cities and towns.

During the 1830s the parish priest of St Nicholas North in the city of Galway became aware of the French Sisters of Charity while on a visit to Paris. There he saw 'the Sisters of Charity doing the work which he dreamed of for Galway city'. *The Connaught Journal* of 29 October 1834 reported that Fr Daly was bringing ladies from Galway to France to be trained as Sisters of Charity; who would then return to Galway and work among the poor there.[11] Two ladies returned in 1835 to a convent owned by Fr Daly. The official title given to the convent was 'The Office of Benevolence of the Sisters of Charity'.[12] 'In 1840 there were five "Sisters" ... they were not religious in the sense that they had taken vows. They were committed lay people, working unselfishly with a total devotion to the sick and poor.'[13] One of these, Anne Pritche O'Briene, joined the Sisters of Mercy when they came to Galway on 8 May 1840 at the request of Fr Daly, and she 'was one of the three professed on 1 October 1841 ... For over fifty years she served in Galway ... thirty-four she spent in the Convent of Mercy'.[14]

Young women from Ireland had joined religious congregations in Europe. According to records thirty Irish women joined the Daughters of Charity at the motherhouse in Paris prior to November 1855, the year the Daughters arrived in Drogheda.[15] The missionary journey had really begun for these Irish girls, their training and formation was through the French language, their companions were from many nationalities and diverse languages. Sisters were frequently missioned from the seminary to distant countries. Sister Teresa O'Callaghan (1820–1909) was sent to work with the poor in Constantinople, Smyrna and to the military hospitals of Lyons and Algiers. Finally she was

---

[9] D.S. Blake CFC, *Servant of the Poor, Mary Aikenhead 1787–1858: Founder of the Religious Sisters of Charity* (Dublin, 2001), p. 22.

[10] J. Prunty, *Margaret Aylward, 1810–1889: Lady of Charity, Sister of Faith]* (Dublin, 1999), p. 22.

[11] Untitled notes by Fr Padraic O'Laoi, Sisters of Mercy, Western Procincial Archives, Galway.

[12] Ibid.

[13] Ibid.

[14] Ibid.

[15] PA:DC/MH (Provincial Archives, Daughters of Charity, Mill Hill, here abbreviated as PA:DC/MH).

asked to lead a group of sisters in the administration of the North Infirmary Hospital in Cork in 1867.[16] Her wealth of experience of hospital administration must have contributed to the quality of the service of the poor in Cork and to the beginnings of the community in Ireland.[17] Sister Bridget Fleming from Duleek, Co. Louth went to Panama in 1886 and was later missioned to Rio de Janeiro in 1889 where she died in 1920. Her sister, Marie Fleming, spent most of her community life in France.

Sister Alice O'Sullivan from Clonmel was directed to the Daughters of Charity by her brother Daniel O'Sullivan CM.[18] She entered the community in 1856, in Paris and was first missioned to Boulogne. Sister O'Sullivan was missioned to China in 1863. She was among the ten Daughters of Charity martyred in Tianjin in 1870.

In fact, there was a continuous presence of Irish Daughters of Charity in China from 1863 until 1952. Following the Boxer Revolution, non-Chinese members of religious communities were forced to withdraw from the country. In total, sixteen Irish Daughters of Charity were missioned to China in the nineteenth and twentieth centuries.[19] As expressed by one author:

> A Sister of Charity may be for years engaged in hospital duty in England, in France, in Germany or in Italy. On a particular morning, she may receive an order to start for China, the following day. No leave-taking of friends, no packing up of luggage, no elaborate arrangements for this long journey of sixteen thousand miles![20]

In the same spirit, the sisters have continued to serve as missionaries in countries such as Albania, Australia, Cook Islands, Ethiopia, China, Japan, Nigeria, Sierra Leone, Romania, Fiji and Kenya. The province of Ireland has also responded to appeals for sisters to engage in humanitarian relief in times of crisis.

Glimpses of the China story

> The arrival of Sr Laporte, the last remaining foreign member of the Sisters of Charity of St Vincent de Paul who was recently expelled from Shanghai, brings the endeavour of a century to a close in China.[21]

---

[16] PA:DC/MH.
[17] Ibid.
[18] Sisters of Charity of St Vincent de Paul, *Pioneer sisters of Charity of St Vincent de Paul in Great Britain and Ireland* (London, 1955), p. 59.
[19] See Appendix I.
[20] J. N. Murphy, 'Les Dames de la Charité', *Terra Incognita* (London, 1873).
[21] W. O'Hara, *The End of a Chapter*, Unpublished, PA:DC/MH2.

The missionary journey began in 1847, when the first group of Daughters of Charity set sail beyond the horizons of previous journeys undertaken by the community, 'The boat from Marseilles to Macau was a long and painful eight months.'[22] One sister died at sea and was buried on Navigator's Island. A second group arrived soon afterwards:

> Misery and uncleanliness reigned; resources were wanting, but despite the difficulties all the Sisters wished to stay. In those first years, four of the twelve sisters missioned to China died, among them Sister Durand, the sister servant, who died shortly after their arrival.[23]

Sister Stephanie Long (1813–94) was missioned to China in 1847. In notes on her life, an example of the extreme poverty of the sisters was recorded: 'Our sisters had no shoes, but the castaway by the Vincentians.'[24] In 1851, the sisters went to Ning Po, under the cover of night.[25] There began the Daughters of Charity presence in mainland China. While in Macau, the sisters had already tried to learn the Chinese language and some of the customs of the local people. They took over the responsibility of the Orphanage of the Holy Childhood in Ning Po. Gradually the Daughters of Charity spread to Shanghai, Peking, Tientsin and other coastal areas.

The sisters who were missioned to China trained in the seminary in Paris, though they were from various countries. This meant that they had at least a working knowledge of the French language. French was the language spoken within the Daughters of Charity community in China. However, in order to work with the people, the sisters had to learn the local language. Some of them did remarkably well. It is said of Sister M. L. Dodot, a native of France (1831–66), missioned to China in 1862, that 'her facility in speaking the language, her knowledge of medicine and her attention to the sick daily attracted a multitude of poor who demanded her attention'.[26] When sisters volunteered for the mission in China, they had to learn French to be able to communicate within the community and the local language in order to work with the people. This was a great challenge for sisters from Ireland. It is said of Sister Bridget Coleman from Co. Wexford, that she had 'very little French and no Chinese'[27] yet she spent seventeen years in Pekin, Shanghai and Tienstsin. She spent many years of loving devoted service in the Holy Childhood Infirmary at the Pekin Orphanage.[28] She died of consumption in 1934.[29]

---

[22] Note on lives of deceased sisters, PA:DC/Taiwan.

[23] Ibid.

[24] Ibid.

[25] Ibid.

[26] Ibid.

[27] Ibid.

[28] M. H. L., *Sister Xavier Berkeley (1861–1944): Sister of Charity of St Vincent de Paul: Fifty-Four Years a Missionary in China* (London, 1949), pp. 119–20.

[29] Notes on the lives of deceased sisters, PA:DC/Taiwan.

Sister Alice O'Sullivan was the first Irish Daughter of Charity to go on mission to China. She was born in the town of Clonmel, Co. Tipperary in 1836, the second youngest of a family of five children. Her parents had moved from Newry, Co. Down to a house near the West Gate in Clonmel. Her mother died soon after the birth of Francis, the youngest child, and the children were cared for by a nurse. Alice was spoiled by the very pious and devoted servant of the family.[30]

Alice attended the Presentation convent schools in Clonmel. Her former teachers 'speak with deep affection of their pupil'. The Sisters of Charity had recently arrived in the town and Alice, who was just ten years old, asked to be admitted as a postulant, but was told she was too young.[31] Alice continued her education at the Dominican Convent in Dún Laoghaire; a former school friend described Alice as 'rather older than most of her companions, small, dark in complexion, not possessing a keen sense of humour, mature common sense and genuine piety'.[32]

In consultation with her brother Daniel, who was a Vincentian priest, she left her family at barely 19 years of age and went to Amiens, in France, for her postulancy. Alice entered the Paris seminary on 30 January 1856. This was a huge step into the unknown, especially because of language and cultural differences. At that time the seminary had over five hundred young sisters coming from many countries. There Sister O'Sullivan met Sister Azais who was for twenty years involved in the seminary formation team in Paris. Sister Azais was missioned to China in 1861 and was the sister visitatrice there until 1870.[33]

Sister O'Sullivan, on receiving the habit of the Daughters of Charity, was missioned for a short while to St Mary's Boulogne in 1857. A letter dated 12 August 1925 from the Maison Sainte-Marie and written by the sister servant, Sister Leplat, includes the following information: 'A Miss Carthwright, an old lady of eighty years, states that she knew Sister O'Sullivan in Boulogne. That she was a happy person, but who wished to be missioned in China and have the grace of martyrdom.'[34]

When Sister O'Sullivan was missioned to Drogheda it must have brought her great joy to return to Ireland. Her love of Drogheda is echoed in later years when she wrote in a letter from Tianjin, China, 'I send you a few lines to remind you of me who has never forgotten you since she was entrusted to your maternal care in dear old Drogheda.'[35] Her five years in Drogheda are reflected

---

[30] Áine M. Chadwick, 'Alice O'Sullivan, Clonmel missionary and martyr (1836–1870)', *Tipperary Historical Journal* (2001).
[31] Ibid.
[32] *Pioneer Sisters of Charity of St. Vincent de Paul*, p. 59.
[33] Notes on lives of deceased sisters, PA:DA/Taiwan.
[34] PA:DC/MH.
[35] Ibid.

in an account by Sister Catherine McGuire (who later led the first group of Daughters of Charity to Australia). She wrote,

> In the early days of the sisters in Drogheda about 1857–58 their work then consisted of visiting the poor and a night school for factory girls. One of the ladies here [Mary Byrne] who was then in Sister O'Sullivan's class is living still and tells us that she was a most generous and self-sacrificing sister, devoted to the girls and she gave them instructions in an old hay loft.[36]

Sister O'Sullivan made her first vows in Drogheda. On leaving Drogheda she was missioned to Bullingham, Hereford for a short while before being chosen in 1863 for the China mission. Sister Alice was not aware of the political turmoil in the Chinese Empire, as a result of the Opium Wars (1837–42). She was unaware of the Treaty of Tientsin in 1857, which gave trading concessions to European companies and allowed Catholic and Protestant missionaries to move from the port areas to places inside the Empire. A group of sisters sailed from Marseilles in 1863, to join an international group of Daughters of Charity already working in China. In a letter to her brother Fr Daniel in St Vincent's Sunday's Well, Cork, dated 6 October 1863 she describes her joy at meeting the Daughters of Charity at Alexandria. She appreciated their hospitality, saying, 'We arrived just in time for breakfast.' In the streets, she explains, she saw 'many asses and camels and women that had their faces quite covered with a black cloth and two holes in it for their eyes'. She wrote about her journey to Cairo passing through the land of the Nile and her first experience of mosquitoes.[37] On board the ship again they continued their voyage to Singapore, Saigon, Hong Kong and then to Shanghai in a smaller boat.

When they arrived in Shanghai the sisters discovered that there were no preparations so they went with the two sisters who welcomed them to Ning Po and awaited developments. Sister Alice discovered that the administrators did not speak French and her superior did not speak English. She became the interpreter, negotiator and peacemaker and she acquired a new name, Sister Gabriel after Gabriel Perboyre, a member of the Congregation of the Mission who was martyred in China on 11 September 1840. Sister O'Sullivan admitted she was a little lonely but refers to a visit from Irish soldiers and gives an account of how thirty soldiers came to see her and gave her £5 for the poor. They went to the chapel and said the rosary and the sister servant gave them pictures of the Pope. At the end of the letter she asks for news of her father.[38]

---

[36] PA:DC/MH.
[37] Sister Alice O'Sullivan to her brother Fr Daniel O'Sullivan CM, PA:CM/Raheny (typed from the handwritten letter by Fr J. Murphy CM).
[38] Ibid.

Her work in Shanghai was successful because eventually the opposition and lack of a warm welcome by the hospital committee was overcome, especially by the sisters' Christian charity and devotion to the poor in the city.[39]

In 1867, Sister O'Sullivan was missioned to Peking, now called Beijing, to the Holy Childhood Orphanage and once again assumed the name Sister Louise. The Society of the Holy Childhood was a missionary society founded during the Pontificate of Pope Pius IX. It was for the welfare of babies and to establish orphanages, schools and workshops to promote the Christian faith. Despite her bright personality and her ease in dealing with difficulties, the continuous tensions caused by political unrest, the demanding work, her homesickness and the overwhelming poverty of life around her took its toll. She wrote to Fr Etienne, the superior general in Paris, and asked to return to France. Her request was granted.[40] Sister Azais, the visitatrice, was about to return to France for the Jubilee celebrations and Sister O'Sullivan was asked to accompany her. They set out on the journey and travelled to Tientsin, to board a ship for Europe.

As in Peking, the sisters in Tientsin were always overwhelmed by work and were short of help. When this Irish sister arrived the sisters saw an answer to prayer in their search for added help in the new foundation of a hospital for Europeans. The sisters begged Sister Alice to stay and help, but she was steadfast in her wish to return to Paris. A visit to the new Church of Notre Dame des Victoires changed Sister Louise's intentions. She hastened to find Sister Azais and tell her that she was at her disposal to remain in China if she thought it was God's will. Sister Azais travelled onwards to Paris leaving Sister O'Sullivan to continue her work in Tientsin.

Tensions were rising in various areas in China between the native Chinese people and the Europeans and as the Daughters of Charity were Europeans they were regarded with suspicion. The work of caring for orphan girls brought further suspicions on the sisters as did their practice of visiting the homes of the poor without a male escort. As tension mounted, the sisters confined their activities to the orphanage and cared for all who came to them for help.[41] During June 1870, the tension gave rise to riots and violence in the city and many Europeans were killed. Members of the Congregation of the Missions, both Chinese and non-Chinese were killed in their church and house. The orphanage was attacked on 21 June in the afternoon. The sisters had attempted to place the children in safety and had gathered in the chapel of the orphanage. Ten members of the Daughters of Charity were killed when the mob broke

---

[39] *The Far East*, July 1919.
[40] Áine M. Chadwick, 'Alice O'Sullivan, Clonmel missionary and martyr', *Tipperary Historical Journal* (2001), p. 86.
[41] *The Far East*, July 1919.

into the compound. Sisters Louise (Alice) O'Sullivan, Josephine Adams (Belgian), Thérèse Lenu (French), Eugénie Pavillon (French), Vittoria Andreoni (Italian), Elizabeth Marquet (Belgian), Vincente Legras (French), Marie Clavelin (French), Louise Violet (French), and Aurélie Tillet (French) were killed as were a number of the children. Some of the Chinese people who had converted to Christianity were also executed during those days.[42] The Revd Charles Henry Butcher MA, British Chaplain at Shanghai writes from there on 6 July 1870:

> The murder of the Sisters of Charity, it is an outrage not on a nation or a church, but on humanity itself. As chaplain to the British Community of Shanghai, I have had opportunities of seeing the noble and devoted work of some of these women, when taking care of the sick at the hospital at this port, before they removed north. One lady, who has been murdered with every circumstance of horror, was an Irish lady whose memory is cherished with affection and gratitude by many of this community.[43]

The Irish lady mentioned was Sister O'Sullivan.

Four years later in 1874, the Daughters of Charity opened a new hospital and dispensary on the site of the destroyed orphanage. Among the first group of Daughters of Charity missioned to Tientsin was Sister Vincent (Catherine) McCarthy from Cork. She was missioned to China from 1873 until her death in 1920 from cholera. Another group of three Irish sisters was missioned to China during the nineteenth century: sisters Jane Murtagh, Marie Ryan and Louise Devane.

The Irish sisters lived in an international community in China. Sister Helen de Jaurias, a French sister called the Heroine of Pe-Tang (1824–1900) is another remarkable missionary. On her journey to China she travelled to London and was welcomed there by the Sisters of Mercy in July 1855 (at that time there was no house of the Daughters of Charity in England) before she embarked on the *Nightingale*, an American vessel bound for China.[44] She spent seven years in Ning Po and was then entrusted with the foundation of a hospital in Shanghai. Having put 'Chinese into her poor brain' she began to study English. Her kindness reached out to Irish soldiers in the English Concession. She was touched by the poverty of their homes and their wives and children. 'Our Irish people gave us consolation. They are so pious, so simply religious!'[45] Her courageous actions during several uprisings and attacks

---

[42] Catholic Truth Society, *Tipperary's Gift to China: Three Apostolic Lives 1863–1898* (Dublin, 1919), pp. 62–4.

[43] *Irish Ecclesiastical Record*, December 1870.

[44] H. Mazeau, *The Heroine of Pe-Tang: Helene de Jaurias, Sister of Charity*, tr. Helené de Jaurias (London, 1928).

[45] Ibid.

saved the lives of many adults and children of all nationalities in her care. Her heroic work in the defence of Pe-Tang eventually took its toll. Soon after the liberation of Pe-Tang she died on 21 August 1900.[46] Sister Helen's letter to Sister O'Sullivan's brother in Cork shows the kindness and concern she showed to members of families who had lost a dear one.[47]

Other sisters too left valuable accounts of their lives and works. The life of Sister Xavier Berkeley, an English sister, gives a detailed account of her contributions to the development of the Holy Childhood works in Ning Po and later in Chusan Island. The remarkable story recorded by Sister Ann Hughes is a good chronicle in the English language of the development of the Company during her life time. Several sisters from Ireland are mentioned, sisters Catherine McCarthy (1841–1920),[48] Margaret Hanley (1876–1924),[49] and Bridget Coleman (1887–1932).[50]

Many Chinese young women joined the Daughters of Charity. The first Chinese Daughter of Charity, Sister Barbara Tchang (1839–1907) was of Tartar origin, of an ancient Christian family. In her seminary training (1864) she quickly mastered the rudiments of the French language and helped in the formation of the Chinese sisters by explaining the rules. During the Boxer Rebellion she helped reorganise the service of the poor in Pekin. She was sincerely grateful to the missionaries 'because without their coming here, I would never perhaps have received the talent of my holy vocation'. Her regret was that she had never seen the motherhouse in Paris.[51] Sister Pauline Souen, who had been a Carmelite sister, felt a strong desire to serve the poor. She was accepted into the Company, but her formation was quickly ended when the Franco-Chinese war broke out. When it was over, a kind French sister gave her lessons in the French language as well as instructions in community spirituality in the Chinese language. Sister Pauline spent most of her life in Chusan with Sister Xavier Berkeley; she died a few months after Sister Berkeley's death on the feast of Our Lady of Mount Carmel.[52] Sister Mary Ou was the first native Chinese sister to die. Her postulancy had been prolonged because of the difficulty she had experienced attempting to learn the French language.

In the twentieth century many more missionary communities went to China including the Missionary Society of St Columban in 1917. In the 1918 edition of *Far East* there is a photograph of Fr Galvin with Sisters of Charity

---

[46] H. Mazeau, *The Heroine of Pe-Tang: Helene de Jaurias, Sister of Charity*, tr. Helené de Jaurias (London, 1928).
[47] PA:CM/Raheny.
[48] M.L.H, *Sister Xavier Berkeley (1861–1944)*.
[49] Ibid.
[50] Ibid.
[51] Notes on lives of deceased sisters, PA:DC/Taiwan.
[52] M.H.L. *Sister Xavier Berkeley (1861–1944)*.

of St Vincent de Paul, and in another edition several Irish sisters are mentioned such as sisters Alice O'Sullivan, Vincent McCarthy, Mary Manning, Margaret Hanley, and Margaret O'Sullivan.[53] In total there were seventeen Irish sisters missioned to China from 1863 onwards.[54]

Other groups of Daughters of Charity arrived in China from the North American provinces. The first sister from the Emmitsburg province to go to China was Sister Catherine Buschman (1868–1926). She travelled to Paris and joined three French sisters on their journey. She died in Shanghai.[55] The second sister was Sister Joanne O'Connell (1862–1921). Her brother was Bishop Denis J. O'Connell who was born in Cork in January 1849; Sister Joanne, however, was born in Columbia, South Carolina. She went to China in 1898 and died in Tientsin in 1921. The first group of American Daughters of Charity left for China in 1922. Others followed and stayed with the French in Shanghai, where they studied the Chinese language and customs.[56] Sister Clara gives a detailed account of their journey to Japan and onwards to Shanghai in 1925. The sisters found that they felt at home with the sisters in Shanghai although 'there were Sisters from nine different nations all living together in perfect harmony and right at home with one another for all the Sisters from Europe spoke French'.[57]

Tension leading to revolution developed across China during the twentieth century. This led to many Daughters of Charity leaving China and returning to their home provinces. By 1952 all the Irish Daughters of Charity had left China and returned to the province of Great Britain and Ireland. Later, as Christianity was suppressed in China, some sisters went on mission for a time to Japan and others to Taiwan. There were 287 Chinese Daughters of Charity and 75 non-Chinese sisters (mostly French) when the Church was suppressed during the 1950s.

---

[53] *The Far East*, February 1918.
[54] See Appendix I.
[55] PA:DC/Emmitsburg/USA.
[56] Clara Groel DC, *White Wings in Bamboo Land* (Emmitsburg, 1973).
[57] Ibid., pp. 20–2.

Appendix I

Irish Daughters of Charity on International Mission

Carmel Ryan DC

Irish Sisters on Mission in China

First Name	Surname	Entered the Community	China Mission	Other Missions
Alice	O'Sullivan (Clonmel)	7 February 1856	1863–1870 (Martyr)	Boulogne, France 1856
Catherine	McCarthy	13 March 1859	1873–1920	
Marie	Ryan	8 March 1873	1882–1882	L'Itay, France 1886
Jane	Murtagh	12 May 1875	1881–1887	Constantinople 1887–1891; Paris 1894–1905
Louise	Devane	27 April 1887	1898–1919	
Alice	O'Sullivan (Cork)	9 August 1895	1906–1942	
Mary	Manning	5 December 1898	1909–1921	Chantilly, France 1906
Margaret	Hanley	6 December 1900	1908–1924	
Margaret	O'Sullivan (Cork)	24 April 1904	1920–1930	
Bridget	Gilmore	6 August 1909	1929–1951	
Susan	Neenan	19 May 1912	1925–1949	
Mary Ellen	O'Connell	1 August 1913	1925–1951	
Bridget	Coleman	30 May 1914	1925–1932	
Pius	Donagh	12 August 1914	1935–1952	
Bridget	Fogarty	24 April 1915	1923–1928	
Margaret	Quinn	2 August 1935	1947–1948	Ismail, 1952; Port Said, Egypt 1952; Italy, 1953; Nazareth, 1964
Louise	O'Connell	3 March 1961	1999–2001	Nigeria 1975–1998; Kenya 2012–Present

Irish Sisters on Mission in Australia

First Name	Surname	Entered the Community	Australian Mission	Other Missions
Catherine	McGuire	26 October 1902	1926–1954	Born in the USA; Pioneer sister on this mission
Elizabeth	Bacon	13 March 1909	1927–1945	
Elizabeth	Fagan	25 January 1914	1926–1959	Pioneer sister on this mission
Marie	Leonard	21 November 1919	1926–1969	Pioneer sister on this mission
Margaret	Brohan	14 August 1914	1927–1949	
Hanorah	Hayes	15 May 1910	1929–1930	
Mary	Minogue	29 January 1911	1929–1952	
Julia	Martin	24 June 1916	1930–1952	
Ellen	Hurley	21 August 1921	1948–1954	
Elizabeth	Barrett	30 January 1923	1936–1979	
Kate	McCarthy	13 August 1923	1929–1935	
Margaret	Roche	8 February 1925	1933–1971	
Margaret	Murphy	6 December 1925	1936–2000	
Johanna	Lyons	16 February 1927	1948–1999	
Mary	Reaper	6 August 1927	1933–1977	
Catherine	Ross	17 July 1927	1933–1986	
Kathleen	Slevin	14 April 1929	1947–1958	
Agnes	Polley	23 March 1931	1936–1954	
Ellen	O'Sullivan	20 December 1931	1954–1963	
Bridget	Cleary	14 February 1938	1946–1972	
Bridget	Coakley	13 January 1936	1949–1989	
Mary	Lambert	1 December 1944	1954–1964	
Jane	Clonan	21 May 1960	1975–1995	

Irish Sisters on Mission in Ethiopia

First Name	Surname	Entered the Community	Ethiopian Mission	Other Missions
Catherine	Tierney	19 June 1940	1990–1993	
Margaret	Cunnane	12 May 1941	1956–1968	Lebanon 1968; Philippines 1968; Bolivia 1969–1970
Catherine	Whelan	9 May 1943	1958–1967	Nigeria 1969–1971; Rue du Bac, Paris 1971
Helen	Lally	30 September 1943	1970–1997	
Barbara	Walsh	7 October 1944	1983–1987	
Teresa	O'Rourke	19 February 1947	1982–1984	
Mary	Dixon	1 December 1948	1968–2001	Nigeria 1965–1967; Kenya 2001–2004
Margaret	Manley	2 March 1949	1986–1988	
Catherine	Gaynor	17 July 1951	1969–2005	Nigeria 1963–1968
Margaret	Twomey	24 November 1951	Summer Schools 1992	Tanzania 1997–1998; Vietnam 2000
Anna	McDonagh	27 April 1956	1970–1974	
Kate	Lehane	23 May 1956	Famine Relief 1985	
Anne	McDermott	6 December 1956	1977–1989	
Margaret	Brady	30 May 1958	1980–1994	
Zoe	O'Neill	19 February 1959	1973–1990	Somalia Relief Work 1992; Sudan Relief Work 1993; Rwanda Relief Work 1995
Rosaleen	Mac Mahon	12 March 1959	1967–1983	
Julie	Ryan	7 March 1961	1989–1990	
Helena	Gormally	16 September 1961	1974–1997	

Irish Sisters on Mission in Ethiopia (cont.)

First Name	Surname	Entered the Community	Ethiopian Mission	Other Missions
Margaret	Coyne	9 August 1962	1983–1991; 1993–2007	
Maeve	Murray	8 March 1963	1974–1977	
Kathleen	Farrelly	15 May 1963	Famine Relief 1985	Sierra Leone 1996–1997
Mary	Mitchell	8 September 1963	1996–Present	
Mai	O'Connor	7 August 1964	1990–1998	
Marguerite	Buckley	5 July 1966	Famine Relief 1984–1985	
Mary	McGrath	10 November 1966	1985–1986	Nigeria 1987–1989
Helen	Byrne	10 November 1966	1994–1995	Nigeria 1987–1989
Olive	Young	7 May 1968	1979–1985	
Anna	Kennedy	12 April 1976	Famine Relief 1984–1985	Nigeria 1990–1995
Brenda	Hunter	1 May 1978	1997–1999	Nigeria 2001–Present

Irish Sisters on Mission in Nigeria

First Name	Surname	Entered the Community	Nigerian Mission	Other Missions
Angela	Gibbons	23 October 1937	1979–1996	
Maeve	O'Sullivan	3 December 1939	1985–1996	
Imelda	McCarthy	4 December 1940	1947–1995	
Catherine	Whelan	9 May 1943	1969–1971	Ethiopia 1958–1967; Rue du Bac, Paris, 1971
Gabriel	Hughes	26 November 1945	1963–1980	Born in Scotland, Pioneer sister in this mission
Magdalen	Higgins	22 June 1946	1979–1993	
Mary	Dixon	1 December 1948	1965–1968	Ethiopia 1968–2001; Kenya 2001–2004
Maura	McCullen	10 February 1950	Relief Work 1984	
Rita	Fallon	10 December 1950	1974–1999	
Paula	Ronayne	13 August 1951	1980–1995	
Pauline	Lawlor	24 November 1951	1973–1976	Rue du Bac, Paris 1991–1997; Canada 1998–2000
Elizabeth	O'Leary	24 November 1951	1977–1991	
Angela	Hender	24 November 1951	1977–2000	
Elma	Hurley	25 November 1952	1977–2003	
Alice	Daly	20 May 1953	1963–1967 1969–1995	Pioneer sister in this mission; Kenya 2001–2014
Bridget	O'Connor	2 December 1954	1970–2003	

Irish Sisters on Mission in Nigeria (cont.)

First Name	Surname	Entered the Community	Nigerian Mission	Other Missions
Rose	Harte	27 January 1956	1978–1982	
Louise	Steen	6 March 1956	1966–1988	
Nora	Lally	25 April 1957	1970–1999	
Bernadette	Fennessy	28 May 1957	1995–1997	
Margaret	Casey	9 April 1958	1972–1985	
Peig	O'Brien	16 June 1960	1972–1997	Kenya 2008–Present
Louise	O'Connell	3 March 1961	1975–1998	China 1999–2001 Kenya 2012–Present
Catherine	Mulligan	8 May 1961	1973–1979	
Caitríona	MacSweeney	7 May 1962	1981–1998	Sudan Relief Work 1999; Iran Relief Work 2004
Christina	Quinn	26 February 1964	1977–2004	
Claire	Sweeney	5 March 1964	1981–1982	
Annette	O'Shea	5 March 1964	1999–2010	Rwanda Relief Work 1994
Helen	Byrne	10 November 1966	1987–1989	Ethiopia 1994–1995
Mary	McGrath	10 November 1966	1987–1989	Ethiopia 1985–1986
Marian	Lucey	5 July 1967	1976–1980	
Geraldine	Naughton	5 May 1967	1979–1988	Sierra Leone 1989–1994
Michelle	Nyhan	5 July 1967	1984–1991	Sudan Relief Work 1993
Geraldine	Henry	14 May 1968	1998–2008	Sierra Leone Relief Work 1996; Romania Relief Work 1998

Irish Sisters on Mission in Nigeria (cont.)

First Name	Surname	Entered the Community	Nigerian Mission	Other Missions
Ann Marie	Moynihan	2 May 1969	2001–2002	
Catherine	Kelly	25 March 1970	1983–1990	
Nora	O'Riordan	27 April 1971	1987–1988	
Angela	Burke	15 March 1974	1995–1997	
Anna	Kennedy	12 April 1976	1990–1995	Ethiopia Relief Work 1984–1986
Mary	O'Toole	13 March 1978	1992–1999	
Brenda	Hunter	1 May 1978	2001–Present	Ethiopia 1997–1999
Anita	Hubrich	27 March 1980	1997–2003	Sierra Leone 1989–1993; Kenya 2005–Present

Irish Sisters on Mission in Sierra Leone

First Name	Surname	Entered the Community	Sierra Leone Mission	Other Missions
Johanna	Twomey	26 February 1943	1994–1995	
Josephine	O'Mahony	10 December 1950	1992–1995	
Joan	Moriarty	25 November 1952	1989; and for two other short periods	Romania 1992, 2001, 2002 for short periods
Catherine	Mathews	20 December 1952	1993–1994	
Patricia	Maxwell	2 December 1954	1989–1997	Fiji 2000
Nuala	Dolan	1 February 1957	Relief Work 1992	
Eileen	O'Callaghan	19 February 1959	1989–1997	Kenya 2001
Carmel	McArdle	18 February 1960	1989–1994	
Nora	Corkery	7 March 1962	1990–1994	
Kathleen	Farrelly	15 May 1963	1996–1997	Ethiopia 1985
Loretto	Kelly	14 June 1964	1989–1991	Rue du Bac 2005–2012
Geraldine	Naughton	5 May 1967	1989–1994	Nigeria 1979–1988
Anna	Byrne	12 April 1976	Relief Work 1993	
Anita	Hubrich	27 March 1980	1989–1993	Nigeria 1997–2003; Kenya 2005–Present

Irish Sisters on Mission in Kenya

First Name	Surname	Entered the Community	Kenya Mission	Other Missions
Mary	Dixon	1 December 1948	2001–2004	Nigeria 1965–1967; Ethiopia 1968–2001
Alice	Daly	20 May 1953	2001–2014	Nigeria 1963–1967; Nigeria 1969–1995
Louise	McEvaddy	30 January 1958	2005 Relief Work	
Éilis	O'Kelly	9 August 1958	2004 Relief Work; 2005–Present	
Eileen	O'Callaghan	19 February 1959	2002–Present	Sierra Leone 1989–1993
Peig	O'Brien	16 June 1960	2008–Present	Nigeria 1972–1997
Louise	O'Connell	3 March 1961	2012–Present	Nigeria 1975–1998; China 1999–2001
Catherine	Mulligan	8 May 1961	2006–Present	Nigeria 1973–1979
Mary Ann	Walsh	29 April 1965	2001–2010	Romania Relief Work 1994; Romania Relief Work 1997
Áine	O'Brien	2 May 1969	2011–Present	
Mary	Holland	23 July 1975	2002–Present	Albania Relief Work 1999
Anita	Hubrich	27 March 1980	2005–Present	Sierra Leone 1989–1993; Nigeria 1997–2003

Irish Sisters on Mission elsewhere overseas

First Name	Surname	Entered the Community	Place of Mission
Margaret	Murphy	2 January 1857	Val de Grace, Paris 1868–1869
Ann	Kavanagh	28 January 1857	Constantinople 1857; Naples, Italy 1860; Cava Hospital 1862
Theresa	Broe	20 February 1857	Amiens, France 1857–1860; Vincennes, France 1860–1863
Mary Anne	Costello	14 March 1858	Val de Grace, Paris 1858–1860
Mary	Kavanagh	21 April 1858	Val de Grace, Paris 1858–1861
Margaret	O'Grady	25 June 1858	La Roche-Guyan, France 1858–1868
Ellen	Doyle	28 June 1858	Enghien, Paris 1859–1860; Paris 1890–1896
Catherine	O'Shea	20 October 1858	Val de Grace, Paris 1859
Anne	Byrne	12 May 1859	Smyrna, Turkey 1859; Madrid, Spain 1864; Burgo d'Osma, Spain 1894; Malaga, Spain
Bridget	Duffy	22 October 1859	Paris 1860–1861; Cádiz Hospital, Spain 1878–1879
Theresa	Caraher	22 December 1859	Naples, Italy 1860–1863; Paris, France 1863; Clichy, France 1864
Jane	Ginaty	7 September 1860	Pernambuco College, Brazil 1860
Catherine	Cody	14 January 1860	Val de Grace, Paris 1860
Catherine	Ward	20 April 1860	Amiens, France 1860–1861; Paris 1888–1891
Johanna	Murphy	27 August 1860	Vincennes, France 1861–1864
Margaret	Halligan	5 October 1862	Constantinople 1877–1882; L'Itay, France 1882–1887
Bridget	Lannan	13 May 1862	Paris 1862–1863
Anastasia	Walsh	11 April 1863	Liscard, Belgium 1863–1864; Celles, Belgium 1864–1901
Margaret	Mackin	7 December 1864	Santiago, Chile 1871
Mary	McGill	14 April 1864	Val de Grace, Paris 1864
Elizabeth	Thompson	3 January 1869	Bournabat, Turkey 1871–1880; Lyons, France 1880
Catherine	Stewart	7 March 1874	Panama 1886

Irish Sisters on Mission elsewhere overseas (cont.)

First Name	Surname	Entered the Community	Place of Mission
Jane	Murtagh	12 May 1875	China 1881–1887; Constantinople 1887–1891; Paris 1894–1905
Bridget	Fleming	8 July 1876	Panama 1886–1889; Rio de Janeiro, Brazil 1889
Marie	Fleming	19 January 1878	Paris 1890–1891; Montolieu, France 1891–1894
Ann	Johnston	24 April 1878	Peru 1890–1897
Margaret Mary	McCarthy	9 November 1878	Paris, France 1897–1899; Clichy, France 1899
Ellen	Sheridan	31 July 1886	Smyrna, Turkey 1892–1908
Emma	Keelty	12 March 1897	Boulogne, France 1898–1903; Constantinople 1913; Spain 1934
Mary	Manning	5 December 1898	Chantilly, France 1906–1909; China 1909–1921
Anne	Meadows	14 July 1907	Chantilly, France 1914; Haifa, Palestine
Kathleen	O'Reilly	24 April 1909	Ismaïlia, Egypt 1919–1927; Bethlehem 1927
Mary Anne	Bryan	21 April 1913	Pol sur Ternoise, France 1913–1914
Emily	Rafferty	19 June 1925	Rue du Bac, Paris 1932–1966
Margaret	Quinn	2 August 1935	China 1947–1952; Ismailia, Egypt 1952; Port Said, Egypt 1952; Italy 1953; Nazareth 1964
Emily	Godson	22 June 1935	Japan 1948–1949; China 1949–1951
Margaret	Cunnane	12 May 1941	Ethiopia 1956; Lebanon 1968; Philippines 1968; Bolivia 1969
Catherine	Whelan	9 May 1944	Ethiopia 1958–1967; Nigeria 1969–1971; Rue du Bac, Paris 1971–1975
Catherine	McCarthy	24 November 1950	Rue du Bac, Paris 1976–1984
Pauline	Lawlor	24 November 1951	Nigeria 1973–1976; Rue du Bac, Paris 1991–1997; Canada 1998–2000

Irish Sisters on Mission elsewhere overseas (cont.)

First Name	Surname	Entered the Community	Place of Mission
Brenda	O'Neill	24 November 1951	Romania
Louise	O'Brien	25 January 1952	Rue du Bac, Paris 1984–1990
Catherine	Ryder	29 April 1953	Sudan Relief Work 1993
Patricia	Maxwell	2 December 1954	Sierra Leone 1989; Fiji 2000
Josephine	Flynn	26 January 1956	Romania 1995–1997
Zoe	O'Neill	19 February 1959	Ethiopia 1973–1990; Somalia Relief Work 1992; Sudan Relief Work 1993; Rwanda Relief Work 1994
Patricia	McLaughlin	4 July 1959	Fiji 2000–2010
Ann	O'Neill	27 September 1960	Romania 1998
Caitríona	MacSweeney	7 May 1962	Nigeria 1981–1998; Sudan Relief Work 1999; Iran Relief Work 2004
Sheila	Browne	8 March 1963	Cook Islands 2005
Loretto	Kelly	14 March 1964	Sierra Leone 1989–1991; Rue du Bac, Paris 2005–2012
Mary Ann	Walsh	29 April 1965	Romania Relief Work; Kenya 2001–2010
Mary	McGrath	10 November 1966	Sudan Relief Work 1993; Ethiopia 1985–1986; Nigeria 1987–1989
Stella	Bracken	14 May 1968	Romania 1993–1996
Áine	Cahalane	27 June 1975	Fiji 2000–2003
Maura	Houlihan	17 July 1975	Sudan Relief Work 1993
Breege	Keenan	1 May 1978	Brussels, Belgium 1995–1998

Appendix II

Irish Women who joined the Daughters of Charity in France before 1855

Carmel Ryan DC

This appendix contains the names of twenty-nine Irish-born women who joined the Daughters of Charity between June 1843 and August 1855, before the Daughters of Charity were established in Ireland. It shows their place of birth and where they died; gives the names of their parents (where available); the date they joined the community; where they postulated and the different places in which they served.

In post-Famine Ireland many young women left to complete their education on the continent. Those who joined the community first met the Daughters of Charity in France.

The age profile of the women ranged from eighteen to thirty-one. Among this group there were three sets of blood sisters: two Morris sisters from Skryne in Co. Meath, the Martins from Dunshaughlin, Co. Meath, and the Behans from Dublin.

These sisters served in France, Egypt, Chile, Spain, Italy, Turkey, Peru, Guatemala, England, Scotland, Brazil, United States and Panama.

The names of young Irish women are recorded among the pioneer sisters in Drogheda, Fairview and North William Street. Altogether thirteen of them returned to Ireland in the final decades of the nineteenth century as the community developed a variety of works.

This resource allows the reader a glimpse of their courage, strength and determination in their endeavours to take the gospel to the ends of the world. They made a commitment to go 'wherever God may wish to send you; to Africa, into Africa, to the army, to the Indies, to whichever places ask for you; it does not matter; you are Daughters of Charity and so you must go.'[1] These twenty-nine women were the prototypes for those who would follow in their footsteps in the ensuing decades.

---

[1] P. Coste CM, *Saint Vincent de Paul: Correspondence, Conferences, Documents,* vol. 1, ed. and tr. Marie Poole DC (New York: New City Press), p. 105.

Irish women who joined the Daughters of Charity in France before 1855

Name	Date of Birth	Place of Birth	Parents' Names	Entered Comm.	Postulated	Placements	Date of Death
Belinda O'Hara	16 Feb. 1816			6 June 1843	St Médard, Paris (Rosalie Rendu, sister servant)	Amiens, France 1844; Charenton, France 1845 (Left the Community in 1848)	
Dorothy Beahan	3 Nov. 1816	Dublin	Andrew Beahan Sara Linchon	10 Sep. 1844	St Médard, Paris (Rosalie Rendu, sister servant)	Bayonne Hospital, France 1845; Alexandria, Egypt 1847; Santiago, Chile 1853	4 October 1873 (Santiago, Chile)
Teresa O'Callaghan	5 May 1820	Finglas, Dublin	Peter O'Callaghan Mary O'Donovan	25 July 1847	Ménages, Paris	Constantinople 1848; Smyrna, Turkey 1857; Lyon Hospital, France 1858; Algiers Hospital, France 1859; North Infirmary Hospital, Cork 1867	17 June 1909 (North Infirmary Hospital, Cork, Ireland)
Mary McGuiness	15 Aug. 1826	Ennis, Clare		30 May 1848	Manchester	Constantinople 1849; Smyrna, Turkey 1856; Turin, Italy 1859; Granada, Spain 1860; Cartagene 1861; Burgo d'Osma, Spain 1866; Paris 1871; London 1872; Dublin 1872; Paris 1877; Bone Hospital 1880	16 July 1883 (France)

Irish women who joined the Daughters of Charity in France before 1855 (cont.)

Name	Date of Birth	Place of Birth	Parents' Names	Entered Comm.	Postulated	Placements	Date of Death
Margaret King	16 Oct. 1826	West-meath		6 Aug. 1849		Nantes, France 1850; St Germain-en-Laye, France 1851; Meaux Hôpital, France 1852; Constantinople 1854; Meaux, France 1856; Trévira, France 1857; Fairview 1858 (Left the Community in 1859)	
Jane O'Brien	16 Sept. 1818	Dublin	Patrick O'Brien Jane O'Leary	6 Aug. 1849	Notre Dame, Paris	Montrouge, Paris 1850; Constantinople 1854	27 Aug. 1887 (Constan-tinople)
Margaret Martin	30 July 1826	Dun-shaughlin, Meath		14 Aug. 1849	St Médard, Paris (Rosalie Rendu, sister servant)	Alexandria, Egypt 1850	12 Aug. 1853 (Egypt)
Elizabeth Crawford	7 July 1827	West-meath	James Crawford Bridget Magor	21 June 1850	Notre Dame, Paris	Aversa, Italy 1851; North William Street, Dublin 1857; Fairview, Dublin 1857; Paris 1859; Sheffield, England 1860	13 Dec. 1897
Catherine Callery	6 Jan. 1833	Kilbarry, Meath		21 Nov. 1850	Paris	Rue du Bac, Paris 1851; Colombines, France 1852; Alexandria, Egypt 1853; Rue du Bac, Paris 1855 (Left the Community in 1855)	

Irish women who joined the Daughters of Charity in France before 1855 (cont.)

Name	Date of Birth	Place of Birth	Parents' Names	Entered Comm.	Postulated	Placements	Date of Death
Brigid Nowlan	30 Jan. 1824	Dublin		25 Jan. 1851	Notre Dame, Paris	Notre Dame, Paris 1852; United States 1852	14 April 1873
Mary Martin	26 Dec. 1827	Dun- shaughlin Meath		27 Jan. 1851	St Médard, Paris (Rosalie Rendu, sister servant)		23 Nov. 1851
Margaret Rath	12 Jan. 1832	Drogheda, Louth	John Rath Margaret Smyth	24 April 1851	Notre Dame, Paris	Aumale, Paris 1854; St Philippe, Paris 1855; Vincennes, France 1859; Necker Hôpital, France 1861; Paris 1862; Dijon, France 1864; Clichy, France 1867; Valparaiso, Chile 1868; Santiago, Chile 1875; Concepcion, Chile 1876; Panama Canal 1882	13 April 1890 (Central Mission, Guatemala)
Mary Malone	15 June 1831	Stamullen, Dublin	John Malone Mary Gough	12 April 1852	Notre Dame de Loretto, Paris	Tourcoing, France 1852; Le Tréport, France 1856; Drogheda, Ireland 1860; London 1861; Belleville, Paris 1863; Lanark, Scotland 1865; Liverpool, England 1868; Buenos Aires, Argentina 1869	9 Dec. 1894 (Buenos Aires)

Irish women who joined the Daughters of Charity in France before 1855 (cont.)

Name	Date of Birth	Place of Birth	Parents' Names	Entered Comm.	Postulated	Placements	Date of Death
Jane Turner	12 Oct. 1829	Dublin	John Turner Ann Brien	12 April 1852	Notre Dame de Loretto, Paris	Rochefort Marine, France 1852; Little Crosby, England 1860; Melun Hospital, France 1866; Fairview 1883	2 March 1905
Ann Farrell	13 Feb. 1832	Brownstown, Meath	John Farrell Julia McNamara	16 Aug. 1852	Amiens, France	Smyrna, Turkey 1853; Sheffield, England 1857; London 1859; Lanark, Scotland 1861	8 Aug. 1913
Jeanne Morris	25 Dec. 1834	Skryne, Meath	Robert Morris Ann O'Carroll	26 Aug. 1952	Amiens, France	Sedan, France 1853; Drogheda, Ireland 1855; North William Street, Dublin 1857; Sheffield, England 1859; Rue du Bac, Paris 1859; Sedan, France 1861	29 June 1899
Helen MacDonnell	18 Feb. 1819	Dublin		3 March 1853	Hospital for the terminally ill, Paris	Le Havre, France 1853	Left the Community in 1854
Brigid Clarke	11 April 1826	Ireland	Hugh Clarke Mary Lynch	22 Aug. 1853	Hotel Dieu, Amiens, France	Boulogne, France 1854; Constantinople 1855; Sheffield, England 1857	5 Jan. 1893

Irish women who joined the Daughters of Charity in France before 1855 (cont.)

Name	Date of Birth	Place of Birth	Parents' Names	Entered Comm.	Postulated	Placements	Date of Death
Mary Ann Behan	25 July 1827	Dublin	Andrew Behan Sara Linchon	5 May 1854	Hotel Dieu, Amiens, France	Boulogne, France 1854; Amiens, France 1856; North William Street, Dublin 1857	13 April 1883
Mary Halligan	14 Dec. 1834	Kilcock, Kildare	Patrick Halligan Ellen Donnelly	18 July 1854		Drogheda 1857; Liverpool, England 1863; Drogheda 1865; Dublin 1868; London 1869; Hereford, England 1875; Beacon Lane, England 1891	21 Nov. 1903
Mary Ann Morris	28 July 1836	Skryne, Meath	Robert Morris Ann O'Carroll	7 Nov. 1854	Sedan, France	St Philippe, Paris, 1855; St Germain, Paris, 1861; Rue du Bac, Paris 1865	20 Nov. 1888 (Rue du Bac, Paris)
Catherine Doyle	31 Dec. 1828	Dublin		10 Aug. 1854	Amiens, France	Amiens, France 1855; North William Street, Dublin 1857	21 Nov. 1864 (North William Street, Dublin)

Irish women who joined the Daughters of Charity in France before 1855 (cont.)

Name	Date of Birth	Place of Birth	Parents' Names	Entered Comm.	Postulated	Placements	Date of Death
Ann Boylan	23 Jan. 1835	Ratoath, Meath	Christopher Boylan Annie McNamara	9 Dec. 1854	Amiens, France	Smyrna, Turkey 1855; Carlisle Place, London 1864; Little Crosby, England 1866; Drogheda, Ireland; 1872	9 July 1876 (Drogheda, Ireland)
Elizabeth Broe	10 April 1832	Celbridge, Kildare	James Broe Mary Dignan	9 Dec. 1854	Hôtel Dieu, Amiens, France	Val de Grace, Paris 1855; Fairview, Dublin 1863; Val de Grace, Paris 1868; Chateaubourg, France 1868; Rochefort Marine, France 1870; Angers, France 1877	9 Dec. 1903 (Angers Hôpital, France)
Ann Carroll	19 Feb. 1835	Louth		9 Dec. 1854	Hôtel Dieu, Amiens, France	Necker Hôpital, Paris 1855	13 Oct. 1858 (Paris)
Susan Farrell	25 Sept. 1831	Kildare	James Farrell Cherry Kelly	9 Dec. 1854	Hôtel Dieu, Amiens, France	Paris 1855; Fairview, Dublin 1857; Vincennes, France 1860; Fairview, Dublin 1868; Sheffield, England 1874; Cette, France 1885; Montolieu, France 1888; Pau Aliènes, France 1888	7 April 1891 (France)

Irish women who joined the Daughters of Charity in France before 1855 (cont.)

Name	Date of Birth	Place of Birth	Parents' Names	Entered Comm.	Postulated	Placements	Date of Death
Sophie MacDonnell	20 Aug. 1832	Armagh	Daniel McDonnell Bridget Bally	9 Dec. 1854	Amiens, France	Chantilly, France 1855; Constantinople 1856; Avignon, France 1856; Rio de Janeiro, Brazil, 1857; Val de Grace, Paris 1859; Clichy, France 1904	8 Dec. 1907 (Clichy, France)
Mary Waters	2 Jan. 1829	Dublin	Jacob Waters Ann	9 Dec. 1854	Hôtel Dieu, Amiens, France	Senlis, France 1855; Lima, Peru 1860; Callao, Peru 1866; Lima, Peru 1871; Callao, Peru 1874	26 May 1888 (Callao, Peru)
Mary Fleming	7 Dec. 1828	Dublin	George Fleming Elizabeth English	13 Aug. 1855	Amiens, France	Rio de Janeiro College, Brazil 1856	30 Aug. 1894 (Rio de Janeiro, Brazil)

Appendix III

Daughters of Charity recorded in the Censuses of Population of 1901 and 1911

Breege Keenan DC

The Daughters of Charity came to Ireland in 1855 and they completed the census for 1861 and 1871, both of which were destroyed. The censuses 'for 1881 and 1891 were pulped during the First World War, probably because of the paper shortage'.[1] The first full records are those for the 1901 census and are available on the National Archives of Ireland website.[2]

The information in this appendix is taken from the original completed censuses. The headings used in the censuses were: Christian Name; Surname; Relation to the head of family; Religious Profession; Education; Age (in 1911 census 'Ages of Females'); Rank, Profession, or Occupation; Where Born; and Irish Language. In the interest of space, the Irish Language heading has been omitted and a note has been added under the Education heading where necessary. The sisters were listed as female, single; none of them was widowed and none had a disability so these headings are omitted in this resource.

Figure III:1 Ages of sisters listed in the census

Ages of sisters	Census 1901	Census 1911
21–30	27	25
31–40	38	51
41–50	23	44
51–60	21	18
61–70	7	18
71–80	1	4
Total number of sisters	117	160

---

[1] Census of Ireland 1901/1911: National Archives,
<http://www.census.nationalarchives.ie/help/history.html> accessed 21 February 2013.
[2] Ibid.

In 1855, four Daughters of Charity arrived in Drogheda, Co. Louth and by 1901, there were 117 sisters: working in parish ministry, with ex-prisoners, in hospitals, in education and in the workhouse system. By 1911, there were 160 sisters working in Ireland and their ages were recorded on the census.

In the 1901 census, the sisters came from twenty-two counties in Ireland and in 1911 from twenty-five counties, as well as from England, France, Germany, Scotland, India, West Indies and the United States of America. The census forms were generally completed by each sister servant, but in the North Infirmary Hospital, Cork, Daniel Murphy is listed first and there was no signature on the form. In Abbeyleix, Michael Maher is the Head of the Family and signed the form while the three sisters were listed at numbers 8, 9 and 10 on it. Daniel Manning, president of Maynooth College is listed as the Head of the Family and he signed the form for the sisters living in Maynooth. The addresses of the houses differed too, for example, Celbridge in 1901 is listed as 35.1 in Big Lane (Celbridge) and in the 1911 census it was entered as 28.2 in Union Lane (Celbridge). The information that follows is transcribed as it was found in the original documents.

Residents of a house 10.1 in Henrietta Street (Inns Quay, Dublin) 1901
Henrietta Street

Christian Name	Surname	Age	Relation to Head of Family	Religious Profession	Birthplace	Rank, Profession, or Occupation	Education
Felicité	Hurley	62	Head of Institution	Roman Catholic	Cork	Sister of Charity	Read & write
Catherine	Condra	47	Member of Community	Roman Catholic	Meath	Sister of Charity	Read & write
Joseph	Bacon	36	Member of Community	Roman Catholic	Westmeath	Sister of Charity	Read & write
Mary	Organ	37	Member of Community	Roman Catholic	England	Sister of Charity	Read & write

Residents of a house 9 in Henrietta St (Inns Quay, Dublin) 1911
Henrietta Street

Christian Name	Surname	Age	Relation to Head of Family	Religious Profession	Birthplace	Rank, Profession, or Occupation	Education
Felicité Bridget	Hurley	72	Sr of Charity	Roman Catholic	Cork	Sister of Charity	Read & write
Jane M	Murtagh	56	Sr of Charity	Roman Catholic	Meath	Sister of Charity	Read & write
Johanna	O'Malley	36	Sr of Charity	Roman Catholic	Limerick	Sister of Charity	Read & write
Mary	O'Donnell	41	Sr of Charity	Roman Catholic	Kerry	Sister of Charity	Read & write
Catherine	Quirke	35	Sr of Charity	Roman Catholic	Tipperary	Sister of Charity	Read & write
Bridget	O'Sullivan	34	Sr of Charity	Roman Catholic	Donegal	Sister of Charity	Read & write
Teresa	Corcoran	37	Sr of Charity	Roman Catholic	Meath	Sister of Charity	Read & write
Margaret Mary	Tracey	26	Sr of Charity	Roman Catholic	Meath	Sister of Charity	Read & write

Residents of a house 47.1 Fair Street (Westgate, Drogheda Town, Louth) 1901
Drogheda

Christian Name	Surname	Age	Relation to Head of Family	Religious Profession	Birthplace	Rank, Profession, or Occupation	Education
Anne	Redman	57	Head of Family	Roman Catholic	England	Sister of Charity	Read & write
Anne	Kavanagh	66	Boarder	Roman Catholic	Wexford	Sister of Charity	Read & write
Catherine	Fagan	41	Boarder	Roman Catholic	Meath	Sister of Charity	Read & write
Ellen	McDermott	41	Boarder	Roman Catholic	Meath	Sister of Charity	Read & write
Mary	Morgan	33	Boarder	Roman Catholic	Cavan	Sister of Charity	Read & write
Elizabeth	Fagan	38	Boarder	Roman Catholic	West-meath	Sister of Charity	Read & write
Margaret	Nolan	31	Boarder	Roman Catholic	Louth	Sister of Charity	Read & write
Teresa	Boyle	27	Boarder	Roman Catholic	London-derry	Sister of Charity	Read & write
Elizabeth	Donavan	28	Boarder	Roman Catholic	Cork	Sister of Charity	Read & write
Margaret	Molloy	21	Boarder	Roman Catholic	Wexford	Sister of Charity	Read & write
Bridget	McNiff	21	Boarder	Roman Catholic	Sligo	Sister of Charity	Read & write

Residents of a house 59.2 in Fair Street (Fair Gate, Louth) 1911
Drogheda

Christian Name	Surname	Age	Relation to Head of Family	Religious Profession	Birthplace	Rank, Profession, or Occupation	Education
Anne	Redman	67	Head of Family	Roman Catholic	England	Sister of Charity	Read & write
Mary	Fagan	51	Boarder	Roman Catholic	Meath	Sister of Charity	Read & write
Helena	McDermott	51	Boarder	Roman Catholic	Meath	Sister of Charity	Read & write
Brigid	Kelly	52	Boarder	Roman Catholic	Meath	Sister of Charity	Read & write
Elizabeth	Fagan	48	Boarder	Roman Catholic	Westmeath	Sister of Charity	Read & write
Margaret	Forrest	42	Boarder	Roman Catholic	Cork	Sister of Charity	Read & write (Irish and English)
Margaret	Nolan	41	Boarder	Roman Catholic	Louth	Sister of Charity	Read & write
Elizabeth	Scott	35	Boarder	Roman Catholic	Kerry	Sister of Charity	Read & write (Irish and English)
Ada	Corrigan	45	Boarder	Roman Catholic	England	Sister of Charity	Read & write
Agnes	Metcalfe	37	Boarder	Roman Catholic	England	Sister of Charity	Read & write
Susan	Ingham	34	Boarder	Roman Catholic	Dublin City	Sister of Charity	Read & write
Frances	Dardis	36	Boarder	Roman Catholic	Donegal	Sister of Charity	Read & write

Residents of a house 44.1 in North William Street (Mountjoy, Dublin) 1901
North William Street

Christian Name	Surname	Age	Relation to Head of Family	Religious Profession	Birthplace	Rank, Profession, or Occupation	Education
Margaret	Barraud	53	Sister Superior	Roman Catholic	England	Sister of Charity	Read & write
Eugénie	Douai	54	Sr of Charity	Roman Catholic	France	Sister of Charity	Read & write
Edith	Hill	51	Sr of Charity	Roman Catholic	England	Sister of Charity	Read & write
Margaret	O Gorman	40	Sr of Charity	Roman Catholic	Armagh	Sister of Charity	Read & write
Margaret	O Mahoney	42	Sr of Charity	Roman Catholic	Cork	Sister of Charity	Read & write
Mary	Cullen	34	Sr of Charity	Roman Catholic	England	Sister of Charity	Read & write
Anna	Klauser	40	Sr of Charity	Roman Catholic	Germany	Sister of Charity	Read & write
Catherine	McCarthy	29	Sr of Charity	Roman Catholic	Kilmurry	Sister of Charity	Read & write
Mary	Gallagher	28	Sr of Charity	Roman Catholic	Sligo	Sister of Charity	Read & write
Bridget	Collins	36	Sr of Charity	Roman Catholic	Cork	Sister of Charity	Read & write
Catherine	Bugler	39	Sr of Charity	Roman Catholic	Galway	Sister of Charity	Read & write
Mary	Manning	40	Sr of Charity	Roman Catholic	Cork	Sister of Charity	Read & write
Mary	Forshaw	30	Sr of Charity	Roman Catholic	England	Sister of Charity	Read & write
Agnes	Metcalfe	27	Sr of Charity	Roman Catholic	England	Sister of Charity	Read & write
Julia	McGuire	25	Sr of Charity	Roman Catholic	Kildare	Sister of Charity	Read & write

Residents of a house 44 in William St North (Mountjoy, Dublin) 1911
North William Street

Christian Name	Surname	Age	Relation to Head of Family	Religious Profession	Birthplace	Rank, Profession, or Occupation	Education
Margaret	Barraud	64	Superioress of the Institution	Roman Catholic	England	Sister of Charity	Read & write
Eugénie	Douai	66	Sr of Charity	Roman Catholic	France	Sister of Charity	Read & write
Edith	Hill	61		Roman Catholic	England	Sister of Charity	Read & write
Brigid	Collins	46	Community	Roman Catholic	Clonakilty	Sister of Charity	Read & write
Mary	Cullen	45	Member of the Community	Roman Catholic	England	Sister of Charity	Read & write
Mary	Walshe	46	Member of the Community	Roman Catholic	Clare	Sister of Charity	Read & write
Evelyn	Fraser	39	Member of the Community	Roman Catholic	London	Sister of Charity	Read & write
Ann	Keane	42	Member of the Community	Roman Catholic	Kerry	Sister of Charity	Read & write
Mary	Gallagher	38	Member of the Community	Roman Catholic	Sligo	Sister of Charity	Read & write
Catherine	Bugler	44	Member of the Community	Roman Catholic	Clare	Sister of Charity	Read & write
Julia	McGuire	35	Member of the Community	Roman Catholic	Kildare	Sister of Charity	Read & write
Mary	McEvoy	30	Member of the Community	Roman Catholic	Dundalk	Sister of Charity	Read & write
Catherine	Meagher	25	Member of the Community	Roman Catholic	Tipperary	Sister of Charity	Read & write
Mary	Sawey	28	Member of the Community	Roman Catholic	Down	Sister of Charity	Read & write
Brigid	Gilmore	24	Member of the Community	Roman Catholic	Mayo	Sister of Charity	Read & write
Mary	Fitzsimons	23	Member of the Community	Roman Catholic	Cavan	Sister of Charity	Read & write
Elizabeth	McKeon	23	Member of the Community	Roman Catholic	Belfast	Sister of Charity	Read & write
Hanorah	Byrne	74	Member of the Community	Roman Catholic	Wicklow	Sister of Charity	Read & write
Annie	Keogh	25	Member of the Community	Roman Catholic	Tullow	Sister of Charity	Read & write

Residents of a house 1.1 in Convent Avenue (Drumcondra, Dublin) 1901
St Vincent's Hosptial, Fairview

Christian Name	Surname	Age	Relation to Head of Family	Religious Profession	Birthplace	Rank, Profession, or Occupation	Education
Teresa	Butti	62	Superioress	Roman Catholic	England	Sister of Charity	Read & write
Jane	Turner	71	Member of Community	Roman Catholic	Dublin	Sister of Charity	Read & write
Mary	Kavanagh	69	Member of Community	Roman Catholic	Wexford	Sister of Charity	Read & write
Sarah	Byrne	65	Member of Community	Roman Catholic	Wicklow	Sister of Charity	Read & write
Mary	Magill	62	Member of Community	Roman Catholic	Louth	Sister of Charity	Read & write
Johanna	O'Connor	55	Member of Community	Roman Catholic	Limerick	Sister of Charity	Read & write
Mary	Lewis	57	Member of Community	Roman Catholic	England	Sister of Charity	Read & write
Anne	O'Grady	54	Member of Community	Roman Catholic	Mayo	Sister of Charity	Read & write (Irish and English)
Henrietta	Reydellet	45	Member of Community	Roman Catholic	France	Sister of Charity	Read & write
Roseanne	Boyle	40	Member of Community	Roman Catholic	Derry	Sister of Charity	Read & write
Mathilde	Flood	37	Member of Community	Roman Catholic	Cavan	Sister of Charity	Read & write
Anne Maria	Moore	38	Member of Community	Roman Catholic	King's Co.	Sister of Charity	Read & write
Hannah	Hurley	35	Member of Community	Roman Catholic	Cork	Sister of Charity	Read & write
Mary	McInernay	36	Member of Community	Roman Catholic	Meath	Sister of Charity	Read & write
Bridget	Scanlon	28	Member of Community	Roman Catholic	Clare	Sister of Charity	Read & write
Margaret	Levey	28	Member of Community	Roman Catholic	Meath	Sister of Charity	Read & write
Emily	Jung	30	Member of Community	Roman Catholic	England	Sister of Charity	Read & write

Residents of a house 6 in Convent Avenue (Drumcondra, Dublin) 1911
St Vincent's Hospital, Fairview

Christian Name	Surname	Age	Relation to Head of Family	Religious Profession	Birthplace	Rank, Profession, or Occupation	Education
Teresa	Butti	72	Superioress	Roman Catholic	England	Sister Superintendent	Read & write
Sarah	Byrne	75	Nurse	Roman Catholic	Wicklow	Nursing Sister	Read & write
Johanna	O'Connor	65	Nurse	Roman Catholic	Limerick	Nursing Sister	Read & write
Blanche	Reydellet	55	Nurse	Roman Catholic	France	Nursing Sister	Read & write
Anne	O'Grady	64	Nurse	Roman Catholic	Sligo	Nursing Sister	Read & write (Irish and English)
Roseanne	Boyle	50	Nurse	Roman Catholic	Derry	Nursing Sister	Read & write
Mathilda	Flood	47	Nurse	Roman Catholic	Cavan	Laundry Sister	Read & write
Anne Mary	Moore	47	Nurse	Roman Catholic	Kings Co.	Nursing Sister	Read & write
Hannah	Hurley	45	Nurse	Roman Catholic	Cork	Nursing Sister	Read & write
Mary	McInernay	46	Nurse	Roman Catholic	Meath	Kitchen Sister	Read & write
Margaret	Levy	38	Nurse	Roman Catholic	Meath	Nursing Sister	Read & write
Bridget	Scanlan	38	Nurse	Roman Catholic	Clare	Nursing Sister	Read & write
Roseanna	Flannagan	38	Nurse	Roman Catholic	Kings Co.	Nursing Sister	Read & write
Frances	Darcy	31	Nurse	Roman Catholic	England	Nursing Sister	Read & write
Mary	Ledwith	32	Nurse	Roman Catholic	Meath	Kitchen Sister	Read & write
Ellen	Brady	33	Nurse	Roman Catholic	Cavan	Nursing Sister	Read & write
Elizabeth	Graham	31	Nurse	Roman Catholic	Carlow	Nursing Sister	Read & write
Ellen	Jones	31	Nurse	Roman Catholic	Tipperary	Nursing Sister	Read & write
Ellen	Kearney	33	Nurse	Roman Catholic	Scotland	Nursing Sister	Read & write

Residents of a house 3.1 in Mulgrave Street (North West Ward, Cork) 1901
North Infirmary Hospital

Christian Name	Surname	Age	Sex	Relation to Head of Family	Religious Profession	Birthplace	Rank, Profession, or Occupation	Education
Daniel	Murphy	36	M	House Surgeon	Roman Catholic	Cork		Read & write (Learning Irish)
Teresa	O'Callaghan	69	F		Roman Catholic	Dublin	Matron	Read & write
Bride	Lenon	51	F		Roman Catholic	Water-ford	Sister of Charity	Read & write
Catherine	Murphy	49	F		Roman Catholic	Dublin	Sister of Charity	Read & write
Lucy	Dodson	45	F		Roman Catholic	London	Sister of Charity	Read & write
Martha	Woolley	41	F		Roman Catholic	Yorkshire	Sister of Charity	Read & write
Bride	Sheridan	38	F		Roman Catholic	Meath	Sister of Charity	Read & write
Margaret	Lane	32	F		Roman Catholic	Meath	Sister of Charity	Read & write
Catherine	Harrington	34	F		Roman Catholic	Cork	Sister of Charity	Read & write
Christina	O'Reilly	30	F		Roman Catholic	Meath	Sister of Charity	Read & write

Residents of a house 7.2 in John Redmond Street (Cork No. 4, Cork) 1911
North Infirmary Hospital

Christian Name	Surname	Age	Relation to Head of Family	Religious Profession	Birthplace	Rank, Profession, or Occupation	Education
Catherine	Murphy	64	Matron	Roman Catholic	Dublin	Nursing Sister	Read & write
Bridget	Lennon	70	Nurse	Roman Catholic	Waterford	Nursing Sister	Read & write
Kate	Fogarty	46	Nurse	Roman Catholic	West-meath	Nursing Sister	Read & write
Martha	Ramsbot-tom	55	Nurse	Roman Catholic	England	Nursing Sister	Read & write
Margaret	Lane	42	Nurse	Roman Catholic	Cork	Nursing Sister	Read & write
Norah	Harrington	44	Bursar	Roman Catholic	Cork	Nursing Sister	Read & write
Florence	Young	41	Nurse	Roman Catholic	London	Nursing Sister	Read & write
Bridget	Duffy	32	Nurse	Roman Catholic	Cavan	Nursing Sister	Read & write
Johanna	Walshe	33	Nurse	Roman Catholic	Cloyne	Nursing Sister	Read & write
Kate	Mullally	40	Supt of Nursing	Roman Catholic	West-meath	Nursing Sister	Read & write
Grace	OSullivan	33	Nurse	Roman Catholic	Donegal	Nursing Sister	Read & write
Annie	Scully	31	Nurse	Roman Catholic	Carlow	Nursing Sister	Read & write

Residents of a house 58.1 in Main Street (Dunmanway, Cork) 1901
Dunmanway

Christian Name	Surname	Age	Relation to Head of Family	Religious Profession	Birthplace	Rank, Profession, or Occupation	Education
Gertrude	Barraud	56	Head & Superioress of Rel. Order	Roman Catholic	London	Sister of Charity	Read & write
Catherine	Knowles	51	Member of Religious Order	Roman Catholic	London	Sister of Charity	Read & write
Frances	Fleming	32	Member of Religious Order	Roman Catholic	Meath	Sister of Charity	Read & write
Clare	Harper	35	Member of Religious Order	Roman Catholic	Scotland	Sister of Charity	Read & write
Josephine	Lavery	32	Member of Religious Order	Roman Catholic	Meath	Sister of Charity	Read & write
Gabriel	Carney	31	Member of Religious Order	Roman Catholic	King's Co.	Sister of Charity	Read & write
Margaret	Fraser	28	Member of Religious Order	Roman Catholic	London	Sister of Charity	Read & write
Anthony	Geraghty	25	Member of Religious Order	Roman Catholic	Meath	Sister of Charity	Read & write
Louisa	Plunkett	31	Member of Religious Order	Roman Catholic	Dublin	Sister of Charity	Read & write
Ursula	Coennett	27	Member of Religious Order	Roman Catholic	London	Sister of Charity	Read & write

Residents of a house 48 in Chapel Street (Dunmanway North, Cork) 1911
Dunmanway

Christian Name	Surname	Age	Relation to Head of Family	Religious Profession	Birthplace	Rank, Profession, or Occupation	Education
Josephine	O'Brien	50	Superioress	Roman Catholic	Dublin	Superior of Sisters of Charity	Read & write
Frances	Fleming	43	Sister	Roman Catholic	Meath	Sister of Charity	Read & write (Irish and English)
Clare	Harper	46	Sister	Roman Catholic	Glasgow	Sister of Charity	Read & write
Minni	Lavery	43	Sister	Roman Catholic	Meath	Sister of Charity	Read & write (Irish and English)
Gabrielle	Carney	44	Sister	Roman Catholic	Louth	Sister of Charity	Read & write (Irish and English)
Louisa	Plunkett	43	Sister	Roman Catholic	Dublin	Sister of Charity	Read & write
Lily	Geraghty	38	Sister	Roman Catholic	Meath	Sister of Charity	Read & write
Agnes	Henry	36	Sister	Roman Catholic	Meath	Sister of Charity	Read & write
Angela	OReilly	32	Sister	Roman Catholic	Dublin	Sister of Charity	Read & write
Clare	Nesdale	21	Sister	Roman Catholic	Cork	Sister of Charity	Read & write

Residents of a house 4 in Brunswick Street North (Arran Quay, Dublin) 1901
North Dublin Union

Christian Name	Surname	Age	Relation to Head of Family	Religious Profession	Birthplace	Rank, Profession, or Occupation	Education
Margaret	O'Grady	59	Superioress	Roman Catholic	Mayo	Sister of Charity	Read & write
Bridget	Duffy	58	Sr of Charity	Roman Catholic	Cavan	Attending Sick Poor	Read & write
Catherine	Kerigan	55	Sr of Charity	Roman Catholic	Dublin City	Attending Sick Poor	Read & write
Mary	Parker	54	Sr of Charity	Roman Catholic	England	Attending Sick Poor	Read & write
Mary Ellen	Gray	53	Sr of Charity	Roman Catholic	Armagh	Attending Sick Poor	Read & write
Margaret	Fitzpatrick	48	Sr of Charity	Roman Catholic	Monaghan	Attending Sick Poor	Read & write
Mary	Lyons	48	Sr of Charity	Roman Catholic	England	Attending Sick Poor	Read & write
Ellen	Moore	43	Sr of Charity	Roman Catholic	King's Co.	Attending Sick Poor	Read & write
Annie	Johnson	43	Sr of Charity	Roman Catholic	Louth	Attending Sick Poor	Read & write
Ellen	Gore	44	Sr of Charity	Roman Catholic	Meath	Attending Sick Poor	Read & write
Bridget	McKenna	40	Sr of Charity	Roman Catholic	Derry	Attending Sick Poor	Read & write
Eliza	Murphy	43	Sr of Charity	Roman Catholic	Cork	Attending Sick Poor	Read & write
Agnes	Mulhall	37	Sr of Charity	Roman Catholic	Queen's Co.	Attending Sick Poor	Read & write
Agnes	Irvine	30	Sr of Charity	Roman Catholic	India	Attending Sick Poor	Read & write
Mary	Whitehill	33	Sr of Charity	Roman Catholic	England	Attending Sick Poor	Read & write
Mary Ann	Dullea	44	Sr of Charity	Roman Catholic	Cork	Attending Sick Poor	Read & write
Margaret	Lombard	37	Sr of Charity	Roman Catholic	Cork	Attending Sick Poor	Read & write
Margaret	Moore	27	Sr of Charity	Roman Catholic	Meath	Attending Sick Poor	Read & write
Elizabeth	O'Donohoe	26	Sr of Charity	Roman Catholic	Mayo	Attending Sick Poor	Read & write
Catherine	Boyle	33	Sr of Charity	Roman Catholic	Derry	Attending Sick Poor	Read & write

Residents of a house 4.2 in Brunswick Street North (Arran Quay, Dublin) 1911
North Dublin Union

Christian Name	Surname	Age	Relation to Head of Family	Religious Profession	Birthplace	Rank, Profession, or Occupation	Education
Margaret	O'Grady	70	Head	Roman Catholic	Mayo	Sister of Charity	Read & write
Brigid	Duffy	70	Sr of Charity	Roman Catholic	Monaghan	Sister of Charity	Read & write
Kate	Kerigan	65	Sr of Charity	Roman Catholic	Dublin City	Sister of Charity	Read & write
Mary E.	Parker	68	Sr of Charity	Roman Catholic	Warickshire, Eng.	Sister of Charity	Read & write
Mary P.	Gray	66	Sr of Charity	Roman Catholic	Armagh	Sister of Charity	Read & write
Margaret	Fitzpatrick	60	Sr of Charity	Roman Catholic	Monaghan	Sister of Charity	Read & write
Mary	Lyons	58	Sr of Charity	Roman Catholic	London	Sister of Charity	Read & write
Ellen	Moore	53	Sr of Charity	Roman Catholic	King's Co.	Sister of Charity	Read & write
Mary	Gore	50	Sr of Charity	Roman Catholic	Meath	Sister of Charity	Read & write
Catherine	Boyle	42	Sr of Charity	Roman Catholic	Derry	Sister of Charity	Read & write
Mary A.	Dullia	55	Sr of Charity	Roman Catholic	Cork	Sister of Charity	Read & write
Margaret	Lombard	47	Sr of Charity	Roman Catholic	Cork	Sister of Charity	Read & write
Agnes	Irvine	41	Sr of Charity	Roman Catholic	India	Sister of Charity	Read & write
Christina M.	O'Rielly	42	Sr of Charity	Roman Catholic	Cavan	Sister of Charity	Read & write
Anne	Wills	49	Sr of Charity	Roman Catholic	London	Sister of Charity	Read & write
Ellen	Campbell	47	Sr of Charity	Roman Catholic	Derry City	Sister of Charity	Read & write
Katie	Mallon	30	Sr of Charity	Roman Catholic	Down	Sister of Charity	Read & write
Nora	Scanlon	29	Sr of Charity	Roman Catholic	Clare	Sister of Charity	Read & write
Agnes	Fay	33	Sr of Charity	Roman Catholic	Louth	Sister of Charity	Read & write

Residents of a house 4.2 in Brunswick Street North (Arran Quay, Dublin) 1911
North Dublin Union (cont.)

Christian Name	Surname	Age	Relation to Head of Family	Religious Profession	Birthplace	Rank, Profession, or Occupation	Education
Kathleen	Burke	31	Sr of Charity	Roman Catholic	Galway	Sister of Charity	Read & write
Teresa	Murphy	35	Sr of Charity	Roman Catholic	Cork	Sister of Charity	Read & write
Catherine	Ryan	29	Sr of Charity	Roman Catholic	Clare	Sister of Charity	Read & write
Mary	Ried	34	Sr of Charity	Roman Catholic	Kildare	Sister of Charity	Read & write
Mary	Feirick	24	Sr of Charity	Roman Catholic	Mayo	Sister of Charity	Read & write
Mary	Wallace	23	Sr of Charity	Roman Catholic	Dublin City	Sister of Charity	Read & write
Brigid	Kelly	22	Female	Roman Catholic	Meath	Sister of Charity	Sr of Charity

Residents of a house 1.1 in Collegeland (Maynooth, Kildare) 1911
Maynooth

Christian Name	Surname	Age	Relation to Head of Family	Religious Profession	Birthplace	Rank, Profession, or Occupation	Education
Daniel	Manning	47	President of College	Catholic	Cork	Provst. President of Maynooth College, DD. LLD	
Elizabeth	Murphy	51	Religious of the Congregation of the French Sisters of Charity DC	Catholic	Cork	Sister of Charity	Read & write
Annie	Johnston	54		Catholic	Louth	Sister of Charity	Read & write
Mary	Harrington	48		Catholic	Cork	Sister of Charity	Read & write
Margaret	Bacon	42		Catholic	West-meath	Sister of Charity	Read & write
Mary K.	Scanlan	34		Catholic	Clare	Sister of Charity	Read & write
Bridget M.	Brady	43		Catholic	Meath	Sister of Charity	Read & write
Mary	O'Flaherty	41		Catholic	Kerry	Sister of Charity	Read & write

Residents of a house 97.1 in Cabragh (Castleknock, Dublin) 1901
Cabra

Christian Name	Surname	Age	Relation to Head of Family	Religious Profession	Birthplace	Rank, Profession, or Occupation	Education
Margaret	Galvin	55	Head	Roman Catholic	King's Co	Superintendant of Institution	Read & write
Anne	Mc Grane	52	Sr of Charity	Roman Catholic	Louth	Visitor	Read & write
Alice M.	Watson	51	Sr of Charity	Roman Catholic	England	Teacher G School	Read & write
Bedelia	Connolly	51	Sr of Charity	Roman Catholic	Galway	Teacher B School	Read & write
Mary	Flanagan	43	Sr of Charity	Roman Catholic	King's Co.	Supt Industrial Work	Read & write
Catherine	Franklin	42	Sr of Charity	Roman Catholic	Cork City	Nurse	Read & write
Margaret	McKenna	41	Sr of Charity	Roman Catholic	Cavan	Teacher G School	Read & write
Elizabeth	Cullen	40	Sr of Charity	Roman Catholic	England	Workroom	Read & write
Mary	Hook	40	Sr of Charity	Roman Catholic	England	Supt of Laundry	Read & write
Margaret	Coakley	30	Sr of Charity	Roman Catholic	Cork	Babies Nursery	Read & write
Teresa	Addis	34	Sr of Charity	Roman Catholic	England	Teacher B School	Read & write
Mary	O'Sullivan	30	Sr of Charity	Roman Catholic	Cork	Teacher B School	Read & write
Mary A.	Garn	25	Sr of Charity	Roman Catholic	Meath	Teacher G School	Read & write
Anne	Hannigan	39	Sr of Charity	Roman Catholic	Cavan	Supt of Kitchen	Read & write
Monica	Markey	29	Sr of Charity	Roman Catholic	Meath	Supt of Dressmaking	Read & write
Mary	Goggins	27	Sr of Charity	Roman Catholic	Cork	Teacher	Read & write
Margaret	Scully	27	Sr of Charity	Roman Catholic	Dublin	Teacher	Read & write

Residents of a house 52.6 in Cabragh (Castleknock, Dublin) 1911
Cabra

Christian Name	Surname	Age	Relation to Head of Family	Religious Profession	Birthplace	Rank, Profession, or Occupation	Education
Margaret	Galvin	65	Superioress	Roman Catholic	King's Co.	Sister of Charity	Read & write
Anne	McGrane	62	Sr of Charity	Roman Catholic	Louth	Sister of Charity	Read & write
Mary	Flannagan	52	Sr of Charity	Roman Catholic	King's Co.	Sister of Charity	Read & write
Bedelia	Connolly	62	Sr of Charity	Roman Catholic	Galway	Sister of Charity	Read & write
Teresa	Addis	45	Sr of Charity	Roman Catholic	Monmonth	Sister of Charity	Read & write
Margaret	McKenna	50	Sr of Charity	Roman Catholic	Cavan	Sister of Charity	Read & write
Elizabeth	Cullen	50	Sr of Charity	Roman Catholic	Manchester	Sister of Charity	Read & write
Mary	O'Sullivan	40	Sr of Charity	Roman Catholic	Cork	Sister of Charity	Read & write
Margaret	Coakley	39	Sr of Charity	Roman Catholic	Cork	Sister of Charity	Read & write
Catherine	Scully	40	Sr of Charity	Roman Catholic	City Dublin	Sister of Charity	Read & write
Margaret	Markey	39	Sr of Charity	Roman Catholic	Meath	Sister of Charity	Read & write
Nora	Giligan	29	Sr Visitor	Roman Catholic	Leitrim	Sister of Charity	Read & write
Annie	Kehoe	26	Sr of Charity	Roman Catholic	Wexford	Sister of Charity	Read & write
Bridget	McNiffe	32	Sr of Charity	Roman Catholic	Sligo	Sister of Charity	Read & write
Bridget	Murray	28	Sr of Charity	Roman Catholic	Cavan	Sister of Charity	Read & write
Hannah	Mulcahy	32	Sr of Charity	Roman Catholic	Cork	Sister of Charity	Read & write
Norah	O'Driscoll	30	Sr of Charity	Roman Catholic	Cork	Sister of Charity	Read & write
Kathleen	O'Shea	23	Sr of Charity	Roman Catholic	Cork	Sister of Charity	Read & write

Residents of a house 1.1 in Oranmore Street (Falls Ward, Antrim) 1901
Belfast

Christian Name	Surname	Age	Relation to Head of Family	Religious Profession	Birthplace	Rank, Profession, or Occupation	Education
Anne Clare	Graham	50	Head	Roman Catholic	Louth	Sister of Charity	Read & write
Ellen	Luciensmith	42	Sister in Religion	Roman Catholic	West Indies	Sister of Charity	Read & write
Mary	O'Donnell	33	Sister in Religion	Roman Catholic	Ireland	Sister of Charity	Read & write
Frances	Hickey	35	Sister in Religion	Roman Catholic	England	Sister of Charity	Read & write
Alice	O'Sullivan	33	Sister in Religion	Roman Catholic	Cork	Sister of Charity	Read & write
Esther	Whitehill	30	Sister in Religion	Roman Catholic	England	Sister of Charity	Read & write

Residents of a house 1.2 in Oranmore Street (Falls, Antrim) 1911
Belfast

Christian Name	Surname	Age	Relation to Head of Family	Religious Profession	Birthplace	Rank, Profession, or Occupation	Education
Mary Josephine	Graham	60	Head of Family	Roman Catholic	Louth	Sister of Charity	Read & write (Irish and English)
Gertrude	Watson	61	Sister in Religion	Roman Catholic	York, England	Sister of Charity	Read & write (Irish and English)
Mary	Madden	53	Sister in Religion	Roman Catholic	Meath	Sister of Charity	Read & write (Irish and English)
Agnes	Mullen	40	Sister in Religion	Roman Catholic	Meath	Sister of Charity	Read & write
Columba	Delacy	38	Sister in Religion	Roman Catholic	Plymouth, England	Sister of Charity	Read & write (Irish and English)
Vincent	Wallace	25	Sister in Religion	Roman Catholic	Dublin City	Sister of Charity	Read & write (Irish and English)
Gabriel	Sammon	23	Sister in Religion	Roman Catholic	Tipperary	Sister of Charity	Read & write (Irish and English)

Residents of a house 5.1 in Knocknamoe (Abbeyleix, Queen's Co.) 1911
Abbeyleix

Christian Name	Surname	Age	Relation to Head of Family	Religious Profession	Birthplace	Rank, Profession, or Occupation	Education
Michael	Maher	40	Head of Family	Roman Catholic	Queen's Co.	Master of Workhouse	Read & write
Margaret M.	Maher	30	Wife	Roman Catholic	Queen's Co.		Read & write
John Patrick	Maher	4 weeks	Son	Roman Catholic	Queen's Co.		Read & write
Johanna	Kavanagh	26		Roman Catholic	Queen's Co.	Matron of the workhouse	Read & write
Mary	McGrath	22		Roman Catholic	Queen's Co.	School Mistress	Read & write
Catherine	Tobin	52		Roman Catholic	King's Co.	Fever hsp Nurse	Read & write
Kate	Byrne	40		Roman Catholic	Queen's Co.	Infirmary Nurse	Read & write
Henrietta	Madden	54	[Not listed as Daughters of Charity]	Roman Catholic	Tipperary	Infirmary Nurse	Read & write
Mary Ann	Buckley	53	[Not listed as Daughters of Charity]	Roman Catholic	Cork	Infirmary Nurse	Read & write
Emma	Keelty	38	[Not listed as Daughters of Charity]	Roman Catholic	Down	Infirmary Nurse	Read & write

Residents of a house 35.1 in Big Lane (Celbridge, Kildare) 1901
Celbridge

Christian Name	Surname	Age	Relation to Head of Family	Religious Profession	Birthplace	Rank, Profession, or Occupation	Education
Mary	Nolan	53	Superioress	Roman Catholic	Carlow	Sister of Charity	Read & write
Martha	Prendergast	52	School Mistress	Roman Catholic	Wicklow	Sister of Charity	Read & write
Evelyn	O'Bryan	41	Nurse	Roman Catholic	Liverpool	Sister of Charity	Read & write
Henrietta	Madden	44	Nurse	Roman Catholic	Tipperary	Sister of Charity	Read & write
Anne	Forge	33	Nurse	Roman Catholic	Hertfordshire	Sister of Charity	Read & write
Elizabeth	O'Brien	33	Nurse	Roman Catholic	Meath	Sister of Charity	Read & write
Catherine	Mullaly	30	Nurse	Roman Catholic	Westmeath	Sister of Charity	Read & write

Residents of a house 28.2 in Union Lane (Celbridge, Kildare) 1911
Celbridge

Christian Name	Surname	Age	Religious Profession	Birthplace	Rank, Profession, or Occupation	Education
Agnes	Mulhall	55	Roman Catholic	Queen's Co.	Sister of Charity	Read & write
Joseph	Prendergast	62	Roman Catholic	Wicklow	Sister of Charity	Read & write
Aloysuis	Whitehill	44	Roman Catholic	Liverpool	Sister of Charity	Read & write
Anthony	Hegarty	38	Roman Catholic	Cork	Sister of Charity	Read & write
Catherine	O Donohoe	36	Roman Catholic	Mayo	Sister of Charity	Read & write
Columba	Caghlan	38	Roman Catholic	Wellington, India	Sister of Charity	Read & write
Angela	Shaw	45	Roman Catholic	Westmeath	Sister of Charity	Read & write
Cecilia	Dooly	34	Roman Catholic	Cork	Sister of Charity	Read & write
Mary	Murphy	37	Roman Catholic	Cork	Sister of Charity	Read & write

Residents of a house 12.5 in Irishtown (Mountmellick Urban, Queen's Co.) 1911
Mountmellick

Christian Name	Surname	Age	Relation to Head of Family	Religion	Birthplace	Rank, Profession, or Occupation	Education
Margaret	O'Mahony	52	Matron	Roman Catholic	Cork	Matron	Read & write
Elizabeth	O'Brien	43	Nursing Sister	Roman Catholic	Meath	Sister Nursing Order	Read & write
Mary	Mullally	40	Nursing Sister	Roman Catholic	West-meath	Sister Nursing Order	Read & write
Hannah	McGuire	35	Nursing	Roman Catholic	Louisville, USA	Sister Nursing Order	Read & write (Irish and English)

Residents of a house 22.3 in Pelletstown (Castleknock, Dublin) 1911
Pelletstown

Christian Name	Surname	Age	Relation to Head of Family	Religious Profession	Birthplace	Rank, Profession, or Occupation	Education
Mary Patrick	McDonnell	42	Superior	Roman Catholic	Louth	Sister of Charity	Read & write
Josephine	Connolly	29	Members of Community	Roman Catholic	Cork	Sister of Charity	Read & write (Irish and English)
Frances	Dooley	33	Members of Community	Roman Catholic	Cork	Sister of Charity	Read & write (Irish and English)
Mary	Brady	33	Members of Community	Roman Catholic	Galway	Sister of Charity	Read & write
Vincent	Cuming	29	Members of Community	Roman Catholic	Armagh	Sister of Charity	Read & write
Magdalen	McCarthy	26	Members of Community	Roman Catholic	Cork	Sister of Charity	Read & write (Irish and English)

Appendix IV

Foundations of the Daughters of Charity in Ireland, 1855–2012

Carmel Ryan DC

Name of Community House	Date of Opening	Diocese	Ministries	Sisters withdrew
St Vincent's, Drogheda, Louth	8 November 1855	Armagh	Parish Ministry, Orphanage, Education	
St Vincent's, North William Street, Dublin	14 May 1857	Dublin	Orphanage, Parish Ministry, Education	
St Vincent's Hospital, Fairview, Dublin	14 May 1857	Dublin	Psychiatric Hospital	19 December 1997
North Infirmary Hospital, Mulgrave Street, Cork	25 January 1867	Cork & Ross	General Hospital	27 November 1987
St Mary's Dunmanway, Cork	8 September 1887	Cork & Ross	Education	8 December 2002
St John's North Dublin Union, North Brunswick Street, Dublin	15 December 1888	Dublin	Workhouse/Hospital	22 February 1929
St Anne's, Celbridge, Kildare	18 June 1892	Dublin	Workhouse/Hospital	13 April 1922
St Vincent's (Cabra), Navan Road, Dublin	7 October 1892	Dublin	Workhouse, work with persons with an Intellectual Disability	
Our Lady's Henrietta Street, Dublin	5 May 1899	Dublin	Home for Released Female Prisoners	
St Vincent's, Clonard Gardens, Belfast	30 April 1900	Down & Connor	Parish Ministry, Education, Hostel for Mill Girls	14 September 1990
St Vincent's Hospital, Abbeyleix, Laois	7 September 1901	Kildare & Leighlin	Workhouse/Hospital	25 May 1934
St Vincent's Hospital, Mountmellick, Laois	10 October 1902	Kildare & Leighlin	Workhouse/Hospital	31 August 1987
Senior Infirmary, Maynooth, Kildare	27 March 1905	Dublin	Infirmary for staff and clerical students	1 September 1998
St Patrick's (Pelletstown), Navan Road, Dublin	17 March 1910	Dublin	Workhouse	3 February 1986

Name of Community House	Date of Opening	Diocese	Ministries	Sisters withdrew
Sacred Heart Home, Drumcondra, Dublin	1 September 1913	Dublin	Orphanage	10 February 1988
St Joseph's Hospital, Coole, Westmeath	29 June 1916	Meath	Hospital and school for children with physical disabilities	7 October 1981
Pigeon House, Ringsend, Dublin	24 November 1918	Dublin	Hospital for patients with tuberculosis	2 August 1955
St Anne's Hospital, Northbrook Road, Dublin	16 July 1919	Dublin	Skin and Cancer Hospital	18 December 1997
St Teresa's, Blackrock, Dublin	22 September 1925	Dublin	Orphanage	
St Brigid's, Kilternan, Dublin	7 October 1927	Dublin	Aftercare of patients from St Anne's Hospital	27 September 1967
St Vincent's Coolarne, Athenry, Galway	17 December 1927	Tuam	Home Economics School and primary education	16 April 1974
St Joseph's, Antrim Town, Antrim	29 March 1928	Down & Connor	Education, Parish Ministry	12 June 1937
St Mary's Hostel, Knock, Mayo	29 July 1931	Tuam	Hostel for pilgrims, Parish Ministry, work in Shrine	
St Philomena's, Stillorgan, Dublin	11 February 1932	Dublin	Orphanage, Education	1 July 1971
Seminary, Blackrock, Dublin	8 September 1932	Dublin	Seminary	
St Louise's Marino, Dublin	4 October, 1934	Dublin	Parish Primary Schools	9 October 1978
St Martha's College, Navan, Meath	18 June 1936	Meath	Home Economics College	11 April 1983
St Catherine's, Dunardagh, Blackrock, Dublin	8 December 1939	Dublin	Seminary, Provincial House	
St Mary's Hostel, Mountjoy Square, Dublin.	1 September 1941	Dublin	Hostel for working young women	7 March 1979
Clonliffe College, Dublin	1 September 1942	Dublin	Infirmary for staff and clerical students	31 August 1985
Immaculate Conception, Mount Prospect Avenue, Clontarf, Dublin	29 December 1942	Dublin	Holiday home for children from North William Street	
St Joseph's, Clonsilla, Dublin	8 September 1945	Dublin	Residence for adults with an intellectual disability	
St Kevin's, Glencree, Wicklow	15 March 1946	Dublin	Care of German refugee children	22 May 1947

Name of Community House	Date of Opening	Diocese	Ministries	Sisters withdrew
Holy Angels, Glenmaroon, Chapelizod, Dublin	1 August 1950	Dublin	Residence for children with an intellectual disability, Education	9 May 2009
St Vincent's, Lisnagry, Limerick	31 March 1952	Limerick	Residence for children with an intellectual disability, Education	
Our Lady's Hospital, Crumlin, Dublin	21 November 1956	Dublin	Hospital for sick children	31 July 1999
St Louise's Drumfinn Road Ballyfermot, Dublin	12 August 1961	Dublin	Education, Parish Ministry	
Eccles Street, Dublin	20 December 1965	Dublin	Hostel for teenage boys	11 February 1974
Springfield, Tallaght, Dublin	1 December 1973	Dublin	Parish Ministry	1 January 1989
Ballymurphy, Belfast	10 February 1974	Down & Connor	Parish Ministry	6 December 2005
Kilmore West, Dublin	7 August 1974	Dublin	Parish Ministry, Education, Sheltered Housing	
St Louise's, Hollyhill, Cork	14 April 1977	Cork & Ross	Parish Ministry, Education, Pre-school education	
Moyard, Belfast	11 October 1977	Down & Connor	Sheltered Housing, Parish Ministry	31 October 2012
Marlborough Street, Dublin	1 January 1978	Dublin	Parish Ministry, Dublin Diocesan Social Services	4 September 1991
St Catherine's, Killinarden, Tallaght, Dublin	6 November 1979	Dublin	Parish Ministry, Education	
Rickard House, Dunardagh Blackrock, Dublin	8 September 1982	Dublin	Care of elderly sisters	13 February 2013
Marillac Balmoral Avenue, Belfast	8 April 1983	Down & Connor	Education	31 January 2003
Carnew, Wicklow	15 August 1983	Dublin	Care of the elderly, Parish Ministry, Education	
Seton House, Northbrook Road, Dublin	2 September 1985	Dublin	Residence	
Rowan Byron, Bray, Wicklow	3 September 1986	Dublin	Work with members of Travelling Community	20 July 1988
Labouré House, Mount Nebo Blarney Street, Cork	25 August 1987	Cork & Ross	Parish Ministry, Nursing	25 November 2011

Name of Community House	Date of Opening	Diocese	Ministries	Sisters withdrew
Belvedere Road, Dublin	14 December 1987	Dublin	Parish Ministry, Education	
Shanliss Drive, Santry, Dublin	10 February 1988	Dublin	Childcare	12 September 2012
Church Road, East Wall, Dublin	14 November 1988	Dublin	Parish Ministry	1 October 2004
Teach Féile, Mulhuddart, Blanchardstown, Dublin	9 June 1989	Dublin	Residence shared with persons with an intellectual disability	1 June 1993
Navan Road, Dublin	1 September 1989	Dublin	Working with persons with an intellectual disability	
Cherry Orchard, Ballyfermot, Dublin	December 2, 1989	Dublin	Parish Ministry	September 18, 2006
St Rosalie's, Portmarnock, Dublin	1 February 1990	Dublin	Sisters working with persons with an intellectual disability	19 September 1997
Glen Road, Belfast	4 July 1990	Down & Connor	Education, Parish Ministry	
Cavendish Street, Belfast	21 September 1985	Down & Connor	Education Parish Ministry	8 September 2006
St Louise's, Dalymount, Phibsborough, Dublin	26 April 1991	Dublin	Parish Ministry	
Killarney Street, Dublin	1 January 1992	Dublin	Parish Ministry	
Maplewood Road, Tallaght, Dublin	2 July 1993	Dublin	Parish Ministry	31 August 1989
Ballymakenny, Drogheda, Louth	10 August 1993	Armagh	Residence	28 May 2003
Maderian Court, Galway	5 October 1995	Galway	Parish Ministry, Work with the Society of St Vincent de Paul	8 December 1998
Bettyglen, Raheny, Dublin	6 October 1995	Dublin	St Francis Hospice	6 February 1998
St Assam's Drive, Raheny, Dublin	1 February 1998	Dublin	St Francis Hospice	
Shantalla, Galway	27 September 1998	Galway	Parish Ministry, Work with the Society of St Vincent de Paul	

APPENDIX V

General and Provincial Superiors of the Company of the Daughters of Charity

Carmel Ryan DC

Superioress General	Superior General	Visitatrice/Provincial	Provincial Director
Elizabeth Montcellet 1851–1857	Jean-Baptiste Etienne 1843–1874		
Augustine Devos 1857–1860			
Elizabeth Montcellet 1860–1866		Marie Chatelain	
Félicité Lequette 1866–1872			
Louise Lequette 1872–1878	Eugéne Boré 1874–1878		
Marie Juhel 1878–1880	Antoine Fiat 1878–1914		
Marie Dérieux 1880–1887		Juliette Minart 1885–1890	William Gavin 1885–1898
Léonide Havard 1887–1893			
Marie Lamartinie 1887–1899		Eugenié Marcellus 1890–1919	
Marie Kieffer 1899–1910			Joseph Walsh 1898–1909
Marie Mauche 1910–1912			William Byrne 1909–1922
Marie-Jeanne Maurice 1912–1918	Emile Villette 1914–1916		
	Alfred Louyick 1916–1918		
Emilie Maurice 1918–1921	Francoise Verdier 1918–1933		
Mathilde Inchelin 1922–1928		Louise Hannezo 1919–1926	Joseph Walsh 1922–1923
		Mary Boyle 1926–1928	John O'Connell 1923–1938

Superioress General	Superior General	Visitatrice/Provincial	Provincial Director
Marie-Anne Lebrun 1928–1934	Charles-Léon Souvay 1933–1939	Anne Thomson 1928–1946	Joseph Sheedy 1938–1952
Marie Chaplain 1934–1940	Edouard Robert 1939–1947	Barbara Burke 1946–1947	
Marie-Laure Decq 1940–1946			
Antoinette Blanchot 1946–1953			
	William Slattery 1947–1969	Mary (Joseph) McGee 1947–1952	
		Margaret Whalen 1952–1966	Patrick Travers 1952–1961
Francine Lepicard 1953–1962		Gertrude Andrew 1966–1970	James Cahalane 1961–1967
Suzanne Guillemin 1962–1968			Felix McAtarsney 1967–1970
Christiane Chiron 1968–1974	James Richardson 1969–1980		
		Catherine Barrett 1970–1976	James Doherty 1970–1974
Lucie Rogé 1974–1985	Richard McCullen 1980–1992	Pauline Lawlor 1976–1985	Frank Mullan 1974–1981
Anne Duzan 1985–1991		Bernadette Mac Mahon 1985–1994	Eamon Cowan 1981–1992
Juana Elizondo 1991–2003		Catherine Mulligan 1994–2004	Jim Touhy 1992–1996
Evelyne Franc 2003–	Robert Maloney 1992–2004		Harry Slowey 1996–2005
	G. Gregory Gay 2004–	Catherine Prendergast 2004–2013	Eamon Flanagan 2005–2011
			Mark Noonan 2011–Present

Bibliography

NEWSPAPERS

Cork Examiner, 25 January 1867.

Eagle Supplement of the Southern Star, 19 January 1889.

The Drogheda Argus, 10 November 1855.

The Freeman's Journal, 13 October 1858; 4 April 1862; 9 June 1887;
    11 October 1888; 3 April 1895.

The Irish Catholic, 26 January 1918.

The Irish News Centenary Edition, 2000.

The Imperial Gazetteer, 1868.

The Kilkenny People, 30 June 1934.

The Leinster Leader, 20 February 1902.

The Leinster Express, 20 February 1902.

JOURNALS

Echoes of the Company of the Daughters of Charity, no. 6, June/July 2003,
    'Marian Spirituality and the Vincentian Charism'.

— no. 1, January/February 2005, 'Mary Immaculate and the Company of the
    Daughters of Charity'.

— no. 2, March/April 2005, 'Marian Vincentian Youth'.

— no. 1, January/February 2007, 'Introduction'.

Irish Ecclesiastical Record, December 1870, vol. xi, July to December 1932.

Irish Nursing News, vol. xix, no. 8, May 1941.

Irish Quarterly Review, vol. viii, part viii, December 1881, James G. Alcorn, 'Discharged Prisoners' Aid Societies'.

Past and Present, 177:1, 2002, Curtis, Sarah A., 'Charitable Ladies: Gender, Class and Religion in Mid Nineteenth-Century Paris'.

The Far East, February 1918; July 1919.

Tipperary Historical Journal 2001, Chadwick, Áine M., 'Alice O'Sullivan, Clonmel missionary and martyr (1836–1870)'.

Vincentiana, 1981, Prager, John, CM, 'Reflections on the Renewal of Vincentian Spirituality'.

REPORTS

Annual Reports of the Dublin Catholic Discharged Female Prisoners' Aid Society, 1906–07, 1909, 1911–13, 1918–20, 1923 (Dublin).

Annual Report of the Inspector of Mental Hospitals for the year 1943, Department of Health (Dublin, 1949).

Annual Reports of the Inspector of Mental Hospitals for the years, 1924–52, Department of Local Government and Public Health (Dublin).

Annual Reports of the Ladies of Charity of St Vincent de Paul (Dublin, 1852–61).

North Dublin Union, Copy of Committee Proceedings, 1910–11, 1927 (Dublin: Dollard).

Report of the Commission of Enquiry on Mental Handicap (Stationery Office, Dublin, 1965).

Report of the Local Government Board of Inspectors (Dublin: Dollard, 1894).

Report of the Reformatories and Industrial Schools Commissioners (1884).

Report from the select committee appointed to inquire into the expediency of making provision for the relief of the lunatic poor in Ireland, 1817, House of Commons (1817), (430) viii.

Report of the Special Commission of the Board of Guardians (Dublin: Dollard, 1907).

WHO, Technical Report Series, no. 75, *The Mentally Subnormal Child* (Geneva), April 1954.

Prisons Act (Ireland) 1877, 40 & 41 Vic., c. 49, sec. 44.

Private Lunatic Asylums (Ireland) Act, 1842, 5 & 6 Vic. c. 123.

An Roinn Oideachais, *Charting our Education Future* (Stationery Office, Dublin, 1995).

PUBLICATIONS

Abelly, Louis, *The Life of the Venerable Servant of God: Vincent De Paul: Founder and First Superior General of the Congregation of the Mission,* 3 vols, iii (New York, 1993).

A Priest of the Mission, *The First Martyrs of the Holy Childhood,* tr. Lady Herbert (Leamington and London, 1900).

Ball, Ann, *Encyclopaedia of Catholic Devotions and Practices* (Indiana, USA, 2003).

Bardon, Jonathan, *Belfast: An Illustrated History* (Belfast, 1982).

Bew, Paul, 'Politics and the Rise of the Skilled Working Man' in J. C. Beckett et al., *Belfast: The Making of the City* (Belfast, 2006).

Bishop of Canea, *Short Histories of Dublin Parishes,* part xii (Dublin, 1913).

Blake, Donal S., CFC, *Servant of the Poor, Mary Aikenhead 1787–1858: Founder of the Religious Sisters of Charity* (Dublin, 2001).

Boyle, Patrick, CM, *St Vincent de Paul and The Vincentians* (London, 1909).

Brennan, Eilis; Cardwell, Evelyn; Gallagher, Carmel; Crawford, Bill; Brown, Deirdre; and Anderson, Andrew, *Linen: Continuity and Change: The Story of the Irish Linen Industry* (Belfast: Ulster Folk and Transport Museum in association with The Irish Linen Guild, 1988).

Burdett, Henry C., *Hospitals and Asylums of the World: Their Origin, History, Construction, Administration and Legislation,* 3 vols, ii (London, 1891).

Carey, Tim, *Mountjoy: The Story of a Prison* (Cork: Collins Press, 2000).

Catechism of the Catholic Church (Dublin: Veritas, 1994).

Catholic Truth Society, *Tipperary's Gift to China: Three Apostolic Lives 1863–1898* (Dublin, 1919).

Common Rules of the Daughters of Charity (London, 1955, private circulation).

Company of the Daughters of Charity of Saint Vincent de Paul, Constitution Statutes (2004, private circulation).

Coste, Pierre, CM, *The Life and Works of St Vincent de Paul*, tr. Joseph Leonard CM, 3 vols (New York: New City Press, 1987).

Coste, Pierre, CM, *Saint Vincent de Paul: Correspondence, Conférences, Documents*, ed. and tr. Marie Poole, 13 vols (New York: New City Press, 1983–2010).

Daughters of Charity, *A Light Shining on the Earth: The Message of the Miraculous Medal: The Fiftieth Anniversary of the Canonization of Saint Catherine Labouré (1947–1997)* (Strasbourg, 1997).

Daughters of Charity, *Among Mary's Gifts: The Green Scapular* (Dublin, 1985).

Daughters of Charity, *The Chapel Pamphlets*
History of the Medal
The Medal a Gift (140 rue du Bac, 2004).

Daughters of Charity, *The Novena in Honour of Our Lady of the Miraculous Medal* (Dublin: Elo Press).

Daughters of Charity, *The Sisters of Charity, Centenary Record, 1857–1957* (Dublin, 1957).

Daughters of Charity of the British Province, *Together Let Us Praise God's Name* (Cambridge, 2003).

Donnelly, James, 'The Peak of Marianism in Ireland, 1930–1960' in S. J. Brown and D. W. Miller, *Piety and Power in Ireland 1760–1960: Essays in Honour of Emmet Larkin* (Belfast, 2000).

Dublin Archdiocese, *The Dublin Diocesan Directory 2013*.

Duggan, Maura, OP, *In Search of Truth: Journeys of Nineteenth Century Irish Dominican Women* (Dublin, 2010).

Esquirol, Jean-Étienne Dominique, *Mental Maladies: A Treatise on Insanity* (Philadelphia, 1845).

Gillespie, Raymond and Royle, Stephen A., *Irish Historic Towns Atlas, No. 12, Belfast, Part I, to 1840* (Royal Irish Academy in Association with Belfast City Council, 2003).

Gobillon, Monsieur, *The Life of Mademoiselle Le Gras,* tr. Daughters of Charity (London, 1984).

Grant, James, *One Hundred Years with the Clonard Redemptorists* (Dublin: Columba Press, 2003).

Green, Marion, *Mill to Millennium* (Belfast, 1996).

Greene, Stephen J., 'The Building of St Agatha's Church' in *Saint Agatha's Church, North William Street: 75 Years Old* (Dublin, 1983)

Gregory, Richard L., ed., *The Oxford Companion to the Mind* (Oxford, 1987).

Groel, Clara, DC, *White Wings in Bamboo Land* (Emmitsburg, Maryland 1959).

Hardy, Horatio Nelson, *The Medical Profession, the National Insurance Act, and the State of Poor Law Dispensaries in Ireland* (1913).

Hare, Edward H., *On the History of Lunacy: The Nineteenth Century and After* (London, 1998).

Hepburn, Anthony C., 'The Catholic Community of Belfast, 1850–1940' in Max Engman, ed., et al., *Ethnic Identity in Urban Europe* (New York, 1992).

Hopkins, Gerald M., 'Sonnet 34', *The Major Poems* (London, 1979).

Hughes, Ann, *History of Drogheda* (Drogheda, 1893).

Inglis, Henry D., *A Journey Through Ireland* (London, 1838).

Field, E. M. 'The Care of Girls Leaving Elementary Schools' in *Women Workers: papers read at a conference convened by the Bristol and Clifton Ladies' Association for the care of girls, in November 1892* (London, 1893).

Flynn, Patrick, 'The Department's Roots and the Jones Years' in Patrick Flynn, ed., *Dalhousie's Department of Psychiatry, A Historical Retrospective* (Halifax, 1999).

Frankl, Victor E., *Man's Search for Meaning: An Introduction to Logotherapy* (New York, 1946).

Kavanagh, Patrick, 'Having Confessed', *Collected Poems* (London: W.W. Norton, 1973).

Kinealy, Christine, 'The Role of the Poor Law during the Famine' in Cathal Poirtéir, *The Great Irish Famine* (Cork: Mercier, 1995).

La Fleur, Kathryn B., SP, *Louise de Marillac: A Light in the Darkness* (New York: New City Press, 1996).

Laurentin, René, *The Life of Catherine Labouré, 1801–1876,* tr. Paul Ingwood (London: Collins, 1983).

Macaulay, Ambrose, *Down and Connor: A Short History* (Du Signe, 2000).

Mac Thormaid, Brendan M., *Deathless Glory* (Dublin, 1966).

Maloney, Robert P., CM, *The Way of Vincent de Paul: A Contemporary Spirituality in the Service of the Poor* (New York: New City Press, 1992).

Maria Immaculata Secondary School Commemorative Booklet: 'A Caring Tradition' (unpublished, 2002).

Mazeau, Henri, *The Heroine of Pe-Tang: Helene de Jaurias, Sister of Charity*, tr. Helené de Jaurias (London, 1928).

M. L. H, *Sister Xavier Berkeley (1861–1944)* (London: Burns & Oates, 1949).

Murphy, John Nicholas, *Terra Incognita or the Convents of the United Kingdom* (London: Longman Green, 1873).

O'Connor, John, *The Workhouses of Ireland: The Fate of Ireland's Poor* (Dublin, 1995).

Pioneer Sisters of Charity of Saint Vincent de Paul in Great Britan and Ireland (Daughters of Charity London, 1955).

Pope Benedict XVI, *Porta Fidei*: Apostolic Letter (Vatican, 2012).

Pope John Paul II, *Christifideles Laici*: Post-Synodal Apostolic Exhortation (Vatican, 1990).

— *Starting Afresh From Christ: A Renewed Committment to Consecrated Life in the Third Millenium*: Instruction for Institutes of Consecrated Life and Societies of Apostolic Life (Vatican, 2002).

— *Novo Millennio Ineunte, At the Beginning of the New Millennium*: Apostolic Letter (Vatican, 2001).

— *Vita Consecrata: The Consecrated Life and its Mission in the Church and the World* (Vatican, 1996).

Pope Paul VI, *Marialis Cultus*: Apostolic Exhortation (Vatican, 1974).

Pope Pius IX, *Ineffabilis Deus*: Apostolic Constitution (Vatican, 1854).

Porter, Roy, *Madness: A Brief History* (Oxford, 2002).

Prendergast, Catherine, DC, 'Deus Caritas Est and the Daughters of Charity: Looking Anew at the Vincentian Charism' in Eoin G. Cassidy, ed., *Who is my Neighbour? Deus Caritas Est: An Encyclical for Our Times?* (Dublin: Veritas, 2009).

Proclamation of the Irish Republic, 1916.

Prunty, Jacinta, *Dublin Slums 1800–1925: A Study in Urban Geography* (Dublin: Irish Academic Press, 1998).

Prunty, Jacinta, *Margaret Aylward, 1810–1889: Lady of Charity, Sister of Faith,* (Dublin: Four Courts Press, 1999).

Reilly, A. J., *Father John Murphy: Famine Priest* (Dublin, 1963).

Renaudin, Paul, *The Sisters of Charity* (Paris: Bloud et Gay, 1930).

Robins, Joseph, *From Rejection to Integration: A Centenary of Service of Daughters of Charity to Persons with a Mental Handicap* (Dublin, 1992).

Robins, Joseph, *Fools and Mad: A History of the Insane in Ireland* (Dublin, 1986).

Román, José María, CM, *St Vincent de Paul: A Biography*, tr. Joyce Howard DC (London: Melisende, 1999).

Royle, Stephen A.; Simms, Anngret, Clarke, H. B., Gillespie, Raymond, eds, *Irish Historic Towns Atlas, No. 12, Belfast, Part I, 1840–1900* (Royal Irish Academy in Association with Belfast City Council, 2007).

Sheedy, Joseph P., CM, *A Short History of the Sisters of Charity of St Vincent de Paul* (London, 1951).

Sullivan, Louise, DC, ed. and tr., *Spiritual Writings of Louise de Marillac: Correspondence and Thoughts* (Brooklyn: New City Press, 1991).

Sullivan, Louise, DC, *Sister Rosalie Rendu: A Daughter of Charity on Fire with Love for the Poor* (Chicago: Vincentian Studies Institute, 2006).

Taylor, Fanny, *Irish Homes and Irish Hearts* (London, 1867).

The Holy Bible, Revised Standard Version Catholic Edition (London: Nelson, 1965).

The Official Handbook of the Legion of Mary, Legio Mariae (Dublin, 2005).

Webb, Sidney, 'Women and the Factory Acts', *Fabian Tract*, 67 (London, 1896).

WEBSITES

Skidmore College [website] <http://www.skidmore.edu> accessed 4 September 2012.

'Education for Persons with Disabilities Bill, 2002' *Houses of the Oireachtas* [website] <http://www.oireachtas.ie/viewdoc.asp?fn=/documents/bills28/bills/2002/1702/b17b02s.pdf> accessed 12 February 2013.

'Pioneer Total Abstinence Association', *University College Dublin* [website] <http://www.ucd.ie/archives/html/collections/pioneer-association.html> accessed 20 March 2013.

The Banford Haughtons: A Family History 1815–1888 [website] <http://www.thebanfordhaughtons.co.uk> accessed 14 March 2013.

'An Excerpt from the History of Drummanway [*sic*], County Cork', *Kaweah* [website] <http://kaweah.com/famtree/stories/donlin/Drummanway.html> accessed 21 March 2013.

FAMVIN [website] <www.famvin.org> accessed 1 May 2014.

CiNews [website] <http://www.cinews.ie> accessed 3 March 2013.

The National Archives of Ireland [website] <http://www.census.nationalarchives.ie> accessed 21 February 2013.

Biographical Notes on the Authors

Byrne, Anna, a Daughter of Charity since 1975, is a native of Kilkenny and has lived in Belfast for over twenty years. Involved in education Anna worked in Navan and Dunmanway before taking up a teaching post in the Geography Department in St Louise's College on the Falls Road, Belfast. Anna obtained teaching qualifications and has a BA Honours degree, Bachelor Theology Honours and a Masters in Educational Management. Presently she ministers as Chaplain in St Louise's Comprehensive College and is qualified in spiritual guidance.

Casey, Carmel, was born in Ballynoe in East Cork. She trained in Child Care and worked in Children's Homes and with young people in Ireland and England. Carmel worked in hostels and she was involved in pastoral care in various parishes including the Parish of the Travelling People. She is presently engaged in pastoral care of the elderly in hospitals in Drogheda, Co. Louth.

Devlin, Eileen, was born in Dublin and entered the Daughters of Charity in 1948. She trained in Child Care and has worked with children in Tollcross (Scotland), Endfield (England), Drogheda, Co. Louth, and the Sacred Heart Home in Dublin. She worked with homeless young men in Henrietta Street, which developed into St Vincent's Trust. She was a recipient of the People of the Year Awards in 1985 for her work with homeless people. Eileen was a member of the first leadership team in the Irish province. She was sister servant in the Sacred Heart Home and in Drogheda. She is currently involved in pastoral care in St Mary's Hospital, Phoenix Park, Dublin.

Dixon, Mary, was born in Lahinch, Co. Clare in 1927. She qualified as a primary school teacher in 1947. She entered the Daughters of Charity in 1948 and taught in St Michael's Special School in Glenmaroon and in St Teresa's School, Blackrock, Co. Dublin. She obtained a certificate for the specialised teaching of children with an intellectual disability from St Patrick's College of Education, Drumcondra, Dublin in 1962 and her Bachelor of Arts in 1965 from University College, Dublin. She was appointed to the new mission of Nigeria in 1965 and she left in 1967 due to the war in Biafra. She was appointed to Ethiopia in 1968. She was one of the pioneer sisters in Kenya in 2001 and served there until 2004. On her return to Ireland, she lived in St Catherine's, Dunardagh, St Louise's, Hollyhill, Cork and Rickard House, Blackrock, Dublin. She died in August 2012. + RIP

Fennessy, Bernadette, was born in Dublin and joined the Daughters of Charity in 1957. Bernadette is a qualified paediatric, general and geriatric nurse. She worked in child care in Gravends in Kent and nursed in Our Lady's Hospital, Crumlin, the North Infirmary, Cork, St Vincent's, Elm Park, Dublin, St Vincent's, Mountmellick, Co. Laois, and with elderly sisters of the Daughters of Charity in Dublin. Bernadette worked for two years with people who were deaf, people with physical disabilities, as well as being involved in pastoral work in Nigeria. She trained in sign language and worked with people who are deaf, and visited them annually on a national level. She currently lives in Henrietta Street, Dublin.

Keenan, Breege, a native of Knock, Co. Mayo, is a qualified social worker and holds an MA in Management from DCU. She has worked with people with an intellectual disability, in an information and advocacy service and in a family resource centre. Breege was involved in the setting up of L'Olivier (Brussels) and the Vincentian Refugee Centre (Dublin), both drop-in services for asylum seekers and refugees. She has nineteen years experience of working with asylum seekers, refugees and victims of human trafficking. She currently works with Crosscare Refugee Service, a project of Crosscare, the Catholic social care agency of the Archdiocese of Dublin.

Mathews, Sheila, was born in Phibsborough, Dublin in 1921. She entered the Daughters of Charity in 1940. She trained as a nurse in the North Infirmary Hospital, Cork. She worked as a nurse in Pinner, England, St Mary's, Lanark, Scotland, Ladbrooke Terrace, London and in St Anne's Skin and Cancer Hospital, Dublin. She was appointed as theatre sister and assistant tutor in the North Infirmary Hospital, Cork in 1963. She served as the sister servant and matron in St Vincent's Hospital Fairview, Dublin. She was the matron in the North Infirmary Hospital when it closed in 1987 and was appointed to Mount Cara Redemption Road, Cork as a nursing sister in 1989. She worked with the elderly in Kilmore West, Dublin for about sixteen years. She lived in Mount Prospect, Dublin while she undertook research for this publication and later in Rickard House, Blackrock. She died in January 2011. + RIP

Neylon, Anne, born in Dublin, taught in St Mary's National School, Fairview, Dublin before she joined the Daughters of Charity in 1983. Her interest in the parish mission stemmed from her teaching experience in St Vincent's Girls

National School, North William Street. She worked as principal in St Louise de Marillac, Junior National School, Ballyfermot. While working with the Vincentian Partnership for Social Justice, Anne received her MA in School Chaplaincy and Pastoral Care. Anne is currently working as a Primary Diocesan Advisor in the Archdiocese of Dublin. She is vocations director for the Daughters of Charity and is editor of the community quarterly journal *New Beginnings*.

O'Brien, Áine, a native of Dunmanway, Co. Cork joined the Daughters of Charity in 1969. She is a qualified primary teacher with a Bachelor Degree in Education. Áine has taught in St Louise's Junior School Ballyfermot, Scoil an Chroí Ró Naofa, Killinarden and in St Vincent's Girls School, North William Street, Dublin. For a number of years she was involved in Vocation Ministry for the Daughters of Charity. She was a member of the leadership team from 2002–10. In 2011, she went to work in Kenya where she is currently working in formation with the seminary sisters.

O'Connell, Louise, was born in Donoughmore, Co. Cork in 1942. Her aunt Louise O'Sullivan was a Daughter of Charity who spent many years in Australia. Louise entered the Company in 1960 and has spent much of her life in the field of education. She has taught in the following primary schools: St Philomena's, Stillorgan; St Vincent's, North William Street; St Michael's, Glenmaroon; St Teresa's, Blackrock; St Mark's, Springfield, Tallaght. She was missioned to Nigeria in 1975, where she worked in formation and education. Louise returned to Ireland in 1998 and was later missioned to China where she taught English for two years. She was then missioned to Knocknaheeny, Cork and to Killinarden to work in a family resource centre. Upon her retirement from the centre she was missioned in the autumn of 2012 to Kiio, Kenya.

O'Mahony, Christina is a Daughter of Charity. For many years, she was engaged in the ministry of post-primary education, teaching Religious Education, French and Irish. Having completed a Masters in Theology and Spirituality and a H.Dip. in Spiritual Guidance, she is now engaged in the ministry of prayer guidance and spiritual direction and with Contemplative Outreach Ireland, which fosters the growth of the method and practice of centering prayer. She is a member of the All Ireland Spiritual Guidance Association (AISGA) and is involved in administration and spiritual direction at All Hallows College, Dublin.

O'Neill, Bríd (Honora Teresa), was born in Rossmore, Clonakilty, Co. Cork and she joined the Daughters of Charity in 1946. Bríd studied home economics in Sion Hill College, Dublin. She has taught housewifery, crafts and needlework, poultry and dairy, as well as butter-making in St Martha's Navan and in Coolarne, Co. Galway, both of which were home economic colleges. She also taught in St Vincent's Trust, Henrietta Street, a centre for homeless young men and women. For a number of years Bríd was responsible for accommodating pilgrims to Knock Shrine who stayed at St Mary's Hostel in Knock. She was sister servant in Coolarne, Navan, Dunmanway and Henrietta Street. She currently lives in Henrietta Street.

Prunty, Dr Jacinta is a Holy Faith sister and senior lecturer in History at NUI Maynooth. She is author of *Margaret Aylward: Lady of Charity, Sister of Faith, 1810–1889* (Dublin: Four Courts Press, 1999) as well as other works on the history of religious orders in nineteenth-century and early-twentieth-century Ireland.

Ryan, Carmel, was born near Cork city and she joined the Daughters of Charity in 1976. Carmel studied in Mater Dei Institute of Education, Dublin and qualified with a Bachelor of Religious Science and holds an MA in School Chaplaincy and Pastoral Care. Carmel spent sixteen years teaching History and Religious Education at Maria Immaculata Secondary School, Dunmanway, Co. Cork. She spent three years as a diocesan advisor for the religious education of the Traveller community in the Archdiocese of Dublin. During her time working with the Travellers she helped in the publication of a textbook and workbook for the religious education of travelling children who are infrequent school attenders. Carmel spent an academic year in Chicago where she was involved in the Vincentian Integration Experience, with a group of Daughters of Charity from the United States, Great Britain and Australia. At present Carmel is School Chaplain in Nagle Community College, Mahon, Cork city.

Sherlock, Olivia, was born in Dublin and entered the Daughters of Charity in May 1956. Olivia began her life of ministry in 1958 in Rosewell, Scotland, caring for people with an intellectual disability. Later she was missioned to London, to minister in a hostel for young girls who came from troubled home backgrounds or recently discharged from childrens' homes. Upon her return to Ireland towards the end of 1968 she served in the finance office of the newly erected province of Ireland. When the new parish mission was opened in 1977, in Hollyhill/Knocknaheeny Olivia was the sister servant of the house. She worked in pastoral care in this newly developing area on the outskirts of Cork city. Olivia was missioned in 1980 to Dublin, to work with one-parent families and their babies. She has served as provincial treasurer from 1983–1994 and as provincial councillor from1995–2001. Olivia worked as the first director of service in the Vincentian Housing Partnership, North William Street (1996–2002). She was appointed sister servant to the local communities in Henrietta Street and Termonfeckin, Drogheda. She completed a second term as provincial treasurer in 2012 and is now a member of the community caring for the older sisters in nursing homes.

Sullivan, Dr Louise, a Daughter of Charity of the province of St Louise, USA, received her Bachelor of Science Degree in Elementary Education and Foreign Language in 1956 from St Joseph's College, Emmitsburg Maryland. She earned her MA in French Language and Literature from the Catholic University of America in 1966 and her doctoral degree in French and Comparative Literature in 1972 from L'Université de Paris IV: Sorbonne. She is the author of several articles and books on Louise de Marillac, the Daughters of Charity, the Core Values of Vincentian Education and the Vincentian Mission in Health Care. She edited and translated from the French *Spiritual Writings of Louise De Marillac: Correspondence and Thoughts* (New York, 1991) (*Sainte Louise de Marillac: Ecrits Spirituels*). She is the author of *Sister Rosalie Rendu: A Daughter of Charity on Fire with Love for the Poor* (Chicago, 2006). She has given numerous talks and presentations in the United States, Canada, Haiti, Ireland, Europe and Asia on Louise de Marillac and the Vincentian charism. She has served as a translator/interpreter at international meetings in Paris and Rome and was the recipient of three grants to study archival material in France relative to Vincentian heritage. She is Professor Emerita of Niagara University, New York State.

Sweeney, Claire, a native of Donegal, joined the Daughters of Charity in 1963. Having qualified as a primary school teacher in 1969, she completed a BA in 1972, H.D.E. in 1973 and M.Ed. in 1985. She is a member of senior faculty of William Glasser International. She did an intensive course in Vincentian spirituality in Chicago 2010/11. She has worked in the field of education in Dublin, Belfast, Dunmanway and Nigeria. She served as principal from 1983 to 1994, first in Caritas College, Ballyfermot and then in Maria Immaculata Secondary School, Dunmanway. She has contributed articles to the William Glasser Institute Ireland Journal, *Irish Perspectives,* to the Irish Learning Support Association Journal, *Learn,* to the Vincentian Partnership for Social Justice website (www.justicematters.ie) and to The Daughters of Charity journal, *New Beginnings.* Her main interests are Vincentian spirituality, special needs in education, the Quality School and 'an Ghaeilge'.

Index